PLANNING IN THE
EARLY MEDIEVAL LANDSCAPE

EXETER STUDIES IN MEDIEVAL EUROPE
History, Society and the Arts

SERIES EDITORS
Oliver Creighton, Anthony Musson,
Fabrizio Nevola and Yolanda Plumley

Planning in the Early Medieval Landscape

John Blair, Stephen Rippon
and Christopher Smart

LIVERPOOL UNIVERSITY PRESS

First published 2020 by
Liverpool University Press
4 Cambridge Street
Liverpool
L69 7ZU

British Library Cataloguing-in-Publication data
A British Library CIP record is available

ISBN 978-1-78962-116-7 cased

Typeset by Carnegie Book Production, Lancaster
Printed and bound by CPI Group (UK) Ltd, Croydon CR0 4YY

Contents

Illustrations

Tables

Preface and acknowledgements

Over the past two decades our knowledge of settlement forms in early England has grown by leaps and bounds. Thanks to the flood of new data about buildings and groups of buildings from developer-led archaeology, and about material culture from the Portable Antiquities Scheme, it is now possible to get a direct grip on problems that hitherto could only be approached speculatively, working backwards from much later patterns. With new evidence, however, come new problems: the more we see of Anglo-Saxon settlements at first hand, the harder it becomes to categorise them, and to elucidate the forces that brought them into being.

This book presents what is still quite a new hypothesis, and a startling one to some colleagues: that certain settlements and building complexes, in certain periods (c.600–800 and then c.940–1000), were laid out in accordance with geometrically accurate grids, the work of surveyors in the tradition of the Roman *agrimensores*. The possibility of a regular, grid-based system underlying some Anglo-Saxon settlements first occurred to John Blair in 2011, during work for a different project. After collecting more examples, and investigating the continental background to the transmission of surveying expertise, he published a preliminary article in 2013. By then it had become clear that the intensive, map-based analysis of the whole country required to take the hypothesis further was beyond the scope of one individual. During informal discussions between John Blair and Stephen Rippon, the idea of the present project was formulated and a successful funding bid to the Leverhulme Trust was launched. It thus became possible to recruit a colleague full-time to undertake the necessary groundwork, and Christopher Smart joined the team.

The three of us have worked together extremely well. The area of study is one that at best cannot avoid some subjective judgements, and at worst risks sailing close to the edge of rational academic enquiry. Helped by our statistician colleagues, we have tried at all stages to maintain high standards of scientific consistency. But it is in the nature of the problem that, while some grid-planned settlements are self-evidently convincing on the evidence available, others are debatable. And debate them we certainly did: it was fascinating to discover the differences between our respective cognitive faculties, often causing one member of the team to respond with derision to cases that looked very convincing to the others. It can at least be said that – at the cost of discarding some cases that are probably in fact genuine – the sites and settlements discussed in this book have passed the test of convincing all of us.

How many readers will be convinced remains to be seen. Reactions so far have been varied, although positive overall: some colleagues have immediately grasped the reality of the organising principles underlying the places discussed here; others have done so after further help and persuasion; and a few have remained resolutely sceptical. This is a microcosm of the variations in human cognition: some people conjure up visual patterns that are fictional ('faces in the clouds'), some readily detect patterns that really do exist, and others cannot see them at all. More specifically, some scholars of medieval rural society have found it hard to swallow the proposition that 'ordinary' settlements were governed by seemingly exotic and rarified patterns. It might help to say at the outset that we do not propose any arcane purpose or mystique in grid-planning: the techniques discussed here derived from a Classical tradition and were promoted by literate specialists, but their application was essentially pragmatic. Our claims are, in fact, a good deal more modest than some readers might initially suppose.

It remains to thank the many people who have helped us along the way. Our foremost gratitude is to the Leverhulme Trust: without the two-year Research Project Grant (Planning in the Early Medieval Landscape: Technology, Society, and Settlement: University of Exeter award RPG-2013-007) the intensive research on which this book is based would have been impossible. We are grateful to the Archaeology Department at the University of Exeter for accommodating and supporting the project, and we also owe a very big debt to Professor Wilfrid Kendall of Warwick University, and his former student Clair Barnes, for their guidance on statistics and for contributing Appendix A: we could not have done without the generous advice and the independent scientific scrutiny that they have afforded. Likewise, the architectural historian Eric Fernie has engaged – in a most helpful and positive spirit – with a theory of medieval planning very different from the one that he has long championed: it was very satisfactory to establish in the end that the two theories are compatible, as Appendix B shows. As the project advanced, it was greatly helped by several meetings of an academic panel, comprising (in addition to those mentioned above) David Hall, Helena Hamerow and David Palliser. We also thank the staff at the various archives that we visited. Turning to personal acknowledgements, JB is grateful to Kanerva, Edward and Ida for putting up with the obsession-inducing topics of grids, perches and modules; they need hear less about them from now on.

Chapter 1

Introduction

ALTHOUGH the English landscape retains few buildings from the early Middle Ages, it was a period in which many of our existing villages, hamlets and farmsteads took shape. Thousands of place-names now attached to settlements appear in Domesday Book, and archaeological excavations in these places are increasingly revealing traces of pre-Conquest occupation. The early medieval period was, however, one when relatively ephemeral timber buildings predominated, and – in contrast to the stability in settlement location and character that our present-day villages represent – the earliest Anglo-Saxon settlements appear to have sprawled across the landscape in a seemingly unconstrained way.

Over the course of the early to central Middle Ages, however, large parts of the landscape were transformed through an intensification of agriculture and – across a broad swathe of central England – the emergence of nucleated villages and open fields. When and why villages and open fields were laid out has been much debated in recent years, whereas the physical processes and techniques used in their creation have seen less attention. By the 1980s the prevailing view was that they formed part of a 'great replanning' of the landscape, and evidence was cited from various places for regular blocks of tenements, suggesting that the villages were laid out according to some grand design. Characteristically, this regularity within village plans took the form of long, narrow strips of land, the croft-and-toft layout that is so familiar in both deserted and still-occupied settlements. In recent years, however, an alternative hypothesis has emerged that argues that these plots resulted from the spread of village settlement across the earlier strips of land within open fields. As other aspects of the 'great replanning' hypothesis have also been challenged, there is an emerging impression of an early medieval landscape that lacks evidence for planned structure, design or regulation.

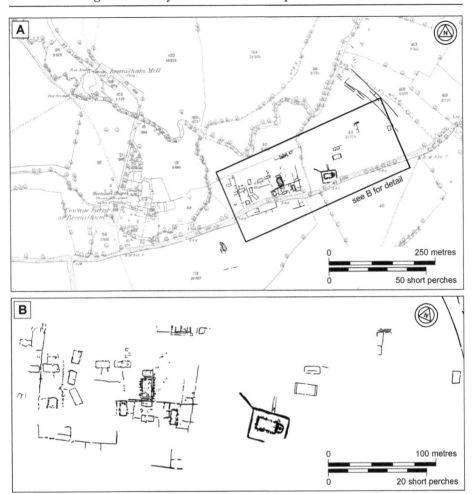

Figure 1.1. The cropmarks of a hall and possible church complex at Cowage Farm, Bremilham, Wiltshire, discussed in chapter 5 (after Hinchcliffe 1986, figs 1 and 6).

A: The cropmarks set within the context of this historic landscape (first edition OS 25-inch base map: © Crown Copyright and Landmark Information Group Limited (2016), all rights reserved, 1886).

B: Detail of the cropmark complex, focusing on the areas where there appears to have been grid-based planning.

C: The first proposed grid orientation (grid of short perches) shown with conforming features, which are predominantly the buildings.

D: The second proposed grid orientation (grid of short perches) shown with conforming features, which are predominantly the enclosure ditches.

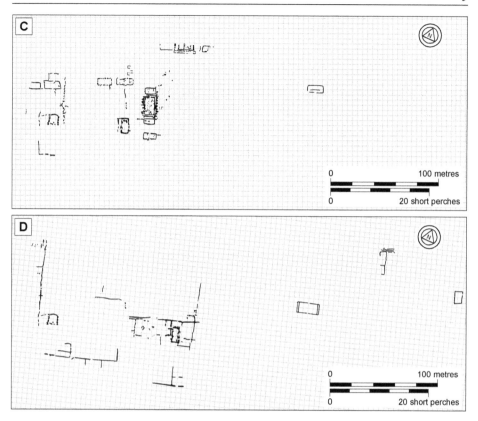

The days when archaeologists and historians referred to the fifth to tenth centuries as the 'Dark Ages' are long gone, and the material culture produced during that period demonstrates a high degree of sophistication. It has also become clear that individual buildings were laid out using specific units and modules, and we are starting to appreciate that buildings constructed of timber are just as likely to have displayed sophisticated design and execution as those built out of stone. But what of settlements and landscapes: is there any evidence for the planned division and organisation of larger areas? During the Roman period, planning was used as an instrument of power on various scales. Across Italy, entire rural landscapes were laid out according to geometrically precise grids of squares – a process known as centuriation – and, while nothing on that scale is known from Britain, all the major towns were divided into *insulae* by grid-planned streets. Grand public buildings were based upon precisely laid-out squares and rectangles, such as the

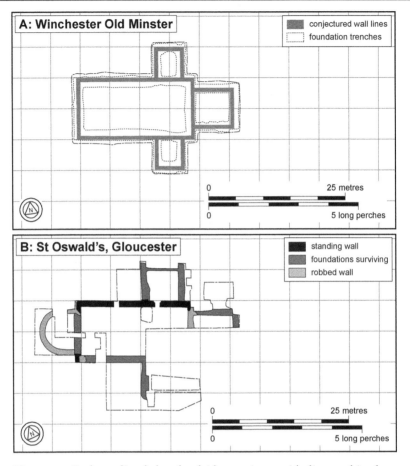

Figure 1.2. Early medieval churches laid out using a grid, discussed in chapter 5.
A: The reconstructed ground plan of Winchester Old Minster overlain
with a grid of long perches (after Kjølbye-Biddle 1986).
B: The known ground plan of the Anglo-Saxon minster church at
St Oswald's Priory, Gloucester, overlain with a grid of long perches
(after Heighway and Bryant 1999, fig. 2.9).

typical Romano-Celtic temple plan that consisted of a square *cella*
set centrally within a square ambulatory.[1] The laying out of space in
a regular way was also widespread in private buildings; for instance,
villas had rectangular ranges grouped formally around courtyards and
the fashion for rigid regularity even extended to funerary monuments

---

[1] For examples of 'square-in-square' temples see Great Chesterford and Harlow
in Essex (France and Gobel 1985; Medlycott 2011).

such as mausoleums.[2] There are non-rectilinear layouts – such as buildings arranged around the edges of trapezoidal-shaped open spaces – but even these show a strong degree of planning.[3] While roundhouses persisted on lower-status rural settlements in some parts of Roman Britain, they became increasingly exceptional, and from the second century rectilinearity was very much the norm.[4]

This regularity in the organisation of space, both in individual buildings and in whole settlements, contrasts strongly with what we see in the fifth to sixth centuries. Very few sub-Roman settlements have been excavated, although in the South West of Britain Romano-British rectilinear enclosures were replaced by curvilinear ones at Poundbury in Dorset and Hayes Farm in Devon.[5] In the east of England the sprawling complexes of post-built halls and *Grubenhäuser* at well-known sites such as Bishopstone (Sussex), Mucking (Essex) and West Stow (Suffolk) are conspicuous in their lack of any evidence for planning, or indeed ditches or fence-lines that marked out property boundaries.[6] It seems that, by the sixth century, the Romano-British fashion for rectilinearity and planning of space within buildings and settlements had been forgotten, had been consciously rejected or proved impossible to continue owing to a lack of professional surveying expertise.

Evidence has now emerged, however, for a hitherto unrecognised episode of sophisticated planning in the early medieval English landscape. This planning appears to have been based upon two principles: first, the use of standardised metrical units; and, secondly, the construction of grids – based on those units – that were then used in the laying out of both individual buildings (e.g. figure 1.2) and whole settlements. Evidence for this planning has been found in a variety of contexts, including the small number of standing buildings that survive from this period; excavated sites (e.g. figures 1.1, 1.3 and 1.4); and the configurations of buildings, roads and property boundaries that survived through to the nineteenth century and appeared on first edition Ordnance Survey maps.

[2] e.g. Bancroft in Buckinghamshire (Williams and Zeepvat 1994).
[3] e.g. Hambledon in Buckinghamshire, Rivenhall in Essex, Welwyn in Hertfordshire (Rodwell and Rodwell 1986, fig. 31), and Gorhambury in Hertfordshire (Neal *et al.* 1990).
[4] Smith *et al.* 2016, 50.
[5] Sparey Green 1987; Simpson *et al.* 1989.
[6] Bell 1977; Hamerow 1993; West 1985.

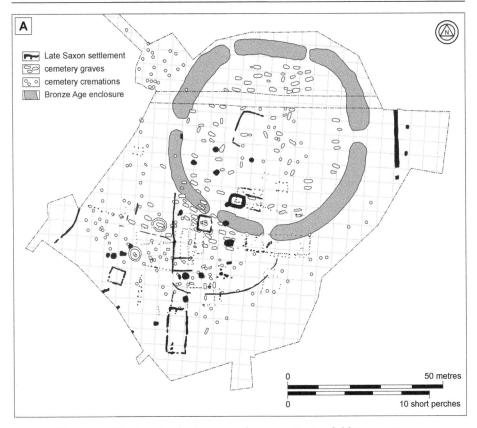

Figure 1.3. The late Anglo-Saxon settlement at Springfield Lyons, Essex, discussed in chapter 2.
　　A: The excavated late Bronze Age ringwork, early Anglo-Saxon cemetery and late Anglo-Saxon settlement, overlain with a grid of short perches (after Tyler and Major 2005, fig. 68).
　　B: All archaeological investigations at Springfield Lyons, shown in relation to the historic landscape (after Tyler and Major 2005, fig. 68; Ennis 2012; 2013; 2014; Pocock 2006; Robertson 2006; first edition OS 25-inch base map: © Crown Copyright and Landmark Information Group Limited (2016), all rights reserved, 1880).
　　C: A detailed plan of the Bronze Age, Roman, late Anglo-Saxon and post-medieval features at Springfield Lyons in relation to the historic landscape, overlain with a grid of short perches.

These phenomena are the focus of the present study, which has four aims: first, to establish the extent of technically precise, grid-based planning and, in particular, to explore whether it is found in all areas that saw the nucleation of settlement into villages; secondly, to determine

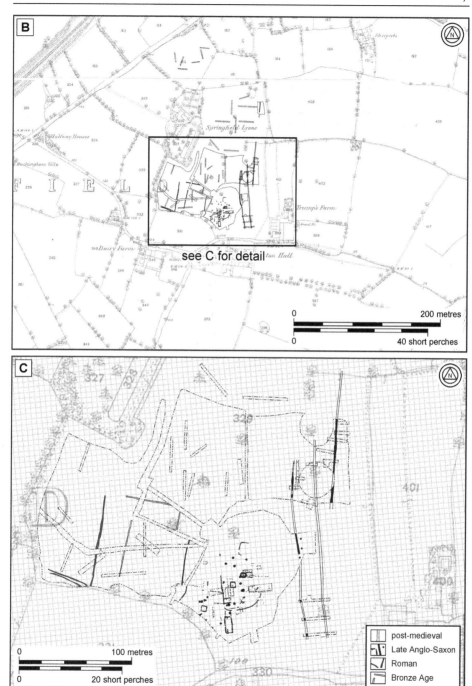

B

see C for detail

0   200 metres

0   40 short perches

C

0   100 metres

0   20 short perches

post-medieval
Late Anglo-Saxon
Roman
Bronze Age

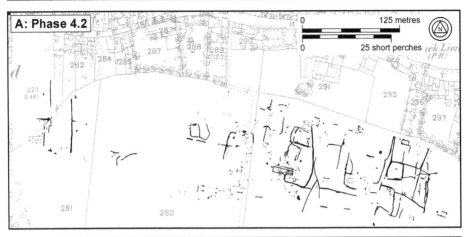

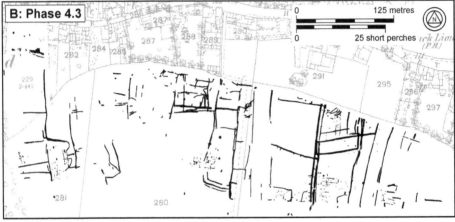

Figure 1.4. The extensive late Anglo-Saxon settlement and enclosure complex at Stotfold, Bedfordshire, discussed in chapter 6 (excavation by Albion Archaeology).
A: Phase 4.2 excavated features (after plan supplied by Drew Shotliffe).
B: Phase 4.3 excavated features (after plan supplied by Drew Shotliffe).
C: Phase 4.2 overlain with a grid of four short perches (after plan supplied by Drew Shotliffe).
D: Phase 4.3 overlain with a grid of four short perches (after plan supplied by Drew Shotliffe).

when grid-based planning was used and, in particular, whether it was a short-lived, culturally specific phenomenon or a long-lived tradition; thirdly, to investigate the tenurial context within which grid-based planning was used – for example, whether it was restricted to particular sections of society, such as the ecclesiastical elites, or spread more widely;

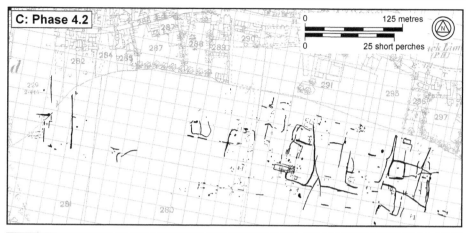

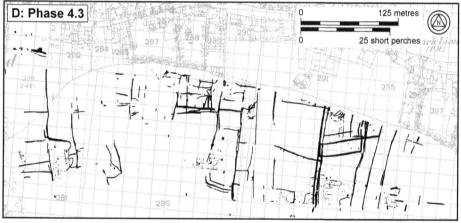

and, finally, to try to establish why this geometrical mode of organising space within buildings and settlements was adopted (or readopted).

Chapter 2 aims to set early medieval planning in context by reviewing past and current ideas on the origins and development of villages and open fields. The 'long eighth century' (the later seventh through to the early ninth century) has often been perceived as a crucial period of economic expansion, and many archaeologists have seen this as the context within which once dispersed settlement patterns were replaced by nucleated villages associated with vast open fields. This 'great replanning' hypothesis has recently been challenged on several fronts, including a rejection of the notion that either villages or open fields show evidence for planning – a debate that this study will address directly.

Chapter 3 outlines the methodology used in this study. We have been well aware that the concept of sophisticated grid-based planning in an early medieval context would prove controversial, and so a wide range of sources have been used (within the framework of a rigorous GIS-based analysis) to establish its overall geographical extent and then investigate potentially gridded places more thoroughly.

In Chapter 4 we explore the history of advanced surveying in Roman and early medieval society. There is no evidence for direct continuity in Roman surveying technology in England, either in the techniques themselves or in landscapes that had been laid out in a regular fashion. In 597, however, the Augustinian mission reconnected England to the Roman world, and the use of grid-based planning appears to have been part of a cultural package that the newly re-established Christian Church, and the secular elite with which it was so closely associated, used to reinforce their legitimacy. Grid-based planning appears initially to have been restricted to elite sites (both ecclesiastical and secular) during the seventh and early eighth centuries, but then went out of fashion between the late eighth and the early tenth centuries. Its revival in the tenth century was apparently associated with the period of monastic reform that saw an influx of new ideas from mainland Europe, and was probably stimulated by the importation of books on surveying. It seems that just two modules were used in early medieval planning: the 'short perch' of 15 imperial feet (4.57m) in eastern and central England, and the 'long perch' of 18 feet (5.5m) in Wessex. This uniformity points to a specialised technology, and to a small group of practitioners with the expertise and training to use standardised linear measures in a precise and consistent fashion.

The various ways in which gridding was used are then explored, first in relation to high-status sites (Chapter 5). The sequence seems to start shortly after 600, with the churches of SS Peter and Paul and St Pancras in St Augustine's monastery at Canterbury. Of particular significance is its use at Yeavering – probably in the early 620s – for the first of the large-scale timber halls and its associated enclosure; remarkably, a surveying instrument (a Roman-style *groma*) was deposited in a grave on the central axis of this complex. During the mid- to late seventh century gridding is found on a series of monastic sites and high-status secular hall complexes. The technique was revived after *c*.940, and can be recognised on some of the reformed monastic sites. A group of grid-planned complexes that probably date from around the mid-eleventh century suggests a final, brief revival in Edward the Confessor's court circle.

Chapter 6 discusses grid-planning on 'ordinary' rural settlements (e.g. figures 1.4 and 1.5), which display the same ninth- to early tenth-century hiatus as the elite ones. In the earlier period grid-planning occurs on a restricted range of sites, mostly in the East Midlands and East Anglia, all or most of which may have been monastic dependencies or possessions. In the period *c.*940–1050 a much larger number of cases can be recognised – many of them still perpetuating their gridded origins in surviving village plans – but there is still a strong concentration in the established 'core' zone of east-central to eastern England. Although a small number of examples have been recognised on monastic estates, most gridded villages were by 1066 in the hands of sokemen, royal officials and minor thegns; there is no direct evidence for who was responsible for planning them, but the groups of free farmers who lived there seem as likely candidates as lords. It is suggested that these villages evolved over a considerable period, and that the original grids framed 'semi-nucleated' settlements of spaced-out farmsteads. Only later did these farmsteads coalesce into smaller, more tightly packed villages, and in some cases it appears that open fields then spread across abandoned areas of the gridded settlement landscape, resulting in strips and furlongs that faintly reflected the regularity of the grid.

Chapter 7 draws some threads together and reflects on the meaning and significance of grid-planning: why did people bother to do it? As it was only in rare cases that the grids were expressed overtly in monumental and symmetrical architectural complexes, the answer to that question is not self-evident. While the process did have the basic practical value of organising space for the construction of any kind of settlement, it seems most likely that it was principally esteemed for its overtones of civilised, Classical and Christian *Romanitas*: the periods and contexts in which Anglo-Saxons aspired to those values are precisely the ones in which we have recognised the technique.

Finally, three appendices explore complementary approaches and provide supporting source material. Since the start of this investigation we have recognised the need for independent statistical scrutiny of what might otherwise seem a rather subjective exercise. John Blair's original paper of 2013 included a statistical appendix kindly supplied by Professor Wilfrid Kendall (University of Warwick), which gave some independent support for a module in the region of the proposed 'short perch'.[7] Professor Kendall maintained a keen and regular involvement in the project, and he and his colleague Clair

---

[7] Blair 2013, 55–7.

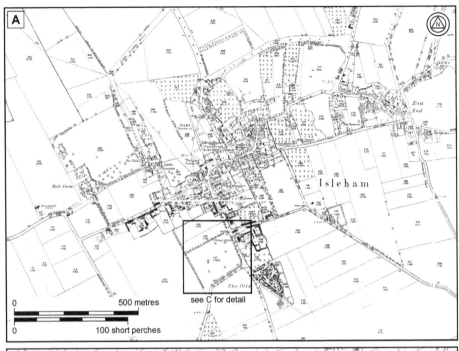

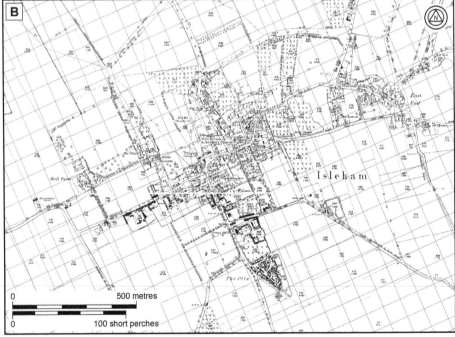

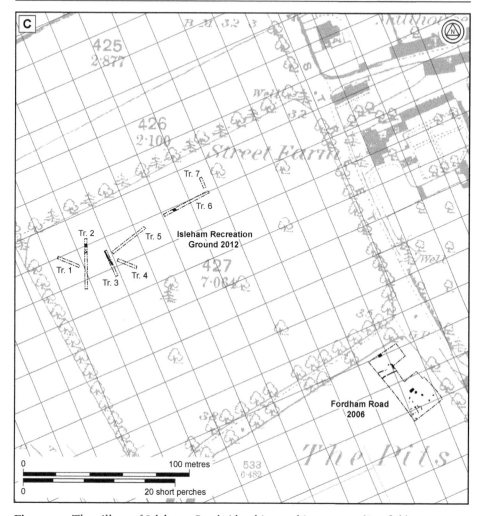

Figure 1.5. The village of Isleham, Cambridgeshire, and its surrounding fields.
A: The late nineteenth-century landscape (first edition OS 25-inch base map: © Crown Copyright and Landmark Information Group Limited (2016), all rights reserved, 1886).
B: The late nineteenth-century landscape overlain with a grid of 16 short perches.
C: Eleventh- to twelfth-century features recorded on the south side of the village, showing general agreement with the orientation of the proposed grid, which here is of four short perches (after Newton 2006; Rees 2012).

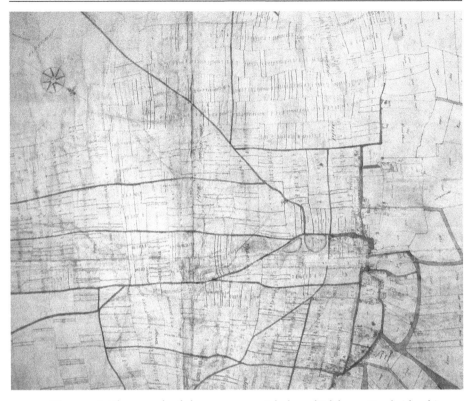

Figure 1.6. Photograph of the 1790 manorial plan of Isleham, Cambridgeshire, showing the pattern of long furlongs that existed prior to enclosure in the nineteenth century (© Cambridge Archives ref. 311 P1; photograph by C. Smart).

Barnes have now contributed to the present volume (Appendix A). While expressing themselves with appropriate professional caution, they offer encouraging intimations that standard modules such as we propose, and regular rectilinear configurations of buildings, may have an objective and verifiable reality. This fruitful interdisciplinary dialogue points the way for future work.

The relationship between land surveying and architectural planning lies at another disciplinary interface. The technology of the western *agrimensores* involved off-setting right angles with rods, not triangulation or proportional geometry. On the other hand, historians of medieval architecture – and pre-eminently Professor Eric Fernie – have argued energetically that architects based their building plans on proportions, notably that between one and the square root of two.

Whether these different approaches could be reconciled, and if so how, remained in a state of uncomfortable irresolution until quite a late stage in the project. Happily, Professor Fernie has engaged fully with the current enquiry, and now shows (Appendix B) how different specialists with different kinds of expertise might have collaborated on the same project: some geometrically planned buildings were probably laid out within pre-surveyed checkerboard grids. Indeed, the hypothesis of a two-stage process – surveyors followed by builders – helps to solve various problems that this project has raised.

Finally, Appendix C lists all the sites, buildings and settlements – whether standing, excavated or known from map evidence – that we accept as convincing or potential cases of grid-planning. Cases are graded (using a combination of number and letter codes) to indicate levels of confidence according to the various criteria. References are given to all analytical plans hitherto published, in the two works by Blair (2013; 2018) and in the present book.

A word is necessary at the outset on our policy for describing linear dimensions. The measuring of land in standard units, or modules based on them, is at the heart of this book. But identifying units of measurement in the Middle Ages, when so many local and customary practices existed, is far from straightforward. In our view it is essential to take no specific units for granted, but instead to adduce recurrent patterns from the physical evidence without importing preconceptions. On that basis we propose the use of modules equivalent to 15 and (less commonly) 18 modern statute feet. But we do not infer that the modern statute foot was necessarily an early medieval unit (even though it sometimes may have been) or make other assertions about how these modules were subdivided. Accordingly, we (and our colleagues who contribute Appendices A and B) follow normal scientific and archaeo-logical practice of expressing measurements in metric units. This may feel alien to the period, but it is more objective, and avoids implying spurious correspondences.

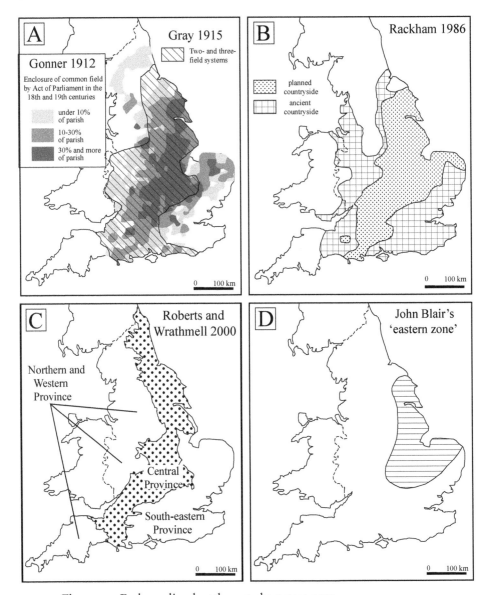

Figure 2.1. Early medieval settlement character zones.
    A: The enclosure of common field by Acts of Parliament in the eighteenth and nineteenth centuries (Gonner 1912), and the region with documentary evidence for regularly arranged two- and three-field systems (Gray 1915).
    B: Rackham's (1986) 'Planned' and 'Ancient Countryside'.
    C: Roberts and Wrathmell's (2000; 2002) 'Provinces'.
    D: John Blair's 'Eastern Zone'.

Chapter 2

Early medieval settlements and field systems

VILLAGES AND OPEN FIELDS were among the most distinctive features of the English landscape, and among the longest-lived. Although open fields have largely now been enclosed, the resulting patterns of field boundaries mean that England's 'Central Province' still has a unique character that led Oliver Rackham to characterise it as 'planned countryside' (Figure 2.1).[1] In coining this term, Rackham was actually referring to the straight-sided fields that were created following parliamentary enclosure of open fields. By the 1980s, however, the prevailing view was that open fields were themselves the result of planning in the landscape, having initially comprised a series of carefully planned 'long furlongs'.

The problem of when villages and open fields originated has been much discussed, with a broad current consensus for a pre-Conquest date. It is also widely believed that there was then a phase of settlement planning, which led to the creation of regularly arranged row-plan villages in northern England following William the Conqueror's 'Harrying of the North'.[2] Overall, there has been an underlying assumption that these distinctive English countrysides characterised by villages and open fields were the product of large-scale landscape reorganisation. Ironically, in the same year that John Blair raised the possibility of another form of early medieval planning – that based upon grids – the prevailing views on village and open-field origins were challenged by Tom Williamson (2013), who argued that these landscapes grew in a more piecemeal fashion. The origins of villages and open fields generally, and the extent of planning in the early medieval landscape specifically, remain one of the most contested areas of landscape studies.

[1] Rackham 1986.
[2] Creighton and Rippon 2017 is a critique of this hypothesis.

Inherited landscapes

Before considering the evidence for planning in the early medieval countryside, the possibility that some regularity was inherited from earlier times needs to be examined. During the prehistoric period there were some impressive feats of planning, most notably the extensive co-axial field systems that are found right across southern England.[3] The earliest of these date to the Middle Bronze Age, and although most of these field systems have long been abandoned and are revealed only as cropmarks, the most famous examples – the Dartmoor reaves in Devon – survive as upstanding earthworks and stone walls.[4] There are around twenty separate reave systems covering up to 3,000 hectares, each representing planning on a grand scale. Although a superficially similar regularity within the modern field-boundary pattern on the lower slopes of Dartmoor led to speculation that some of the Bronze Age reaves may have survived in use through to the present day,[5] it is far more likely that this regularity in the historic landscape results from field systems having been laid out alongside a series of long, sinuous medieval droveways that linked the summer pastures on Dartmoor with settlements in the surrounding lowlands.[6]

During the Late Bronze Age this widespread tradition of landscape planning appears to have ended, although a second form of co-axial landscape was recognised during the 1980s and ascribed to the later Iron Age. Of these co-axials, preserved in today's historic landscape and described by Andrew Fleming as 'perpetuated' systems,[7] the most famous is Tom Williamson's 'Scole–Dickleborough' system in southern Norfolk,[8] the dating of which relied upon the inference that it is overlain by a Roman road (although Williamson has himself now called this into question).[9] Similar co-axial systems have been recorded across southern England; the dating evidence is generally poor, but several others appear to pre-date Roman roads. One – at Cheshunt in Hertfordshire – has been dated through excavation to the Late Iron Age or Roman period,[10]

---

[3] Yates 2007.
[4] Fleming 2008.
[5] e.g. Fleming 1988, 109.
[6] Fox 2012.
[7] Fleming 2008, 176–85.
[8] Williamson 1987.
[9] Williamson 2008.
[10] Bryant *et al.* 2005.

and the extensive system that covers the London Clay basin in southern Essex can now be dated firmly to the early Roman period.[11] While it has traditionally been assumed that these long-lasting co-axial landscapes were deliberately planned, at least some of their regularity may result from fields having been laid out between a series of roughly parallel droveways linking resources in environmentally contrasting areas, as is the case around Dartmoor (above).[12] Overall, these 'perpetuated co-axial systems' are not a single phenomenon, do not all date from the same period and (unlike the Late Bronze Age field systems) are not necessarily the result of deliberate planning.

It is easy to assume that the Roman period saw extensive planning in the British landscape, but in fact this was not the case. It was only the major towns that had planned street systems and, although these were clearly grid-based – and as such could have provided an inspiration for early medieval planning – none of them appears to have survived into the medieval period.[13] Roman Cambridge, for example, lies at the heart of a region with several examples of early medieval grid-plan villages, and is unusual as a smaller town that had a regularly laid-out street system, yet these streets survived into the medieval period only where their line was constrained by the need to pass through gateways in the defensive circuit.[14] In the countryside of Roman Britain a number of scholars have argued for the survival of grid-based field systems known as centuriation,[15] but none of the suggested examples is convincing. These ideas have often been based on measurements taken from inappropriate sources, such as the Ordnance Survey two and a half inch series[16] as opposed to larger-scale maps, while in some cases the apparent regularity in the historic landscape is probably due to an underlying pattern of furlong boundaries within former open fields.[17]

---

[11] Rippon *et al.* 2015.

[12] Williamson 2008; 2013, 94.

[13] Burnham and Wacher 1990; Wacher 1995.

[14] Alexander and Pullinger 1999; Evans and Ten Harkel 2010.

[15] Near Colchester in Essex (Haverfield 1921; Christy 1921; Cole 1935; 1939; Astbury 1980; Jones and Mattingly 1990, map 7.5), at Cliffe in Kent (Nightingale 1952), around Cirencester in Gloucestershire (Rawes 1979), in Norfolk (Ward 1932–4; Applebaum 1981; Peterson 1988), in Hertfordshire (Sharpe 1918; Applebaum 1972, 90–4; Peterson 1990), and around Ripe in Sussex (Margary 1940).

[16] e.g. Astbury 1980, 269.

[17] Bradford 1957, 46–9; Richmond 1963, 16; Dilke 1971, 188–95; Fulford 1990, 26; Martin and Satchell 2008, 214–16.

Although there is no convincing evidence for centuriated landscapes in the Romano-British countryside, let alone their survival through to the medieval period, the *Fields of Britannia* project has recently demonstrated that other field systems do show a surprising degree of potential continuity from the Roman through to the medieval period.[18] In some cases evidence for the survival of Romano-British field systems is clear, such as where there are sequences of ditch cuts with Roman, early medieval and later medieval pottery. More usually, however, it takes the less direct form of common orientations shared by late Roman field systems and medieval fields (the latter known either from excavations, from open-field furlongs visible in earthworks or on maps or from old enclosures in the historic landscape and depicted on first edition Ordnance Survey maps). The degree of similarity between the orientation of late Roman and medieval systems is striking: across all lowland regions the figure is 64 per cent, with most areas close to this figure (the South East 63 per cent; the Central Zone 70 per cent;[19] East Anglia 73 per cent; the Western Lowlands 59 per cent; the North East Lowlands 67 per cent), and it is only the South West that is significantly lower (38 per cent).[20]

Some will no doubt argue that this similarity in the orientation of Romano-British and medieval field systems was determined by topography: land could be laid out within a field system in the Roman period, abandoned in the fifth century, and then cleared of woodland and a new field system established on the same orientation as the abandoned Roman one. This argument can, however, be dismissed for two reasons. First, the clearance of woodland is a destructive process as the tree trunks have to be dragged away and the stumps grubbed out, and it seems implausible that the relatively slight earthworks of a field system could have survived such processes. Secondly, pollen evidence shows quite clearly that there was no widespread woodland regeneration at the end of the Roman period. Across all lowland regions, trees accounted for 26 per cent of the 'Total Land Pollen' in the Roman period,[21] rising to 33 per cent in the fifth century and

[18] Rippon *et al.* 2015, 318–19.

[19] The *Fields of Britannia*'s Central Zone is broadly similar to Roberts and Wrathmell's (2000; 2002) 'Central Province'.

[20] Rippon *et al.* 2015, tab. 3.7.

[21] These percentages relate to the proportions of pollen grains within an assemblage and cannot be translated into the areas occupied by particular land uses, as some types of plant (e.g. trees and grasses) produce far greater amounts of pollen than others (e.g. arable crops).

rapidly falling back to 29 per cent in the sixth to ninth centuries.[22] This overall figure, however, masks important regional variations: whereas in the South East tree pollen increased from 31 per cent in the Roman period to 39 per cent in the fifth century, it was virtually unchanged in the Central Zone (increasing from 14 per cent to 15 per cent).[23] Trees produce vast amounts of pollen: an increase of 1 per cent is simply not significant, and could easily be accounted for by a failure to maintain coppiced woodland and laid hedges.[24] Arable pollen levels were remarkably stable, with plants indicative of cultivation forming 4 per cent of the 'Total Land Pollen' across lowland Britain as a whole in both the Roman period and the fifth century, although improved pasture fell from 49 per cent to 40 per cent.

Overall, the combination of the pollen evidence and the relationship between Romano-British and medieval field systems suggests that there was no widespread woodland regeneration in the early post-Roman period and that, while there may have been a decline in the intensity of land use, most fields remained in some form of agricultural production. Indeed, experiments at Rothamsted Experimental Station have shown that woodland regeneration on former arable fields will occur within 10 to 30 years, and a comparison of sequences of Ordnance Survey maps in areas of abandoned agricultural land confirms that woodland regeneration can indeed happen as quickly as this.[25] The significance of this in the context of the present study is that medieval field systems that demonstrate a degree of regularity could potentially have been laid out during the Roman period and simply survived through to the later period. Crucially, however, these inherited field systems were not based on grid-planning.

[22] Rippon *et al.* 2015, tab. 3.2.

[23] Rippon *et al.* 2015, tabs 4.2 and 6.2.

[24] Coppicing and laying prevents trees from growing to maturity and so producing pollen, and so a failure to maintain this management regime will eventually lead to mature trees that do produce pollen.

[25] Harmer *et al.* 2001; Rippon 2012.

Early medieval landscapes: the 'great replanning' hypothesis and its critics

During the fifth and sixth centuries planning was not a feature of the British landscape. The dominant model of Early Anglo-Saxon settlement, as formulated by Helena Hamerow with Mucking (Essex) as the type-site, presents typical settlements of that period as loose clusters of ground-level rectangular 'halls' and sunken-featured buildings, which moved around within their landscapes and lacked ditched boundaries or other apparent modes of structuring.[26] Dominic Powlesland has questioned that model in the light of his field project in the Vale of Pickering (Yorkshire), where he interprets the settlement pattern as altogether denser, more stable and more regular.[27] For two reasons, this contrast may be over-drawn. First, the Vale of Pickering is in one of the regions where archaeologically visible Anglo-Saxon settlement is densest, whereas in the Thames estuary, where Mucking lies, settlement was perhaps sparser, and is certainly harder for archaeologists to perceive. Secondly, the apparent structuring of the Vale of Pickering settlements owes a great deal to ladder-pattern earthworks surviving from the Romano-British period, and only after 600 were coherent new systems of ditched enclosures created.

The reappearance of ditched property boundaries within and around settlements was one of several profound changes in the landscape in a period that also saw an expansion of agricultural production and manufacturing.[28] This transformative era has been characterised as the 'long eighth century',[29] although some of the major changes may have begun as early as the middle and later thirds of the seventh. This period also saw an intensification in land use, reflected in palaeoenvironmental sequences where arable-indicative pollen increases around the eighth century[30] and in a wide range of archaeological discoveries that illustrate how landowners had increasing resources at their disposal and were using these resources to expand production. At Ebbsfleet in Kent, for example, a tidal mill was constructed *c.*691–2 (a dendrochronological date), while another mill is recorded at Chart (also in Kent) in a charter of 762.[31] At Tamworth,

---

[26] Hamerow 2012, 67–72.
[27] Powlesland 2014.
[28] Reynolds 2003; Blair 2018, 246–54.
[29] e.g. Wickham 2005.
[30] Rippon *et al.* 2015.
[31] Andrews *et al.* 2011; Sawyer 1968, S 25.

a watermill with a leat probably some 500m long was constructed at the Mercian royal centre in the mid-ninth century or earlier.[32] Such major feats of engineering reflect many things, including a landowner's command of human and material resources, and they reflect planning in the sense of landowners' increasing ability to deploy resources in an ordered fashion. A combination of written, topographical and place-name evidence shows that in Mercia – followed probably by both Wessex and Northumbria – during c.740–840 the imposition of the services of bridge-building and fort-building resulted in a network of strong-points linked and supported by better communications and a more coherent infrastructure.[33] Other impressive infrastructural developments at this time included causeways crossing the Thames at Oxford, linking Mersea Island to the mainland of Essex, and linking Glastonbury and Street in the Somerset Levels.[34] The supreme example of planning – in the sense of the ability to command and organise resources – was the construction of Offa's Dyke, Wat's Dyke, Wansdyke (probably marking the frontier between Wessex and Mercia) and the Cambridgeshire Dykes (perhaps marking the south-western limit of the East Anglian kingdom).[35] Major investments such as these were made possible by the increased centralisation of resources seen at sites such as Hereford, where two large corn-drying ovens were constructed during the eighth century,[36] and at Ramsbury in Wiltshire, where a late eighth- or early ninth-century iron-working site was drawing its iron ore from up to 30km away.[37]

Integral to this package of transformations were the first stages of the process whereby villages and open fields were created. There has been much debate about when, how and why villages and open fields appeared, and as there have been several excellent historiographies of this debate[38] a brief summary can suffice here. Until the mid-twentieth

---

[32] Rahtz and Meeson 1992.

[33] Blair 2018, chapters 6 and 7.

[34] Durham 1977; Crummy *et al.* 1982; Brunning 2014.

[35] Hill and Worthington 2003; Ray and Bapty 2016; Reynolds and Langlands 2006; Rippon 2018. Grigg 2015 makes a sharp distinction, both chronologically and functionally, between the major continuous dykes and examples consisting of short lengths.

[36] Shoesmith 1982; Thomas and Boucher 2002.

[37] Haslam 1980.

[38] Dodgshon 1980, 1–28; Fox 1981, 68–72; Lewis *et al.* 1997, 9–21; Roberts and Wrathmell 2002; Williamson 2003, 8–21; Jones and Page 2006, 1–15, 79–83; Williamson 2013, 135–40; Williamson *et al.* 2013, 5–19; Hall 2014, 176–81.

century the prevailing view was that villages and open fields were a mode of managing the landscape that was introduced into England by Anglo-Saxon invaders. This 'introduction hypothesis', which reflected the prevailing culture-historical approach in archaeological thought, argued that major changes in material culture, technology and landscape were introduced by migrants from mainland Europe.[39] In the 1960s, however, there was a paradigm shift, as archaeological excavations of fifth- to seventh-century Anglo-Saxon settlements showed that they were very different in character from later medieval villages – most notably in their lack of defined property boundaries and planned division of space – and were also located in different parts of the landscape. Historians started to argue that open fields were created in a piecemeal fashion, through modifications to existing field systems and the gradual assarting of waste as late as the twelfth or thirteenth centuries,[40] while archaeologists and historical geographers started to argue that villages were also created in the post-Conquest period.[41]

By the 1970s this 'evolutionary' hypothesis, with its relatively late chronology for the origins of villages and open fields, was firmly embedded,[42] but during the 1980s it was in turn replaced by one of a 'great replanning' of the landscape around the eighth century.[43] According to this model (largely based upon evidence from Northamptonshire) a dispersed settlement pattern of isolated farmsteads and small hamlets associated with Early to Middle Anglo-Saxon pottery – examples of which had been located through fieldwalking, settlement-indicative furlong names and increasingly through excavations – was typically abandoned in favour of a single nucleated settlement, whose plan was often then restructured a few centuries later. It was thought that the field systems associated with these dispersed settlements were swept away and replaced by open fields at the same time (Figure 2.2).[44] The earliest evidence for this 'great replanning' was ascribed to parishes associated with royal

[39] e.g. Gray 1915.

[40] e.g. Thirsk 1964, 8–9; 1966.

[41] Dodgshon 1980; Taylor 1983, 112.

[42] e.g. Taylor 1975; 1983; see Fox 1981, 70 for some early concerns about the suggested post-Conquest date.

[43] Foard 1978; Hall 1981a; 1982; 1983; Brown and Foard 1998; Rippon 2008; Foard *et al.* 2009; Partida *et al.* 2013.

[44] Hall 1981a; 1982; Foard *et al.* 2009; Partida *et al.* 2013.

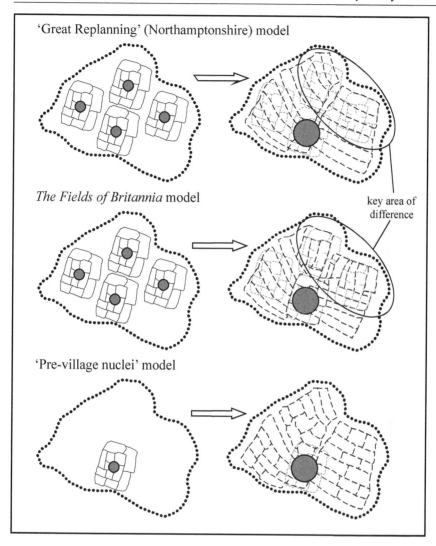

Figure 2.2. Alternative models for the origins of villages and open fields. In the 'great replanning' model, a series of isolated farmsteads, each with its own field system, were brought together in a nucleated single village surrounded by an open-field system that often consisted of a series of 'long furlongs'. In the light of the findings of *The Fields of Britannia*, there may have been greater continuity between the open fields and the boundaries that preceded them. In the 'pre-village nuclei' model there was never more than one early medieval settlement within a vill, and it was from this that villages developed; 'long furlongs' are argued to have developed in a gradual way.

centres or important churches, although it was argued that this approach towards structuring the landscape soon spread right across the Northamptonshire landscape and beyond.[45]

Some archaeologists and historians, while accepting the idea that villages were created through the nucleation of a formerly dispersed settlement pattern, have remained persuaded by the later chronology – in the mid-ninth to twelfth centuries – for this 'village moment', as

> the excavation of more and more deserted and shrunken villages which showed very little evidence for occupation earlier than the eleventh or twelfth century, and the discovery of a growing number of hamlets and farmsteads of the pre-Conquest period which had been abandoned by the ninth century, seemed to push forward the origin of the large nucleated village to the period between about 850 and 1200.[46]

There are, however, a number of problems. First, if villages were created in 'the mid-ninth to twelfth centuries', but the preceding dispersed settlement pattern 'had been abandoned by the ninth century' (emphasis added), then where did people live between these two events? One solution to this dilemma was to recognise that some villages do have evidence for pre-mid-ninth-century occupation beneath them and that, while in the past this has been dismissed as being 'of a formless nature and unrelated in morphology to the subsequent layout',[47] it could actually indicate that village formation was at least a two-stage process, with initial nucleation followed by settlement restructuring.[48] A second problem with the late chronology, however, is that until quite recently the only villages that had seen excavation were those that were deserted, a proportion of which were not parochial centres but secondary settlements probably founded at a later date.[49] Many of these 'villages' are, therefore, best regarded

---

[45] Brown and Foard 1998, 75–6, 80.

[46] Lewis *et al.* 1997, 3; and see Everson *et al.* 1991, 13; Jones and Page 2006; Thomas 2008.

[47] Taylor 1983, 112.

[48] e.g. Lewis *et al.* 1997, 23; Brown and Foard 1998.

[49] e.g. Caldecote that was carved out of Newnham (Hertfordshire) (Beresford 2009); Goltho in Bullington (Lincolnshire) (Beresford 1975); Hatch (Hampshire) (Fasham and Keevill 1995); Moreton in Compton Martin (Somerset) (Rahtz and Greenfield 1977); Upton in Blockley (Gloucestershire) (Hilton and Rahtz 1966; Rahtz 1969; Watts and Rahtz 1984); West Cotton in Raunds (Northamptonshire) (Chapman 2010); Walton in Milton Keynes (Buckinghamshire) (Croft and Mynard

as secondary hamlets, a status often reflected in their locations in somewhat marginal situations.[50]

Since 1991, as a result of PPG16 and its successors, a crucial development has been extensive excavations within currently occupied medieval villages (see Chapter 6 for the relevance of this to the search for gridded settlement plans). There are examples where 'Middle Saxon' occupation appears to have been unrelated to the later village plan, as at Chesterton, in Cambridgeshire, where various excavations have revealed residual Middle Saxon pottery, with the first ditched enclosures and stratified occupation deposits dating from the Late Saxon period.[51] There are, however, a growing number of Middle Saxon settlements that do have key elements of a village, such as regularly arranged ditched property boundaries. At West Fen Road in Ely, for example, an extensive village-like settlement was laid out in the early eighth century, and the way that tenements and furlong boundaries within the open fields that covered Ely in the medieval period were on the same orientation suggests that the whole landscape was planned out at the same time.[52] Even if West Fen Road was a somewhat untypical settlement, associated with the nearby monastery founded c.672, it still shows that the concept of planned and at least semi-nucleated settlements existed in this region at that time. In nearby Cottenham a cluster of ditched settlement enclosures was laid out during the seventh or eighth century, although this was replaced in the eighth or ninth century by a radially arranged series of ditched tenement plots.[53] At Hinxton, also in Cambridgeshire, a single farmstead was occupied between the late sixth/early seventh and eighth centuries, when it was replaced by a series of timber buildings set within ditched enclosures. These are suggestive of a series of adjacent farmsteads that also appear to represent the beginnings of the village; in the eleventh century they were replaced by the present planned settlement.[54] At nearby Cherry Hinton extensive excavations have revealed a spread of Middle Saxon pottery and a series of ditches containing domestic refuse, replaced

---

1993; Mynard 1994); Westbury in Shenley (Buckinghamshire) (Croft and Mynard 1993; Ivens *et al.* 1995).

[50] e.g. the place-name Moreton, in Compton Martin (Somerset) means 'farm on swampy ground' (Rahtz and Greenfield 1977, 91).

[51] Cessford 2004.

[52] Hall 1996, 40; Mortimer *et al.* 2005, 4, 144–8.

[53] Mortimer 2000.

[54] Taylor *et al.* 1994; Taylor 2002, 55–6.

in the late ninth or early tenth century by a large, possibly manorial, enclosure associated with a church.[55]

Duncan Wright has recently reviewed the evidence for late seventh- to early ninth-century occupation within currently occupied medieval villages, and found that, in a sample of five counties within regions that have recognisable Middle Saxon pottery (Norfolk, Cambridgeshire, Northamptonshire, Oxfordshire and Wiltshire), not only is occupation of that date found in more than a third of cases but the nature of that occupation shares many of the characteristics of villages – for example, ditched property boundaries laid out in regular arrangements, as at Fordham in Cambridgeshire, Whissonsett in Norfolk, and Warmington in Northamptonshire.[56] That some villages in East Anglia and the East Midlands do appear to have originated in the seventh to eighth centuries does not, however, necessarily mean that all villages in all regions developed at this time.

In the 'great replanning' hypothesis it was argued that both the Early to Middle Saxon farmsteads and small hamlets and the field systems with which they were associated were replaced by open fields that initially consisted of carefully planned 'long furlongs'; in this model it was only later that they were sub-divided into the complex patterns of small furlongs that survived as ridge and furrow and on early maps. An example was Wadenhoe, in Northamptonshire, where one 'long furlong' stretched for *c.*2,500m.[57] Across Northamptonshire, 65 townships out of 399 (16 per cent) have three or more adjacent furlongs in the same alignment, and in ten townships there are as many as 10 such aligned furlongs.[58] Other 'great furlong layouts' have been identified in the Midlands (Bedfordshire, Berkshire, Buckinghamshire, Cambridgeshire, Leicestershire, Lincolnshire, Nottinghamshire, Oxfordshire, Rutland and Warwickshire),[59] Derbyshire,[60] Holderness,[61] the Wolds and Vale of Pickering in Yorkshire,[62] Fenland[63] and Pembrokeshire.[64] Of these various examples of 'long furlongs' that

[55] Cessford 2005, 51–3.
[56] Wright 2015a; 2015b. Cf. Blair 2018, 322.
[57] Hall 1982, 47; Hall 1983; Partida *et al.* 2013, 35.
[58] Partida *et al.* 2013, 35, fig. 26.
[59] Hartley 1983; 1987; Hall 2014, 187.
[60] Roberts 1987, fig. 10.4.
[61] Harvey 1978; 1980; 1981; 1982; 1983; Hall 2014, 46.
[62] Hall 1982, 47; Roberts 2008, fig. 4.6; Hall 2012; 2014, 46–52.
[63] Hall 1981b; Silvester 1988; Gardiner 2009.
[64] Roberts 1987, figs 3.13 and 10.4.

have been identified in the past, it should be noted that they probably have several origins. While those in Midland counties may relate to the eighth- to tenth-century 'great replanning' of the arable landscape and were subsequently subject to fragmentation, those in Yorkshire were not broken up to the same extent. While it is tempting to suggest that the latter were therefore later in origin, perhaps resulting from a post-Conquest replanning of the landscape following the Harrying of the North,[65] it is very striking that Holderness was one of very few parts of lowland Yorkshire in which there were almost no vills described as 'waste' in Domesday.[66] The plan of the Pembrokeshire landscapes are very similar to Dutch and Flemish wetland reclamations of the same date (such as Assendelft: see Chapter 4), and they may relate to the well-dated settlement of Flemings in this region during the early twelfth century.[67]

In addition to the 'long furlongs', another central plank in the 'great replanning' paradigm was that many villages also had a planned layout. Christopher Taylor, for example, argued that

> one of the most notable of recent advances in our understanding of the origins and development of English villages has been the recognition that a very large proportion of them acquired their present shape not in early Saxon times, but in the tenth–twelfth centuries and even later, and as a result of conscious planning.[68]

In Northamptonshire, for example, Taylor argued that 23 per cent of villages had planned origins, with apparently 14 examples that may have involved the use of a grid (although there is little discussion and no illustrations of these).[69] In the West Lindsey district of Lincolnshire Everson *et al.* suggested that a 'large proportion of the sites examined, both of totally deserted and merely shrunken villages, have their street systems, house sites and associated crofts or closes arranged in such a way as to indicate that the overall plan was the result of conscious and deliberate actions',[70] and they also argue that several

---

[65] e.g. Lewis *et al.* 1997, 17, 23.

[66] Darby 1977, fig. 83.

[67] Van der Linden 1982; Besteman and Guiran 1987; Rippon 2008.

[68] Taylor 1989, 71; for other examples of the 'planning hypothesis' for village origins see Everson *et al.* 1991 for Lincolnshire, Ellison 1983 for Somerset and Lewis *et al.* 1997, 7 for the East Midlands.

[69] Taylor 1983, 133–48.

[70] Everson *et al.* 1991, 14.

villages had grid-based plans. That may in fact be true, even though the plans fall short of the criteria adopted for the present project.[71] Settlement morphology has been mapped in detail for Buckinghamshire, Bedfordshire, Northamptonshire, Leicestershire, Rutland and the Soke of Peterborough, revealing that supposedly planned 'regular row' villages were found right across this region (with the exception of the Chilterns), and, although not quantified, it appears from the published maps that *c.*20–30 per cent of the settlements were of this form.[72]

By the 1990s the 'great replanning' hypothesis – in both its chronological variants – was widely known and accepted. It suggested that early medieval society was capable of planning in many senses: in the laying out, in a regular fashion, of individual settlements and field systems, but also in conceiving 'a total reorganisation of almost the entire landscape'.[73] In recent years, however, the paradigm has come under attack, most notably by Tom Williamson. He has dismissed the idea that villages were planned by returning to a well-known observation that some of the apparent regularity in village plans resulted from the expansion of tenements across pre-existing strips within open field furlongs.[74] The examples he presents are convincing in themselves, but this explanation cannot be extended to all regular villages, and least of all to the grid-based regularity that is presented in this study.

Other scholars have rejected the 'nucleation' element of the 'great replanning' paradigm in favour of one that sees villages as having developed gradually from 'pre-village nuclei'. An early example of this argument came with the results of the Whittlewood Project, where fieldwalking in a number of parishes failed to find many scatters of fifth- to eighth-century pottery outside the later village cores[75] (although this can easily be explained by the marginal nature of this area of high ground, whose very heavy soils saw extensive post-Roman woodland regeneration). In contrast, fieldwalking in parishes in the lower-lying

---

[71] e.g. Bishop Norton, Brattleby, Broxholme, Linwood and Upton (Everson *et al.* 1991, 15 and fig. 14).

[72] Lewis *et al.* 1997, figs 2.7, 2.10, 2.11 and 2.14.

[73] Brown and Foard 1998, 67.

[74] e.g. Lilbourn in Northamptonshire (RCHME 1981, 129); Riseholme in West Lindsey (Everson *et al.* 1991, 155–9); Everson *et al.* (1991, 13) suggest that a large number of deserted villages in West Lindsey overlie ridge and furrow; and see Williamson *et al.* 2013, 78–87.

[75] Jones and Page 2006; Williamson 2013; Williamson *et al.* 2013.

east of the study area, such as Leckhampstead, did reveal several scatters of fifth- to eighth-century pottery outside the later village cores. Williamson and his colleagues have gone on, however, to argue that relatively few parishes across Northamptonshire as a whole have evidence for a dispersed fifth- to eighth-century settlement pattern,[76] suggesting that in 51 per cent of parishes there are no known sites associated with Early to Middle Saxon pottery, while in 28 per cent of parishes there is just one.[77] At face value these data do appear to suggest that the widely accepted 'Northamptonshire model' for settlement nucleation could only work in the remaining 21 per cent of parishes, although in order to make this case we need to know how much of each parish has actually been fieldwalked, and the type of fieldwalking that was used: grid-walking, for example, should have detected every site, although widely spaced line-walking is bound to have missed some sites. If, for example, only 25 per cent of a parish was actually walked, yielding just one site with fifth- to eighth-century pottery (the remaining areas being pasture, woodland and under modern settlement), then statistically there are potentially four sites associated with pottery of that date in that parish. The hypothesis that there was no process of settlement nucleation is, therefore, unproven until we know the proportion of the landscape that has actually been walked, although, as it is impossible to walk an entire parish, it is very likely that some of the 28 per cent of parishes with only one known site actually had more.

A nother argument put forward to counter the 'nucleation hypothesis' – or 'nucleation myth',[78] as some would have it – is that where fifth- to eighth-century pottery has been recovered from within extant villages in Whittlewood it either represents occupation that is unrelated to the later village[79] or covers such a small area (*c*.1–2 ha, 3–5 acres) that it can only represent a very small number of farmsteads and not an entire village.[80] It is important to appreciate, however, that in addition to Whittlewood being a physically relatively marginal landscape where settlement expansion is likely to have been later than in the lower-lying surrounding areas, this reconstruction of the extent of the 'pre-village nuclei' is based upon small-scale test-pitting within extant villages as

[76] Williamson *et al.* 2013, 54–9.
[77] Williamson *et al.* 2013, 54–9.
[78] Williamson 2013, 162.
[79] Taylor 1983, 112.
[80] Jones and Page 2006, 88, 101; Williamson 2013, 164; Williamson *et al.* 2013, 45–9.

opposed to fieldwalking, and the relatively small amounts of pottery associated with fifth- to eighth-century settlements could easily have been missed by a 1m × 1m test pit.

Williamson and his colleagues have also called into question whether open fields were originally laid out in a planned fashion. The recent mapping of the open fields across the whole of Northamptonshire has for the first time allowed the extent of the 'long furlongs' to be determined: this has revealed that they are not particularly widespread, being more common in the north and east than in the south and west of the county.[81] It now seems possible that most open fields did not develop from planned landscapes based upon 'long furlongs', an observation that is entirely in keeping with the conclusions of the *Fields of Britannia* project, which showed that even in England's central zone there is a strong physical relationship between Romano-British and medieval field systems.[82] Williamson has also argued that the 'long furlong' field systems that have been identified were not planned out in a single exercise but instead developed in a gradual, piecemeal fashion, perhaps as late as the twelfth century.[83] This argument is not, however, very convincing, as it seems difficult to believe that sets of parallel field boundaries *c.*2,500m long could have been laid out in a piecemeal fashion without there being tell-tale signs such as slight changes of direction.[84]

Another central element of the 'great replanning' hypothesis was that the context for the reorganisation of landscapes in the late first millennium AD was a profound change in landownership. There is general agreement about a broad trajectory whereby large territories (*regiones*) were gradually annexed by kings as a basis for economic support and political control, were divided or moulded into large estates (initially for monastic foundations but increasingly, from the late eighth century onwards, for the laity) and were often then further subdivided to produce the tenurial geography portrayed in detail by Domesday Book. Behind many of the different ideas about how villages and open fields came into being there is, however, an underlying disagreement about whether the prime movers in instigating and carrying out landscape change were the landowning elite who held

[81]   Partida *et al.* 2013, 35–6, fig. 26.
[82]   Rippon *et al.* 2015.
[83]   Williamson *et al.* 2013, 105.
[84]   And see Foard *et al.* 2009, 36; Hall 2014, 191.

these estates or the rural communities that farmed the land on a daily basis.[85] It has been argued by many scholars

> that the upheaval involved in forming a new settlement for an existing population needed the dictatorial powers of a lord, who could compel peasants to uproot themselves and move to a central settlement, and that a coherent plan is more likely to be formulated successfully by a single authority than by a committee.[86]

In contrast, Williamson and his colleagues have argued that

> It might be suggested that the tendency for landscape historians and others to see 'planning' as the sole explanation for apparent regularities in village forms partly reflects the influence of certain widely held assumptions about the role of lordship in the day-to-day administration of rural life in the Middle Ages – assumptions which are not necessarily supported, for example, in any evidence for the standardization of agricultural routines across medieval estates.[87]

While it is certainly true that landscape change can be initiated by communities, it is wrong to dismiss the possibility that lordship did play a significant, indeed dominant, role in at least some cases. David Hall, for example, has shown that across Northamptonshire there is a strong correlation between the numbers of customary peasant holdings (virgates or yardlands) and the number of Domesday hides, there commonly being 8, 10, 12 or 16 yardlands per hide,[88] and it is difficult to see how this could have arisen without some central guiding hand. While commoners may have divided up the previously unenclosed backfens of Lincolnshire during the twelfth century,[89] this does not necessarily mean that rural communities in eighth-century England were capable of reorganising existing arable fields. Similarly, while the villagers of Segenhoe in Bedfordshire were capable of restructuring their open fields in the 1160s,[90] that does not mean that a community would have been capable, several centuries earlier, of sweeping away a fieldscape held in severalty, or a multiplicity of

---

[85] Hall 1981a; Dyer 1985; Harvey 1989; Lewis *et al.* 1997, 18.
[86] Lewis *et al.* 1997, 173.
[87] Williamson *et al.* 2013, 98.
[88] Hall 1995, 82–6, 115–22.
[89] Gardiner 2009.
[90] Fox 1981, 96–7.

small communal fields, and replacing them with two or three vast open fields.[91]

The most recent contribution to the debate over the origins of villages and open fields has been John Blair's.[92] First, he proposes a developmental sequence for English regionality that differs from the Roberts and Wrathmell model, with its 'Central Province'. He points out that the excavated evidence for Anglo-Saxon settlement between 600 and 900 concentrates heavily in an easterly zone comprising northern East Anglia, the East Midlands, Lincolnshire and eastern Yorkshire (essentially the drainage basins of the Wash and Humber). Whereas Roberts and Wrathmell envisage an outwards advance of what they call the 'townfield system' from a core zone in the Central to South Midlands,[93] Blair proposes a south-westwards expansion of his 'eastern zone' – with population growth and increased pressure on the land – transforming it into the eventual 'Central Province'. Secondly, he recognises a distinctive material culture in that zone, visible especially in metal-detected finds but also in the use of distinctive ceramics, that suggests a prosperous and probably free farming society co-existing with the major monastic proprietors. The eastern zone is essentially undocumented, and it may be wrong to extrapolate social models (for instance, of a dependent peasantry) from better-recorded Wessex. It follows from this perspective that we should envisage not a single uniform 'replanning' but regional modes of settlement – probably more organised and more tightly structured in the eastern zone – that were disseminated more widely over time.

In Blair's model, moreover, the basic settlement form was not a compact 'village' in the later sense, but a loosely clustered group of independent, though associated, farmsteads (a 'semi-nucleation' in his terminology), sited in the core arable area of the community's territory: nucleation in the usual sense was essentially a post-Conquest development. This model is relevant to the present project in two ways. First, it is in the eastern zone that our evidence for gridded settlements concentrates; and, secondly, it may well have been to this kind of structured 'semi-nucleation' that the technique of gridding was most frequently applied.

---

[91]   See also Lewis *et al.* 1997, 172–9 for an excellent discussion of these issues.
[92]   Blair 2018.
[93]   Roberts and Wrathmell 2002, fig. 5.11; cf. Rippon 2008, 17–20.

Other forms of planning: radially arranged field systems, radially planned circular settlements and row-plan villages

Most of this recent debate about the origin of villages has focused on the process of nucleation: when it occurred (if it occurred), the extent to which villages were created (or existing, more loosely arranged settlements were restructured) in a planned fashion and whether the restructuring of landscapes was the result of lordly intervention or community action. There has also been a more or less explicit assumption that the evidence from Northamptonshire can be applied across much of the 'Central Province' (south of Yorkshire), and that in northern England a separate process of landscape replanning followed the Harrying of the North. The vast majority of village planning that has been identified was based upon various linear row-plan forms, and while those in northern England are extremely distinctive – in having a central rectangular green – and were very clearly planned, many of those in Midland and southern England are represented by blocks of long, narrow tofts of which at least some do appear to represent the expansion of villages across the strips within former open fields.

There are, however, other forms of landscape planning in the early medieval period. The village of Cottenham, in Cambridgeshire, was referred to above as an example of an eighth-century settlement with a clearly planned layout. A distinctive element of its plan, however, is its radial layout, which, although not common, is found elsewhere. At Shoebury, in southern Essex – well outside the 'Central Province' – the historic landscape has a distinctive radial layout that can be firmly dated to the early medieval period. It overlies and is on a different orientation from an extensive late Romano-British field system the ditches of which have 'Early Saxon' pottery in their upper fills, whereas the eleventh-century (or earlier) manorial complex at North Shoebury clearly fits into – and clearly post-dates – the radial layout.[94] At nearby Clements Park[95] no Romano-British features were recorded across an extensive excavation, suggesting that the area was open, unenclosed pasture; but an extensive fifth- to sixth- (or possibly seventh-)century settlement was on a different orientation to the historic landscape,[96] suggesting a seventh-century or later date for its radial layout. At Great Wakering

---

[94] Rippon 1991; Wymer and Brown 1995; Rippon *et al.* 2015.
[95] In the grey literature report (Wessex Archaeology 2007) referred to in Rippon *et al.* 2015, the site was called the B&Q/Comet Site.
[96] Chaffey *et al.* 2013.

church a number of Late Iron Age and early Roman ditches were on a different orientation to the historic landscape, whereas the boundary complex associated with an eighth-century minster church conforms to the layout of the historic landscape.[97] It has always been thought that there was very little open-field arable in the south-east of Essex,[98] although early maps of this Shoebury landscape reveal many examples of long, narrow fields with a reversed-S plan.[99] Along with a series of closely spaced medieval ditches *c.*6m apart and containing a few sherds of 'Saxon' and twelfth-/thirteenth-century pottery that were excavated at Milton Close, south of Great Wakering village,[100] this is suggestive of former open-field land. The way that the copyhold lands in North Shoebury Hall[101] were scattered across the northern part of the parish, and included a number of the long, narrow fields, may reflect enclosure by agreement of tenants' strips that had been scattered across open field. The survey of the Manor of Wakering Hill in 1598 includes a field-name 'Furlongs al[ia]s forlands'.[102]

To the north of Shoebury, between the Roach and the Crouch estuaries, a second radial arrangement of roads and fields is preserved in the historic landscape that is morphologically identical to that at Shoebury[103] and can now be dated to the post-Roman period, as the late fourth-century enclosure complex at Bray's Lane in Rochford is on a different orientation.[104]

Another field system that may have been laid out in a radial fashion can be identified to the east of Cuton Hall in Springfield, near Chelmsford in Essex (Figure 1.3). This provides the context for the well-known Late Saxon settlement excavated at Springfield Lyons and, although the published report does little to contextualise the site,[105] a series of more recent evaluations have shed important light on the surrounding landscape.[106] To the west of the Late Saxon settlement

---

[97] Dale *et al.* 2010.

[98] e.g. Martin and Satchell 2008, 225; Hall 2014, 258–61.

[99] e.g. east of Beauchamps in Shopland on the estate map of 1755 (Essex Record Office, D/DU 628/1), and on the first edition Ordnance Survey (1873) map south of Winter's in Great Wakering and south of Crouchmans in North Shoebury.

[100] Reidy 1997.

[101] Essex Record Office, D/DU 663/3.

[102] Essex Record Office, T/Z 38/67.

[103] Rippon 1991.

[104] Miciak and Atkinson 2014.

[105] Tyler and Major 2005.

[106] Pocock 2006; Robertson 2006; Ennis 2012; 2013; 2014.

there is broad correspondence between Bronze Age, Romano-British and Late Saxon ditches, all broadly orientated north-north-east to south-south-west, while to the east of the settlement a series of Late Saxon ditches forms a group of narrow strip-like fields laid out between long, curving and broadly east–west boundaries that survived in the historic landscape into the twentieth century. The latter has the appearance of an open field, like that at Shoebury.

It is likely that early medieval planning techniques used in England included the construction of sub-circular and polygonal forms by surveying radii outwards from a central point – a technique certainly used in later medieval France.[107] This is probably the explanation for a number of Anglo-Saxon minster enclosures, and some secular ones perhaps modelled on them, that take a basically circular form but with the perimeter formed of short straight lengths.[108] The practice may originate in Irish conceptions of concentric sacred space, and is essentially different from the rectilinear modes explored by the present project.

That finally brings us to another very important group of planned villages, mentioned several times already: those comprising distinctive rows of long narrow plots that are found across northern England (e.g. Figure 3.7)[109] and have often been ascribed to replanning following William I's Harrying of the North in 1069–70.[110] This has traditionally been seen as a 'cataclysmic' event,[111] 'perhaps the most destructive single campaign in England's history'.[112] It is widely thought to have been the cause of the many references in Domesday Book to 'waste'. This has been challenged on the grounds of the disorganisation, inconsistency and incompleteness of the Domesday folios on Yorkshire,[113] although other historians continue to argue that Domesday does indeed record very widespread devastation.[114] It is true that the distribution of places that Domesday records as 'waste' bears little resemblance to the probable routes taken by the Norman armies, being focused instead around the upland fringes.[115] It

---

[107] Querrien 2008.

[108] Blair 2018, 143–8.

[109] Sheppard 1966; 1973; 1974; 1976; Allerston 1970; Harvey 1981; 1983; Roberts 1987, 84; 2008, 188–222; Aalen 2006, 71, 203, 207–8.

[110] The following is a summary of Creighton and Rippon 2017.

[111] Roberts and Wrathmell 2002, 12.

[112] McCord and Thompson 1998, 22.

[113] Palliser 1993; Dalton 1994, 23–5.

[114] Palmer 1998.

[115] Darby 1962, figs 131–2; 1977, fig. 83; Palliser 1993, 10–12.

has also been argued that 'small companies of soldiers were the means to subdue or empty' the countryside, which is why there are not particular concentrations of 'waste' along the probable routes taken by William's army.[116] It is possible that this spatial patterning indicates that the 'waste' was at most an indirect result of the Harrying, caused perhaps by the depopulation of upland areas in order to recolonise more productive lowland estates.[117]

Archaeologically, the hypothesis that regular row-plan villages were created as areas wasted during the Harrying of the North were recolonised has proved difficult to test. Settlement nucleation and the laying out of more compact and structured villages do appear to pre-date the Conquest in some parts of northern England – for example, at Wharram Percy[118] – but there is currently no evidence for regular row-plan layouts at that date. There have been a significant number of excavations within row-plan villages, but in most cases there is very little evidence for eleventh- to early twelfth-century activity – usually just a few sherds of unstratified or residual pottery – and the villages in their present-day form can be dated only to the later twelfth or thirteenth centuries.[119] Elsewhere, the dating evidence points to an origin somewhere within the twelfth century, although it is impossible to be more precise.[120] Indeed, while bearing in mind the usual focus of excavations upon houses as opposed to whole tofts, the limited stratigraphy that is found within rural settlements, the poor preservation of the earliest phases and the very limited amount of Saxo-Norman pottery that appears on rural sites in this region, it is striking just how slight the evidence is for pre-Conquest occupation beneath these row-plan villages (where the earliest stratified phases are associated with twelfth-century pottery rather than Saxo-Norman wares). The absence of evidence for a major episode of burning within the early phases of these villages may also be significant, although if

[116] Palmer 1998, 264.

[117] Bishop 1948; cf. Palmer 1998, 264–5.

[118] Wrathmell 2012.

[119] e.g. Kilton (Daniels 1990); Thrislington (Austin 1989); West Hartburn and Thornton (County Durham) (Pallister and Wrathmell 1990; Vyner 2003); Wawne, Cowlam, Sherburn and Sprotbrough (Yorkshire) (Wilson and Hurst 1962–3, 343–5; Hayfield 1984; Brewster and Hayfield 1994; Fenton-Thomas 2007); West Whelpington (Northumberland) (Evans and Jarrett 1987).

[120] e.g. Castle Eden (County Durham) (Austin 1987); Tollesby, Skelton, Long Marston and High Worsall (Yorkshire) (Heslop and Aberg 1990; Screeton 2001; Sherlock 2004; Daniels 2009).

row-plan villages did replace settlements destroyed in the Harrying of the North they could have been rebuilt in different locations.

Overall, the archaeological evidence for the relationship between regular row-plan villages and the Harrying of the North remains inconclusive. While some row-plan villages could date to the first half of the twelfth century, others appear to be later. Rather than a coherent and rapid replanning of the landscape in the wake of the Harrying, it is more likely that they represent the emergence of a regionally distinctive tradition of settlement morphology that developed throughout the twelfth century and was used over a long period of time (and so was potentially in response to the regular devastations that the north of England experienced). The relative uniformity of the village plan may reflect the involvement of experienced surveyors, or the northern English equivalent of *locatores* (colonists/village planners) that are known to have been employed in mainland Europe and in areas of Anglo-Norman Flemish colonisation such as Pembrokeshire.[121]

Conclusion

There has been much debate about the origins of villages and open fields, with a series of paradigm shifts: from the conception that this approach towards structuring the countryside was introduced by Anglo-Saxon immigrants in the fifth and sixth centuries through an 'evolutionary' model with a very late (post-Conquest) date for the development of open fields and nucleated villages to the 'great replanning' and 'village moment' of the Middle and Late Saxon periods respectively. The recent work of Williamson and his colleagues rejects the idea that there was significant planning in the early medieval landscape, returns to a post-Conquest date for village origins and the laying out of open fields and argues that the regularity in village plans results from their having spread across open-field strips and furlongs. It does seem to be the case that the 'great replanning' hypothesis of 'a total reorganisation of almost the entire landscape'[122] took the argument too far, as even Taylor – a great proponent of a planned origin for villages – found evidence for regular arrangements in only 23 per cent of Northamptonshire's villages. There has also been a tendency to apply the evidence from Northamptonshire right across England's 'Central Province' in the form

[121] Rippon 2008, 227–49.
[122] Brown and Foard 1998, 67.

of a universal model, whereas in practice it is likely that the evolution of settlement and field systems will have proceeded at different paces in different regions: we should not take the 'Northamptonshire' model and apply it uncritically elsewhere, but equally we should not take evidence from regions such as Whittlewood – that were physically marginal and so not typical of adjacent lower-lying areas – and apply that to other areas either.

Notwithstanding all the reservations, there is little doubt that in some favoured settlement areas there was indeed a scattered Early–Middle Saxon settlement pattern that was eventually abandoned in favour of living within nucleated settlements. It is also increasingly clear that a significant proportion of our currently occupied medieval villages have evidence for settlement dating back to the Middle Saxon period. While in some cases the form of that occupation may have been less structured than was later to be the case, there are a growing number of instances in which the initial Middle Saxon phases of occupation show some of the characteristics of a village, such as the structured division of space. The 'great replanning' model also suggested large-scale reorganisation of the arable land and, while the mapping of field systems across the whole of Northamptonshire reveals that they are present in only about 16 per cent of parishes, the argument that even these 'long furlong' landscapes could have developed in a piecemeal fashion is not convincing.

For the purposes of the present investigation, the message we take from this recent work is that there is indeed evidence for planning in the layout of both settlements and field systems in early medieval England, but that the planning was both more varied and less comprehensive than some scholars have argued. The hypothesis of technically precise grid-planning introduces a hitherto unsuspected factor, and we now turn to exploring its possibilities.

Chapter 3

Identifying planning in the early medieval landscape

THE IDENTIFICATION of grid-based planning in the early medieval landscape required an interdisciplinary approach, combining a broad assessment of its possible extent across England as a whole with detailed investigation of sites where it has been found. It is also important to adopt a consistent approach, applying the same criteria to all sites and investigating regions with equal thoroughness, whether or not they were already perceived to contain grid-planned sites.

The first stage was therefore a rapid assessment of the geographical extent of potential grid-based planning using a dataset of uniform quality across all England: the later nineteenth-century first edition Ordnance Survey maps. This stage used GIS (Geographical Information Systems) to examine the morphology of all settlements identifiable as medieval parochial centres in order to identify those places that may have been laid out using a grid.

The second stage was to investigate the possible examples of gridded settlements more thoroughly, using a wider range of source material. Although nineteenth-century Ordnance Survey maps have been used extensively in landscape research, including Brian Roberts and Stuart Wrathmell's *Atlas of Rural Settlement in England*,[1] it must be remembered that they reflect the character of the landscape at the time of their compilation: settlement morphology may or may not have been similar in the medieval period. The potential problems in trying to understand village histories from nineteenth-century maps have been explored as part of the Whittlewood Project, an examination of a series of parishes on the Buckinghamshire/Northamptonshire border.[2] For six villages the available evidence included both extensive

[1] Roberts and Wrathmell 2000; 2002.
[2] Jones and Page 2006; Page and Jones 2007.

cartographic and documentary sources and archaeological fieldwork, including test pitting, that allowed areas of medieval and later occupation to be mapped. Within three parishes (Leckhampstead, Silverstone and Whittlebury) the village plan was found to have been broadly stable from the Middle Ages to the nineteenth century, with periodic expansion and contraction occurring within the same basic framework. In contrast, the evidence in the other three cases suggested that there had been important changes in the village plan of which there was no indication on the nineteenth-century maps. At Akeley, for example, it was realised that a road linking two parts of the village is not medieval, and, although this does not profoundly alter the interpretation of this settlement as a polyfocal village, it does remind us that even major elements of a village plan can be relatively recent. The extent to which the layout of Lillingstone Lovell village was reorganised, including the complete abandonment of a manorial complex, was similarly unsuspected. At Wicken the changes were even more profound: while the eighteenth and nineteenth centuries saw considerable stability in the village plan, the tenth to sixteenth centuries witnessed major changes that could not have been predicted from the early Ordnance Survey maps, including its fission into two separate manorial and parochial centres and a later reamalgamation into a single village. The careful integration of archaeological, cartographic and documentary evidence with morphological analysis in these six villages has therefore shown that while nineteenth-century maps are usually a good guide to the broad character of medieval settlement patterns – whether nucleated or dispersed – they can hide a long history of change within the individual components of the village plan.

For this project, therefore, a wide range of source material was gathered for each of the potentially gridded villages identified in Stage 1 of this study (see below), with the aim of shedding light on the pre-nineteenth-century settlement plan. In this second stage four sources, where available, were consulted for each village: LiDAR; early aerial photographs; pre-nineteenth-century maps; and features recorded in excavations. The first two sources reveal elements of the earlier village plan that had gone out of use before the nineteenth-century Ordnance Survey maps were drawn up but which are preserved as earthworks. With all these sources the aim was to see whether they revealed any components of the village plan that had been abandoned, and so were not shown on the Ordnance Survey maps. If such features were on the same orientation or alignment as the gridded elements this would reinforce the interpretation of these villages as planned, whereas if these earlier features were on a different orientation/alignment it might weaken the hypothesis of grid-based planning.

The third stage explored the extent to which this distribution of potentially gridded villages evident on the nineteenth-century mapping reflects their distribution in the early medieval period. While the work carried out at Stage 2 was important for understanding individual settlement histories, it did nothing to confirm whether the overall distribution of grid-based settlement planning established in Stage 1 was reliable: it is quite possible that a village plan was initially laid out based upon a grid, but that subsequent evolution had completely obscured that evidence for planning by the nineteenth century. To assess the reliability of the Stage 1 distribution map, a sample of village plans that did not appear to have been gridded according to the map evidence was therefore explored in the same way as the gridded settlements in Stage 2.

The fourth stage of the project was to explore villages that were severely shrunken or deserted by the time of the nineteenth-century Ordnance Survey mapping, but preserved as the earthworks of 'deserted medieval villages' (DMVs). There is no single archive of DMV earthwork plans, so a sample was investigated through the published literature. The earthworks of DMVs relate mostly to the latest phases of occupation, which in many cases will be late medieval or early post-medieval in date. They also typically comprise spread and eroded banks and hollow-ways, without clear edges suitable for precise metrical analysis. For both these reasons, village earthworks on their own proved to be of limited value for these purposes.

The fifth stage involved the assessment of excavated features that appear to belong to grid-based layouts but which have left no trace in the post-medieval landscape and do not relate to grid-based settlements identified from map evidence. Some of these sites (for instance, Stratton near Biggleswade) were first identified as part of John Blair's (2013) initial work, but more were identified during the present project (for instance, Catholme and Brandon). In some cases it was possible for separate phases to be disaggregated. This demonstrates the existence – possibly widespread across eastern England – of grid-planned sites for which no evidence remains above ground.

The sixth stage was to explore the early medieval landownership of each settlement with a potentially grid-based plan. Usually there is no evidence for who owned places before Domesday Book (1086), although in a few cases earlier documentary evidence – notably charters – does reveal something of early medieval ownership. Where this analysis revealed that certain major landowners – all ecclesiastical, including

Peterborough, Ely and Ramsey – held potentially grid-planned villages, the other properties of those landowners were identified and those villages re-examined to see whether evidence for grid-based planning – missed during the initial assessment – would emerge on closer scrutiny. Reassuringly, this exercise revealed only two new potential examples of gridding, at Exning in Suffolk (Ely property) and Ringstead in Norfolk (Ramsey property), and we feel that it was worthwhile methodologically.

Finally, in the seventh stage, we specifically targeted some places based on their known origins or character – major monastic sites, emporia and places listed in the Burghal Hidage – to look for evidence of grid-planning. This paid dividends at the Northumbrian royal centre of Yeavering – where grid-based planning was recognised for the first time on this crucially important site – whereas it was absent at a range of other places (most notably the Burghal Hidage forts, where we were expecting to find it). Work such as this, leading to an understanding of where grid-planning is *not* found, has helped to clarify the social context in which it was used.

During each stage, the three authors of this book spent many hours debating difficult cases, sometimes heatedly. We all came to realise that there is subjectivity and variation in what the eye sees. Some of us privileged the underlying traces of potentially earlier phases over the dominant structure of the village, others less so. All of us, at various times, accepted with reluctance the inclusion or rejection of examples. The three of us, however, assented to each decision, and we stand confidently by the stronger cases. In a pioneer study it seemed best to err on the side of caution: we acknowledge that we may well have rejected cases that, with new evidence or even seen by different pairs of eyes, will be regarded as grid-planned in the future. All sites and buildings for which we collectively believe that a reasonable case can be made are included in the catalogue at the end of this book (Appendix C).

Mapping the data: the GIS

Central to the research was the creation of a GIS (using ArcGIS software) within which the various datasets could be related to each other. This was based upon modern Ordnance Survey mapping (from Edina Digimap), and first edition Ordnance Survey six- and 25-inch to the mile map sheets (also from Edina Digimap). The data were supplied as GIS-ready tiles which were combined into mosaic datasets in the GIS so that the maps for each county could be viewed as a single entity. These were overlain with county and parish boundaries transcribed from the tithe surveys of *c.*1840 by Kain and Oliver[3] and digitised by the Department of Geography at the University of Portsmouth.[4] The available raw 1-m resolution LiDAR data (supplied by the Environment Agency) was processed to create a shaded hillslope model and added to the GIS for the villages that appear to have been based upon a gridded plan.

Building the database

A Microsoft Excel spreadsheet was used to record data for each village that appeared to show evidence for grid-based planning. This included a note of whether there is LiDAR data, whether any pre-nineteenth-century maps were identified and whether there have been any excavations within the village core; early aerial photographs at the Historic England Archive (formerly the National Monuments Record) in Swindon were consulted for all suspected places. Where these sources existed, a note was also made in the database as to whether they revealed any features that conform to the grid first identified on the first edition Ordnance Survey mapping, or any features that do not conform. These new data then formed the basis for a second grading of the evidence for grid-based planning within each village. The original assessment – based purely upon an assessment of the first edition Ordnance Survey mapping – was, however, retained, as that was the only source that is available for all villages and therefore the only assessment that is based upon consistent source material.

Stage 1: establishing the extent of grid-based planning

In order to explore the extent to which settlements appear to have been laid out according to grid-based planning, a rapid assessment was carried out of all rural settlements associated with parish/township churches across the whole of England based upon the first edition Ordnance Survey six- and 25-inch mapping (Figure 3.1). At this stage the aim was simply to identify settlements that may originally have been laid out using a grid, irrespective of the module(s) potentially used, although a grid based upon modules of four short perches was used as a starting point because this has previously been identified by John Blair as prevalent during the early medieval period (Figures 3.2–3.3).[5] This grid

---

[3] Kain and Oliver 1995; 2001.
[4] Southall and Burton 2004.
[5] Blair 2013.

was created in the GIS in such a way that it could be superimposed over the first edition Ordnance Survey mapping and rotated as required. The GIS-based grid could also be resized to best fit on a case-by-case basis, and the dimensions of the grid recorded. Each settlement was attributed to one of four types, three of which were nucleated (including two planned forms).

Type I: potentially grid-based settlements
Identified on the basis of their regular morphology, with elements (roads, property boundaries and buildings) at right angles to each other and based on a grid of squares. Elements of this grid-planning were also sometimes fossilised in the surrounding pattern of fields. There were four categories of confidence, based upon the evidence on the first edition Ordnance Survey mapping (Table 3.1):

1. Probable: strong evidence of gridding, with numerous components conforming, and many of the elements that do not conform appearing to be later. These include roads that have clearly been diverted, as they run across the grain of earlier property boundaries, areas of parkland inserted within villages and areas of nineteenth-century housing development, all of which can be thought of as 'foreground noise' that should not distract from the underlying regular plan in the background (e.g. Hempsted: Figure 3.4).[6]

2. Plausible: some evidence of gridding, but with many components on different alignments and so not conforming (e.g. Great Hale: Figure 3.5).

3. Possible: some components perpendicular to each other and regularly spaced, within a village plan of predominantly irregular layout that could represent a heavily degraded grid-based plan (e.g. Stow: Figure 3.6).

4. Not categorised: for some other villages we debated energetically whether there was sufficient evidence to suggest grid-based planning, but on balance it was decided that these cases were not strong enough to be regarded as even 'possible'.

In total, 9 settlements are Category 1 (probable), 34 Category 2 (plausible), and 33 Category 3 (possible). Although further work was

---

[6] The most detailed example of village plan analysis is Shapwick in Somerset: Gerrard with Aston 2007; Aston and Gerrard 2013.

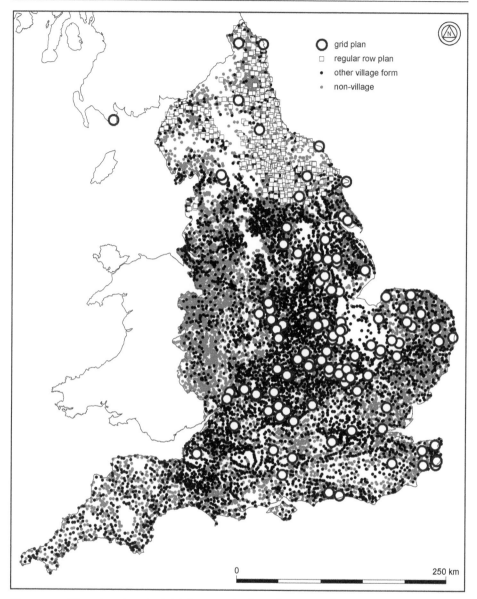

Figure 3.1. Map showing the initial categorisation of nineteenth-century settlement morphology undertaken by the *Planning in the Early Medieval Landscape* project, based on first edition OS 25-inch maps.

carried out on all Category 1–3 village plans using a variety of other sources (see Stage 2 below), a record of the initial grading was kept in the database.

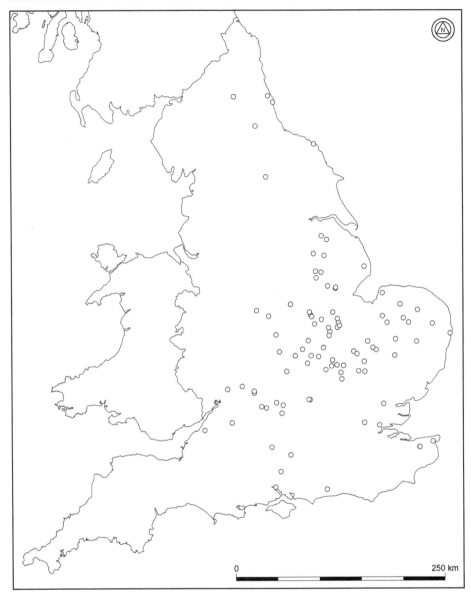

Figure 3.2. Map showing the distribution of potentially gridded places identified by John Blair in his initial work (see Blair 2013) and prior to the beginning of the *Planning in the Early Medieval Landscape* project.

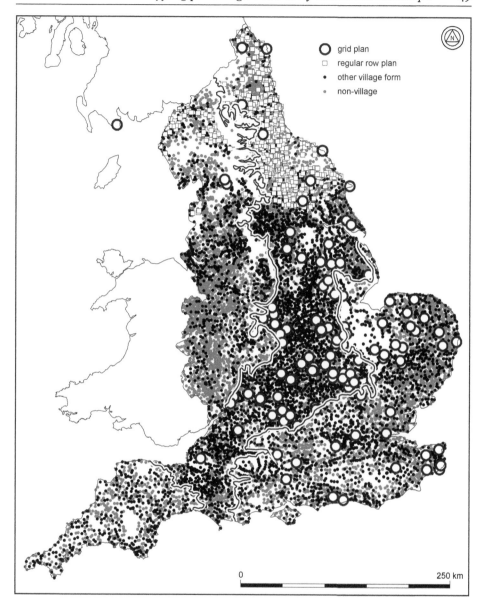

Figure 3.3. Map showing the project's initial categorisation of nineteenth-century settlement morphology (based on first edition OS 25-inch maps) and the 'Central Province' proposed by Roberts and Wrathmell (after Roberts and Wrathmell 2000, fig. 1).

Table 3.1. List of places where evidence of early medieval gridding has been identified

Place-name	County	Settlement or building
Clapham	Bedfordshire	Settlement (extant)
Howbury, Renhold	Bedfordshire	Settlement (excavation only)
Kempston Up End	Bedfordshire	Settlement (extant)
Northill	Bedfordshire	Settlement (extant)
Podington	Bedfordshire	Settlement (extant)
Stotfold	Bedfordshire	Settlement (excavation only)
Stratton, Biggleswade	Bedfordshire	Settlement (excavation only)
Tempsford/Tempsford Park	Bedfordshire	Settlement (extant)
Wrestlingworth	Bedfordshire	Settlement (extant)
Marcham	Berkshire	Settlement (extant)
Stoke Mandeville	Buckinghamshire	Settlement (extant)
Walton, Aylesbury	Buckinghamshire	Settlement (excavation only)
West Fen Road, Ely	Cambridgeshire	Settlement (excavation only)
Fen Drayton	Cambridgeshire	Settlement (extant)
Fordham	Cambridgeshire	Settlement (extant)
Gamlingay	Cambridgeshire	Settlement (extant)
Hinxton	Cambridgeshire	Settlement (extant)
Isleham	Cambridgeshire	Settlement (extant)
Steeple Morden	Cambridgeshire	Settlement (extant)
Hartshorn	Derbyshire	Settlement (extant)
Repton	Derbyshire	Settlement (excavation only)
Whithorn	Dumfries and Galloway	Settlement (excavation only)
Escomb church	Co Durham	Building (standing)
Horndon on the Hill	Essex	Settlement (extant)
Springfield Lyons	Essex	Settlement (excavation only)
Bishop's Norton	Gloucestershire	Settlement (extant)
Bourton on the Water	Gloucestershire	Settlement (extant)
Hempsted	Gloucestershire	Settlement (extant)

	C19 settlement plan				
Grading based on 1st edn OS	Contribution of excavated evidence	Contribution of aerial photos	Contribution of pre-1st edn OS maps	Contribution of LiDAR	Final grade
2	No	No	No	Slight	B
n/a					B
2	Moderate	Moderate	No	No	B
2	No	No	No	Strong	B
3	No	No	No	No	C
n/a					A
n/a					A
2	Strong	No	No	No	A
3	No	No	No	No	C
3	No	Moderate	No	Slight	B
2	No	No	No	No	B
n/a					B
n/a					A
3	No	Moderate	No	No	C
2	Strong	Slight	Moderate	No	A
3	Slight	Moderate	No	No	C
3	Complicated and await publication	Slight	Slight	No	C
1	Moderate	No	Strong	Strong	A
2	No	Slight	No	No	B
1	No	Moderate	No	No	A
n/a					B
n/a					C
n/a					A
2	No	No	No	No	B
n/a					A
3	No	No	No	No	C
2	No	No	No	No	B
1	No	Slight	No	No	A

Table 3.1. *continued*

Place-name	County	Settlement or building
Lower Slaughter	Gloucestershire	Settlement (extant)
Winchcombe	Gloucestershire	Settlement (extant)
Faccombe Netherton	Hampshire	Settlement (excavation only)
Hatch Warren	Hampshire	Settlement (excavation only)
Winchester, Old Minster	Hampshire	Building (excavated)
Westmill	Hertfordshire	Settlement (extant)
Glatton	Huntingdonshire	Settlement (extant)
Orton Longueville, Botolph Bridge	Huntingdonshire	Settlement (excavation only)
Canterbury, St Pancras (St Augustines)	Kent	Building (excavated)
Canterbury, St Peter and St Paul (St Augustines)	Kent	Building (excavated)
Dover	Kent	Building (excavated)
East Langdon	Kent	Settlement (extant)
Lyminge	Kent	Buildings (excavated)
Minster in Thanet	Kent	Settlement (extant)
Staplehurst	Kent	Settlement (extant)
Dadlington	Leicestershire	Settlement (extant)
Desford	Leicestershire	Settlement (extant)
Snarestone	Leicestershire	Settlement (excavation only)
Brant Broughton	Lincolnshire	Settlement (extant)
Candlesby	Lincolnshire	Settlement (extant)
Coleby	Lincolnshire	Settlement (extant)
Goltho	Lincolnshire	Buildings (excavated)
Great Hale	Lincolnshire	Settlement (extant)
Hibaldstow	Lincolnshire	Settlement (extant)
Holton	Lincolnshire	Settlement (extant)
Quarrington	Lincolnshire	Settlement (excavation only)
Stow	Lincolnshire	Settlement (extant)
Welton	Lincolnshire	Settlement (extant)

C19 settlement plan					Final grade
Grading based on 1st edn OS	Contribution of excavated evidence	Contribution of aerial photos	Contribution of pre-1st edn OS maps	Contribution of LiDAR	
3	No	No	No	No	C
2	No	No	No	No	B
n/a					B
n/a					B
n/a					A
2	No	Slight	No	No	B
3	No	No	No	No	C
n/a					B
n/a					A
n/a					B
n/a					B
3	No	Moderate	No	No	C
n/a					A
2	No	No	No	No	B
3	No	No	No	No	C
1	No	No	No	No	A
1	No	No	No	No	A
n/a					B
1	No	Slight	No	Strong	A
2	No	No	No	No	B
3	No	No	No	No	C
n/a					B
2	No	No	No	No	B
3	No	No	No	No	C
2	No	Negative evidence	No	No	C
n/a					C
3	No	Slight	No	No	C
2	Moderate	No	No	No	B

Table 3.1. *continued*

Place-name	County	Settlement or building
Westminster Abbey	London	Building (extant)
Shepperton	Middlesex	Settlement (excavation only)
Attlebridge	Norfolk	Settlement (excavation only)
Bergh/Burgh Apton	Norfolk	Settlement (extant)
Field Dalling	Norfolk	Settlement (extant)
Hingham	Norfolk	Settlement (extant)
Sedgeford	Norfolk	Settlement (extant)
Shipdham	Norfolk	Settlement (extant)
Thetford, Brandon Road	Norfolk	Settlement (excavation only)
Watlington	Norfolk	Settlement (extant)
Whissonsett	Norfolk	Settlement (extant)
Brixworth church	Northamptonshire	Building (standing)
Hackleton	Northamptonshire	Settlement (extant)
Little Brington	Northamptonshire	Settlement (extant)
Little Houghton	Northamptonshire	Settlement (extant)
Peakirk	Northamptonshire	Settlement (extant)
Peterborough	Northamptonshire	Settlement
Polebrook	Northamptonshire	Settlement (excavation only)
Preston Deanery	Northamptonshire	Settlement (earthworks)
Raunds Furnells and Langham Road	Northamptonshire	Settlement (excavation only)
Raunds, West Cotton	Northamptonshire	Settlement (excavated)
Sulgrave	Northamptonshire	Settlement (extant)
Thorpe Mandeville	Northamptonshire	Settlement (extant)
Warmington	Northamptonshire	Settlement (extant)
Beadnall	Northumbria	Settlement (extant)
Hexham	Northumbria	Building (standing)
Yeavering	Northumbria	Building (excavated)
Torworth	Nottinghamshire	Settlement (extant)
Bampton	Oxfordshire	Settlement (extant)
Benson	Oxfordshire	Settlement (extant)

	C19 settlement plan				Final grade
Grading based on 1st edn OS	Contribution of excavated evidence	Contribution of aerial photos	Contribution of pre-1st edn OS maps	Contribution of LiDAR	
n/a					A
n/a					B
n/a					C
3	No	Slight	No	No	C
3	No	Slight	Slight	No	C
3	No	No	No	No	C
3	Slight	Slight	Slight	No	C
2	Strong	Strong	Slight	No	A
n/a					A
1	No	Moderate	Slight	Strong	A
2	Strong	Slight	Slight	No	A
n/a					A
2	No	Moderate	No	Slight	B
2	No	Slight	Moderate	No	B
3	No	No	No	No	C
3	No	No	No	No	C
2	Moderate	No	No	No	A
n/a					B
n/a					B
n/a					A
n/a					A
2	No	No	Slight	No	B
3	No	No	No	No	C
3	No	No	No	No	C
2	No	No	No	No	B
n/a					A
n/a					A
3	No	No	No	No	C
3	No	Slight	No	Slight	C
3	No	No	No	No	C

Table 3.1. *continued*

Place-name	County	Settlement or building
Church Enstone	Oxfordshire	Settlement (extant)
Eynsham	Oxfordshire	Settlement (extant)
Iffley	Oxfordshire	Settlement (extant)
Glaston	Rutland	Settlement (extant)
Ketton Quarry	Rutland	Settlement (excavation only)
Manton	Rutland	Settlement (extant)
Whissendine [east]	Rutland	Settlement (extant)
Whissendine [west]	Rutland	Settlement (extant)
Wing	Rutland	Settlement (extant)
Cheddar	Somerset	Building (excavated)
Catholme	Staffordshire	Settlement (excavation only)
Bloodmoor Hill	Suffolk	Settlement (excavation only)
Brandon	Suffolk	Settlement (excavation only)
Bury St Edmunds	Suffolk	Settlement
Fornham All Saints	Suffolk	Settlement (extant)
Ilketshall St Margaret	Suffolk	Settlement (extant)
Broadwater	Sussex	Settlement (extant)
Burpham	Sussex	Building (excavated)
Fenny Compton	Warwickshire	Settlement (extant)
Wolvey	Warwickshire	Settlement (extant)
Cowage Farm, Bremilham	Wiltshire	Settlement (cropmarks)
Flamborough	Yorkshire (E. Riding)	Settlement (extant)
Keyingham	Yorkshire (E. Riding)	Settlement (extant)
Preston	Yorkshire (E. Riding)	Settlement (extant)
Chapel le Dale	Yorkshire (N. Riding)	Building (excavated)
Clapham Bottoms	Yorkshire (N. Riding)	Building (excavated)
Dunnington	Yorkshire (N. Riding)	Settlement (extant)
Great Habton	Yorkshire (N. Riding)	Settlement (extant)
Kirk Smeaton	Yorkshire (N. Riding)	Settlement (extant)
Whitby	Yorkshire (N. Riding)	Settlement (excavation only)
Hooton Roberts	Yorkshire (W. Riding)	Settlement (extant)

C19 settlement plan					Final grade
Grading based on 1st edn OS	Contribution of excavated evidence	Contribution of aerial photos	Contribution of pre-1st edn OS maps	Contribution of LiDAR	
1	No	No	No	No	A
2	Strong	No	No	No	A
3	No	Slight	No	No	C
2	Moderate	No	No	No	B
	n/a				B
3	No	No	No	No	C
3	Moderate	No	No	No	B
2	No	No	No	No	B
2	No	No	No	No	B
	n/a				B
	n/a				A
	n/a				C
	n/a				A
3	n/a	n/a	n/a	n/a	C
3	No	No	No	No	C
2	No	Moderate	No	Slight	B
1	No	No	No	No	A
	n/a				B
3	No	No	No	No	C
3	No	No	Slight	No	C
	n/a				A
2	No	Slight	Moderate	No	B
2	No	Moderate	Moderate	No	B
3	No	No	No	No	C
	n/a				B
	n/a				B
2	No	Slight	No	No	B
2	No	No	No	No	B
2	No	No	No	No	B
	n/a				B
2	No	No	No	No	B

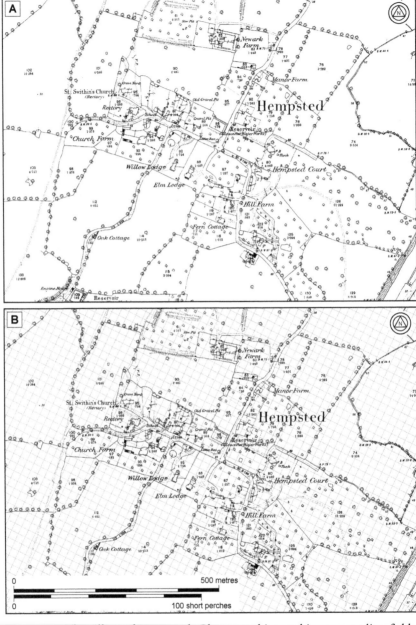

Figure 3.4. The village of Hempsted, Gloucestershire, and its surrounding fields.
A: The late nineteenth-century landscape (first edition OS 25-inch base map:
© Crown Copyright and Landmark Information Group Limited (2016), all
rights reserved, 1884).
B: The late nineteenth-century landscape overlain with a grid of four short
perches. The high degree on conformity of components of the village with
the proposed grid has ranked this example as a Category 1 site.

Figure 3.5. The village of Great Hale, Lincolnshire, and its surrounding fields.
A: The late nineteenth-century landscape (first edition OS 25-inch base map:
© Crown Copyright and Landmark Information Group Limited (2016), all
rights reserved, 1889).
B: The late nineteenth-century landscape overlain with a grid of four short
perches. The moderate degree on conformity of components of the village
with the proposed grid has ranked this example as a Category 2 site.

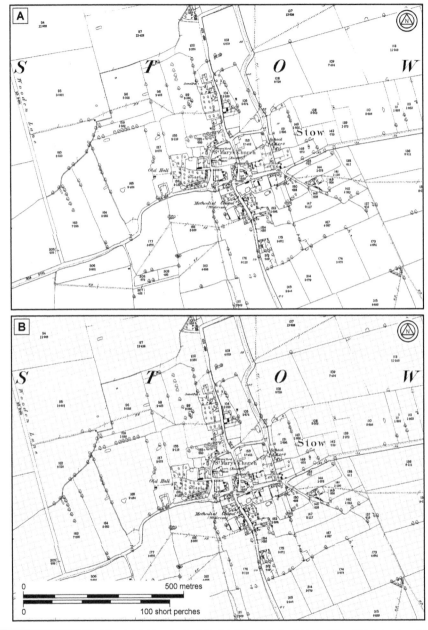

Figure 3.6. The village of Stow, Lincolnshire, and its surrounding fields.
    A: The late nineteenth-century landscape (first edition OS 25-inch base map:
    © Crown Copyright and Landmark Information Group Limited (2016), all
    rights reserved, 1886).
    B: The late nineteenth-century landscape overlain with a grid of four short
    perches. The lesser degree on conformity of components of the village with
    the proposed grid has ranked this example as a Category 3 site.

Type II: regular row-plan villages

This distinctive form of planned settlement, found extensively across the north of England (e.g. Carthorpe: Figure 3.7). Traditionally they have been attributed to the post-Harrying of the North recolonisation, although an assessment of recent excavations suggest that they represent a long-lived way of planning new settlements that continued into the late twelfth and the thirteenth centuries (see Chapter 2). The character-defining feature of these villages is a series of tightly packed houses facing onto a straight stretch of road or rectangular green (although there are some polygonal row-plan villages with, for example, three rows of tenements around a triangular green). Buildings are typically placed with their long axis facing onto the road/green (although there are a few examples where buildings are placed with their gable-ends facing the street/green in order to face south). This is, therefore, a much narrower definition of 'row-plan' than Brian Roberts uses in *Making of the English Village*[7] (which includes any settlement that is strung along a principal road or roads), but corresponds to his 'regular row-plan' form.

Type III: nucleated settlement with no evidence of grid-based planning

It was important to map these villages in order to determine whether the distribution of potentially grid-based settlements simply reflects that of nucleated villages as a whole, or whether they are found only in parts of the areas across which villages were common. This proved to be an important exercise, since potentially grid-based plans do indeed have a more restricted distribution than that of all nucleated villages.

Type IV: no nucleated settlement at the parish centre

Not surprisingly, these were predominantly found in the South East, the South West and the West of England, reflecting the dispersed settlement patterns of these regions, although there are examples in areas with large numbers of nucleated villages that reflect desertion or severe shrinkage in specific cases. In East Anglia another process was at work: the migration of settlement away from parish churches and towards commons that started in the tenth century and continued into the twelfth. This was a piecemeal process, and no evidence for grid-based planning is found in these sprawling green-side villages.[8]

This work was carried out before the various examples originally identified by Blair[9] (largely based upon excavated settlements and a few

[7] Roberts 1987.
[8] e.g. Wade-Martins 1980; Davison 1990; Davison *et al.* 1993.
[9] Blair 2013.

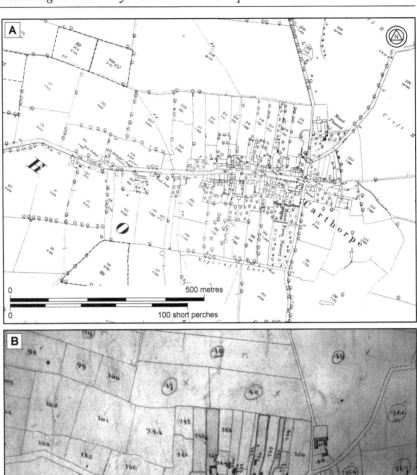

Figure 3.7. The 'row-plan' village of Carthorpe, North Yorkshire, and its surrounding fields.

A: The late nineteenth-century landscape (first edition OS 25-inch base map: © Crown Copyright and Landmark Information Group Limited (2016), all rights reserved, 1892).

B: The 1839 parish tithe map (© North Yorkshire County Record Office ref. PR/BUE 11/2/2; photograph by C. Smart).

possible examples identified on first edition Ordnance Survey maps) were plotted, in order to avoid biasing the investigation towards areas already perceived to be rich in grid-planned sites. When plotted on a single map, the distribution of settlement Types I–III (the nucleated forms) was found – not surprisingly – to show some correspondence with England's 'Central Province' as mapped by Roberts and Wrathmell (Figure 3.3). The distribution of potentially gridded villages (Category 1), however, shows that they are not found across the whole of the 'Central Province', being mostly in eastern and central England (a distribution that corresponds to the excavated examples: see below). It must be stressed that this mapping gives a *minimum* extent of early medieval gridded settlements: there are likely to be cases of villages initially laid out on a grid where all evidence of regularity has been lost during a thousand years or more of landscape change, or as a result of severe shrinkage or desertion of the village. An attempt to assess the extent to which this was the case was carried out in Stage 3 (below).

Stage 2: exploring the plans of potentially grid-based settlements

The next stage was to explore the plans of the potentially gridded settlements more thoroughly, using the four separate datasets described below.

LiDAR
The Environment Agency supplied the project with 1-m resolution raw LiDAR data for all areas where it exists, although unfortunately it does not cover all places of interest. For each potentially gridded place where 1-m LiDAR exists the data have been modelled to create a shaded terrain model that was overlain on the first edition Ordnance Survey mapping. Initially, it was hoped that LiDAR would add important information on elements of early village plans that had been abandoned before the nineteenth century but which survive as earthworks, but unfortunately this rarely proved to be the case, as recent housing development has usually destroyed any such evidence. A notable exception was Watlington, where the LiDAR reveals extensive areas of earthworks that conform to the gridded layout of the landscape and supplement components shown on the first edition Ordnance Survey map (Figure 3.8; see Chapter 6). Where any useful information was gained from the LiDAR data, a note was made in the project's database entry for that village.

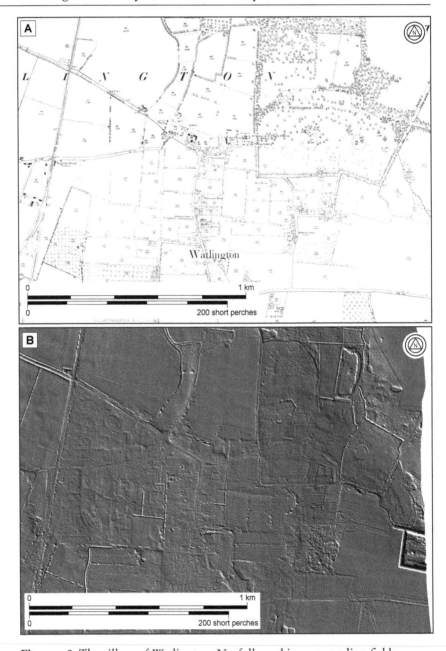

Figure 3.8. The village of Watlington, Norfolk, and its surrounding fields.
A: The late nineteenth-century landscape (first edition OS 25-inch base map:
© Crown Copyright and Landmark Information Group Limited (2016), all
rights reserved, 1885).
B: A hillshade model of 1m resolution LiDAR data for the same area as
shown in A (© Environment Agency copyright and/or database right 2015.
All rights reserved).

C: The late nineteenth-century landscape overlain with a grid of four short perches.

D: The late nineteenth-century landscape overlain with a grid of four short perches and with landscape components and features showing on the LiDAR data that conform to the proposed grid emboldened.

Late 1940s aerial photographs

The vertical aerial photographs taken by the RAF in the late 1940s and 1950s and held at the Historic England Archive (formerly the National Monuments Record) in Swindon were consulted for each of the potentially gridded villages identified in Stage 1 (Categories 1–3). This did reveal a number of examples of earthworks and soilmarks that conform to the gridded village plan and represent features that had gone out of use before the mid-nineteenth century or that have been destroyed through ploughing or housing development since the aerial photographs were taken (e.g. Shipdham: Figure 3.9). Where any useful information was gained from these early aerial photographs, a note was made in the project's database entry for that village.

Pre-nineteenth-century maps

In order to assess any changes to village plans before they were systematically mapped in the nineteenth century an attempt was made to locate any earlier maps of the potentially gridded examples in a sample of counties.[10] While these earlier maps were not necessarily accurately surveyed or proportionately correct in their depiction (e.g. Flamborough: Figure 3.10), they sometimes show features that had disappeared by the time of the first edition Ordnance Survey mapping and allow features that were recent at that point to be eliminated, thus bringing us a little closer to the original village plan. Where any useful information was gained from these early maps, a note was made in the project's database entry for that village. Tracking down the earlier maps of potentially gridded villages, however, proved difficult and not very rewarding. It was found that online catalogues and the A2A website[11] omitted many of the maps preserved in county record offices and other archives, and these required direct contacts to locate them. Where earlier maps were located, most were no earlier than the late eighteenth or early nineteenth century, and only a few examples contained useful information (e.g. Sompting, Figure 6.20). In the light of this somewhat disappointing result, the only further work on pre-Ordnance Survey mapping was carried out where copies of relevant maps were already held by members of the project team and its Advisory Board members.[12]

---

[10] Leicestershire and Rutland, North Yorkshire, East Riding of Yorkshire, Lincolnshire, Bedfordshire, Cambridge, Norfolk, Warwickshire, Derbyshire.

[11] http://discovery.nationalarchives.gov.uk/.

[12] We are grateful to David Hall for sending copies of several maps of Northamptonshire villages.

Evidence from excavations

The published literature, Archaeology Data Service (ADS) Grey Literature Library[13] and the Archaeological Investigations Project (AIP)[14] were searched and reports obtained for all the potentially gridded villages identified in Stage 1 in order to identify the layout of features securely dated to the early medieval period and to determine their relationship to the grid-based layout evident on the first edition Ordnance Survey mapping. A note was also made of features of any period that conformed to the grid (e.g. Shipdham, Figure 3.9; Whissonsett, Figure 3.11), since chronologies in evaluation reports are sometimes open to question: for example, ditches ascribed by excavators to the Roman period on the basis of residual sherds may in fact be early medieval.[15] Many of the clearest excavated cases had already been picked up by Blair (2013).

Regrading of settlements

Having completed the data collection and analysis in Stage 2, the initial grading of villages into Categories 1–3, as proposed in Stage 1, was revised in the light of this new evidence (see Table 3.1 and Appendix C). This provided each potentially gridded village with three classifications: the first (by Arabic numeral) based on the Ordnance Survey evidence alone (since this source is consistent for every place); the second (by bold Roman numeral) giving an assessment of the persuasiveness of excavated evidence (strong, moderate or slight); and the third (by letter) offering an overall assessment that takes into account any LiDAR, early aerial photographs, earlier maps and excavation evidence (in other words, data available for some but not all places). A settlement graded 2/-/A, for example, looked only plausibly gridded on the basis of the Ordnance Survey data alone and provides no excavated evidence, but looks probably gridded when other data (e.g. earthworks and earlier maps) providing further features in conformity with the grid are taken into account. A grade of 3/I/A denotes a place that is only 'possible' on map evidence alone, but raised by excavated evidence into the 'probable' category. A settlement graded 3/-/C, however, still only looks 'possible' after the other data have been taken in account.

---

[13] http://archaeologydataservice.ac.uk/archives/view/greylit/query.cfm.

[14] https://archaeologydataservice.ac.uk/archives/view/aip_he_2018/.

[15] This is discussed in Rippon *et al.* 2015, 109–10, 332–4, particularly the examples of Bishop Burton College and Sleighford.

Figure 3.9. The village of Shipdham, Norfolk, and its surrounding fields.
A: The late nineteenth-century landscape (first edition OS 25-inch base map:
© Crown Copyright and Landmark Information Group Limited (2016), all
rights reserved, 1884).
B: The late nineteenth-century landscape overlain with a grid of four short
perches.
C: A detailed extract from the late nineteenth-century Ordnance Survey
mapping of the south-west side of the village showing the areas excavated

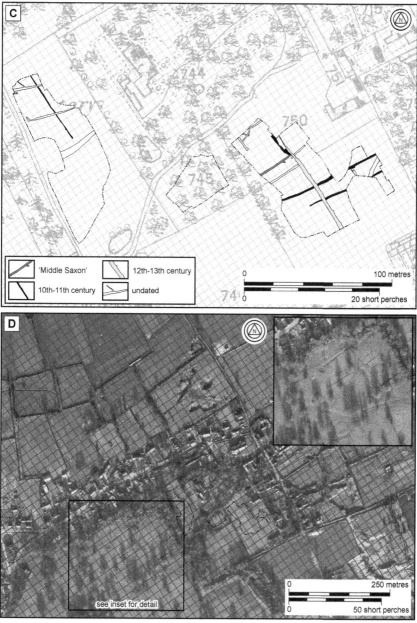

by Norfolk Archaeological Unit and the conformity of Middle Saxon, Late Saxon and post-Conquest ditches to the proposed grid of short perches (after Ames and Phelps 2008, fig. 3; Ames *et al.* 2009, fig. 2).
D: A detailed extract of a 1946 Royal Air Force vertical aerial photograph showing a series of earthwork anomalies on the south-west side of the village which conform to the orientation and positioning of the proposed grid. A grid of four short perches is shown overlaying this photograph (© Historic England: RAF 3G TUD UK 52 V 5143 31 January 1946).

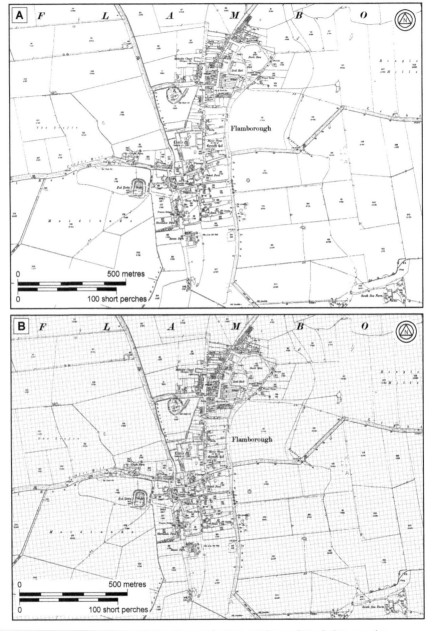

Figure 3.10. The village of Flamborough, East Riding of Yorkshire, and its surrounding fields.

    A: The late nineteenth-century landscape (first edition OS 25-inch base map: © Crown Copyright and Landmark Information Group Limited (2016), all rights reserved, 1891).

    B: The late nineteenth-century landscape overlain with a grid of four short perches.

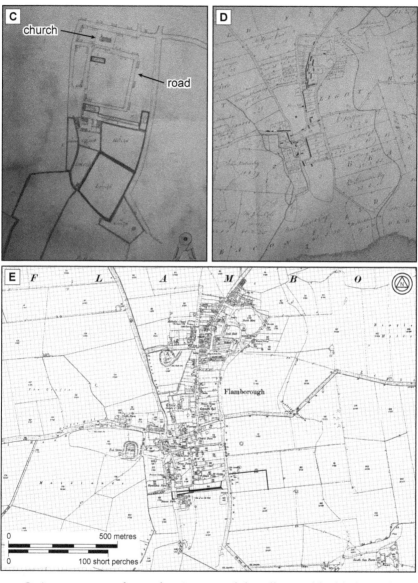

C: An estate map of 1761 showing part of the village and highlighting the position of a presumed cartographic error: the road south-east of the church by Grove Farm is shown on the map has having been aligned with Tower Street directly to the north, whereas the late nineteenth-century Ordnance Survey mapping shows it *c.*70m to the west (© East Riding Archives and Local Studies ref: DDHU/20/1).

D: The parish enclosure map of *c.*1767 showing parts of the village (© East Riding Archives and Local Studies ref: IA/64).

E: The late nineteenth-century landscape with additional boundaries transcribed from the 1767 map, overlain with a grid of four short perches.

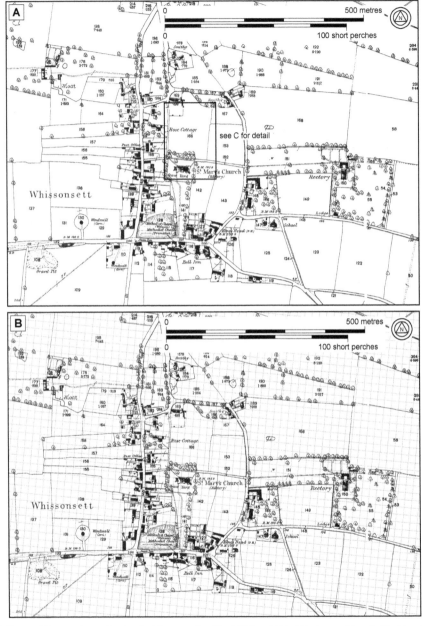

Figure 3.11. The village of Whissonsett, Norfolk, and its surrounding fields.
A: The late nineteenth-century landscape (first edition OS 25-inch base map:
© Crown Copyright and Landmark Information Group Limited (2016), all
rights reserved, 1886).
B: The late nineteenth-century landscape overlain with a grid of four short
perches.

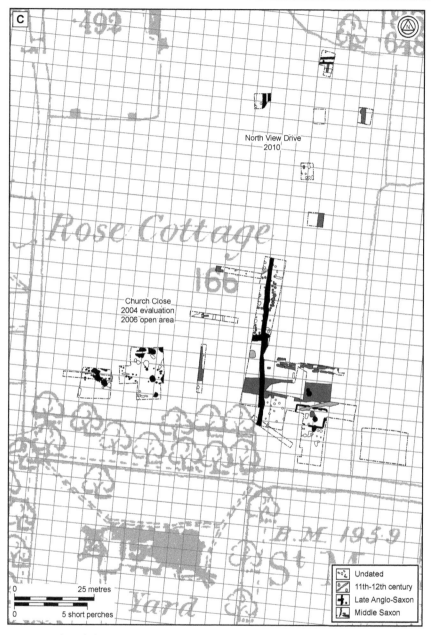

C: A detailed extract from late nineteenth-century Ordnance Survey
mapping of the north-east part of Whissonsett, Norfolk, showing the areas
excavated by Norfolk Archaeological Unit and Archaeological Project
Services and the conformity of Middle Saxon, Late Saxon and possible
post-Conquest ditches to the proposed grid, here shown as a grid of short
perches (after Trimble 2006, figs 3–6; Trimble and Hoggett 2010, figs 2, 3, 6,
11, 13 and 15; Mellor 2004, fig. 4).

Stage 3: the control sample

If a settlement based upon a grid was laid out in, say, the eighth century, and has been continuously occupied ever since, there will have been some 1,200 years of evolution within the village plan that could have erased most or all traces of the original layout. To explore the potential extent of this kind of loss, two lines of enquiry were followed. First, a sample of villages was examined whose nineteenth-century plans (based upon the first edition Ordnance Survey mapping) show no evidence of a grid-based layout but which have seen extensive excavations. This sample – 59 sites – was identified simply by trawling through a sample of published county and period-specific journals in order to provide a representative sample of major excavations within currently occupied village cores.[16] The sample counties examined included those with a significant number of potentially gridded villages (e.g. Cambridgeshire), ones elsewhere within England's 'Central Province' that do not show much evidence for gridding within villages (e.g. Oxfordshire), and some that lie outside the 'Central Province' (e.g. Kent). Secondly, a sample of earlier maps was examined for non-gridded villages in each of the record offices that were visited.

It seems significant that not a single further example of a possibly grid-based village was identified by these means. This might suggest that the total erasure of grid-based layouts by later change and development is not especially common, even though some of our best early examples – such as Ely, Quarrington and Stratton – are illustrations of precisely that process. It is of course possible that a much higher proportion of the post-940 grids than of the pre-800 ones remain perceptible in the modern landscape. It is at any rate reassuring that this exercise did nothing to undermine the hypothesis that the region where a tradition of grid-planning is apparent from nineteenth-century maps is indeed an accurate reflection of that tradition's original extent.

Stage 4: deserted, or severely shrunken, medieval villages (earthwork sites)

A sample of deserted medieval villages preserved as earthworks was also examined, including those that previous studies have suggested

---

[16] In the counties of Buckinghamshire, Cambridgeshire, Gloucestershire, Hertfordshire, Huntingdonshire, Kent, Leicestershire, Norfolk, Northamptonshire, Oxfordshire, Surrey, Sussex, Warwickshire, Worcestershire and Yorkshire.

may have been grid-based. In Northamptonshire, for example, Taylor identified 14 examples that may have involved the use of a grid (although there is little discussion and no illustrations of these).[17] In the West Lindsey district of Lincolnshire, Everson *et al.* suggested that several villages had grid-based plans,[18] but although this could be true in some cases the evidence does not meet the criteria adopted for this project. This may be more a methodological problem than a reflection of reality: the spread banks and relict ditches of earthworks leave too wide a range of interpretation for precise metrical analysis to be very convincing. Just one wholly deserted earthwork site (Preston Deanery: Figure 3.12) has been accepted as providing persuasive evidence for grid-planning.

Stage 5: early medieval settlements (excavated sites)

It was John Blair's recognition that some extensively excavated early medieval settlements have grid-planned layouts that laid the initial groundwork for this project.[19] The original analysis was carried out by simply placing a grid drawn on a sheet of clear film on top of the excavation plans that had been enlarged or reduced to a common scale using a Xerox machine. As part of this present study all these excavated sites were re-examined using the project's GIS, which allowed the excavated features to be placed accurately within the wider context of the nineteenth-century landscape and any features showing on LiDAR, and were graded using bold Roman numerals as described above.

Stage 6: exploring landownership

For places identified in Stage 1 as potentially having an underlying grid (i.e. Categories 1–3), Domesday Book was checked for evidence of proprietorship in 1066 and 1086. While this information was helpful in certain cases (see Figure 6.4), it was overall of less value than might have been hoped. Most of the relevant places are in the East Midlands and East Anglia, where the land market was probably fluid in the late Anglo-Saxon period, and tenure was certainly fragmented. By 1066 many of the grid-planned places were in the hands of minor individuals who may well have played no part in their original

---

[17] Taylor 1983, 133–48.
[18] Above, p. 30 note 71.
[19] Blair 2013.

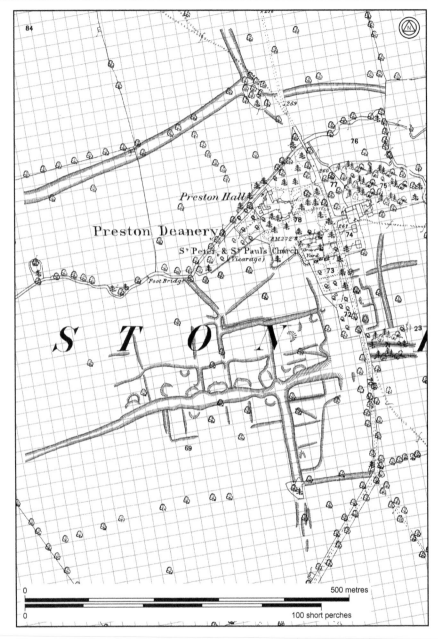

Figure 3.12. The undated earthworks of a deserted settlement at Preston Deanery, Northamptonshire, overlain with a grid of four short perches (after RCHME 1979, fig. 62).

construction. It is only rarely possible to trace their history further back, as those regions of England are also very poorly provided with Anglo-Saxon charters. The only exceptions are properties of a small number of major reformed monasteries – notably Ely, Bury and Peterborough – whose archives survive. So far as it goes, this limited evidence is consistent with the hypothesis of monastic influence in the background of many grid-planned places, although the Domesday data also offer slight suggestions of a correlation with properties of Edward the Confessor's earls.

Stage 7: places of high status

An important exception to this lack of documentation is the category of major monastic sites, both from the first monastic 'golden age' (*c*.660–750) and from the tenth-century Benedictine reform period, several of which were grid-planned. These provide the strongest evidence for the social and cultural contexts of the introduction and revival of the technology, as is explored further in Chapter 5.

Two other categories of site capable of precise definition – the eighth-century commercial emporia and the heterogeneous group of places listed in the Burghal Hidage – were also examined, but with more limited results. The emporium of *Hamwic* shows evidence for the short-perch module and for rectilinear planning of some kind, although that may have been defined in strips rather than squares; in *Lundenwic* the long perch can be identified, but so far no evidence of formal planning (below, Chapter 5). Elements of possible grid-planning were initially proposed in each of the four Burghal Hidage sites that are superficially rectilinear (Wareham, Cricklade, Oxford and Wallingford), but in the end they were all rejected after further analysis and discussion. These results are interesting in themselves: they suggest that the technique was not mainstream practice for all mid- to late Anglo-Saxon construction projects supported by high-level patrons, but was specific to certain kinds of cultural context and probably to specific periods.

Conclusion

The methodology adopted in this study was designed to determine the spatial extent of grid-based planning in the early medieval landscape and then to explore the form that it took in individual villages. The aim was to be systematic and rigorous, in the first instance by carrying out

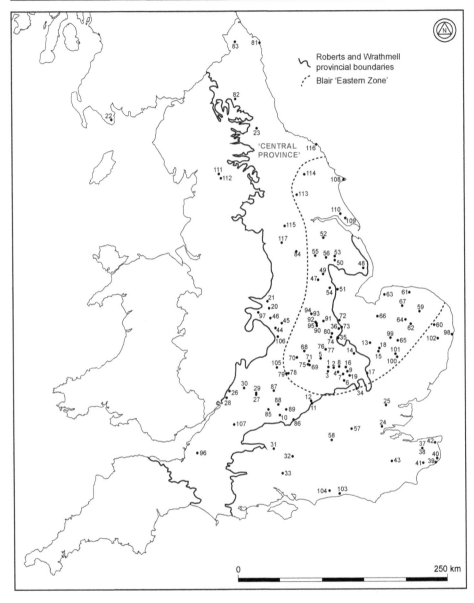

Figure 3.13. Distribution map of all places where the *Planning in the Early Medieval Landscape* project has identified possible grid-planning.

1. Clapham, Bedfordshire
2. Howbury, Renhold, Bedfordshire
3. Kempston Up End, Bedfordshire
4. Northill, Bedfordshire
5. Podington, Bedfordshire
6. Stotfold, Bedfordshire
7. Stratton, Biggleswade, Bedfordshire
8. Tempsford/Tempsford Park, Bedfordshire
9. Wrestlingworth, Bedfordshire
10. Marcham, Berkshire
11. Stoke Mandeville, Buckinghamshire
12. Walton, Aylesbury, Buckinghamshire
13. Ely, West Fen Road, Cambridgeshire
14. Fen Drayton, Cambridgeshire
15. Fordham Cambridgeshire
16. Gamlingay, Cambridgeshire
17. Hinxton, Cambridgeshire
18. Isleham, Cambridgeshire
19. Steeple Morden, Cambridgeshire
20. Hartshorn, Derbyshire
21. Repton, Derbyshire
22. Whithorn, Dumfries and Galloway
23. Escomb church, Co Durham
24. Horndon on the Hill, Essex
25. Springfield Lyons, Essex
26. Bishop's Norton, Gloucestershire
27. Bourton on the Water Gloucestershire
28. Hempsted, Gloucestershire
29. Lower Slaughter, Gloucestershire
30. Winchcombe, Gloucestershire
31. Faccombe Netherton, Hampshire
32. Hatch Warren, Hampshire
33. Winchester, Old Minster, Hampshire
34. Westmill, Hertfordshire
35. Glatton, Huntingdonshire
36. Orton Longueville, Huntingdonshire
37. Canterbury, St Pancras, Kent
38. Canterbury, St Peter and St Paul, Kent
39. Dover, Kent
40. East Langdon, Kent
41. Lyminge, Kent

42. Minster in Thanet, Kent
43. Staplehurst, Kent
44. Dadlington, Leicestershire
45. Desford, Leicestershire
46. Snarestone, Leicestershire
47. Brant Broughton, Lincolnshire
48. Candlesby, Lincolnshire
49. Coleby, Lincolnshire
50. Goltho, Lincolnshire
51. Great Hale, Lincolnshire
52. Hibaldstow, Lincolnshire
53. Holton, Lincolnshire
54. Quarrington, Lincolnshire
55. Stow, Lincolnshire
56. Welton, Lincolnshire
57. Westminster Abbey, London
58. Shepperton, Middlesex
59. Attlebridge, Norfolk
60. Bergh/Burgh Apton, Norfolk
61. Field Dalling, Norfolk
62. Hingham, Norfolk
63. Sedgeford, Norfolk
64. Shipdham, Norfolk
65. Thetford, Brandon Road, Norfolk
66. Watlington, Norfolk
67. Whissonsett, Norfolk
68. Brixworth church, Northamptonshire
69. Hackleton, Northamptonshire
70. Little Brington, Northamptonshire
71. Little Houghton, Northamptonshire
72. Peakirk, Northamptonshire
73. Peterborough, Northamptonshire
74. Polebrook, Northamptonshire
75. Preston Deanery, Northamptonshire
76. Raunds, Furnells and Langham Road, Northamptonshire
77. Raunds, West Cotton, Northamptonshire
78. Sulgrave, Northamptonshire
79. Thorpe Mandeville, Northamptonshire
80. Warmington, Northamptonshire
81. Beadnall, Northumberland
82. Hexham, Northumberland

83. Yeavering, Northumberland
84. Torworth, Nottinghamshire
85. Bampton, Oxfordshire
86. Benson, Oxfordshire
87. Church Enstone, Oxfordshire
88. Eynsham, Oxfordshire
89. Iffley, Oxfordshire
90. Glaston, Rutland
91. Ketton Quarry, Rutland
92. Manton, Rutland
93. Whissendine [east], Rutland
94. Whissendine [west], Rutland
95. Wing, Rutland
96. Cheddar, Somerset
97. Catholme, Staffordshire
98. Bloodmoor Hill, Carlton Colville, Suffolk
99. Brandon, Suffolk
100. Bury St Edmunds, Suffolk
101. Fornham All Saints, Suffolk
102. Ilketshall St Margaret, Suffolk
103. Broadwater, Sussex
104. Burpham, Sussex
105. Fenny Compton, Warwickshire
106. Wolvey, Warwickshire
107. Cowage Farm, Bremilham, Wiltshire
108. Flamborough, E. Riding of Yorkshire
109. Keyingham, E.Riding of Yorkshire
110. Preston, E. Riding of Yorkshire
111. Chapel le Dale, N. Riding of Yorkshire
112. Clapham Bottoms, N. Riding of Yorkshire
113. Dunnington, N. Riding of Yorkshire
114. Great Habton, N. Riding of Yorkshire
115. Kirk Smeaton, N. Riding of Yorkshire
116. Whitby, N. Riding of Yorkshire
117. Hooton Roberts, W. Riding of Yorkshire

an initial assessment of village morphology across the whole of England on the basis of a single cartographic source. The decision to take account of all nucleated villages, whether showing evidence for grid-planning or not, was fundamental. However, nineteenth-century maps are not always a reliable guide to either the form or the distribution of medieval settlement: by adding the evidence of aerial photographs, LiDAR and excavations we aimed to assess the extent to which village grids may have been initially established but then effaced during over a thousand years of evolution.

We believe that the methodology outlined above has given us an objective and consistent body of data: the corpus of potentially gridded places that were finally accepted on the basis of these criteria and are catalogued in Table 3.1 and Appendix C. It is upon this body of evidence that the rest of the book is based and, as both the dating and the distribution of sites are fundamental to what follows, we present at the outset the broad picture in a series of distribution maps (Figures 3.13–3.18).

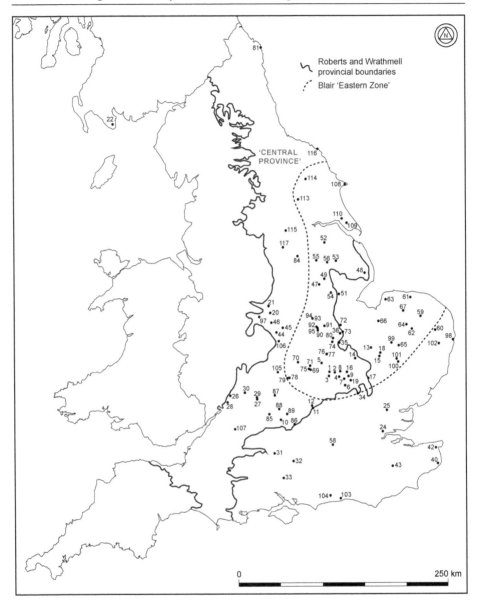

Figure 3.14. Distribution map of all places where grid-planning is possibly evidenced across whole settlements in relation to Roberts and Wrathmell's 'Central Province' and Blair's 'Eastern Zone'.

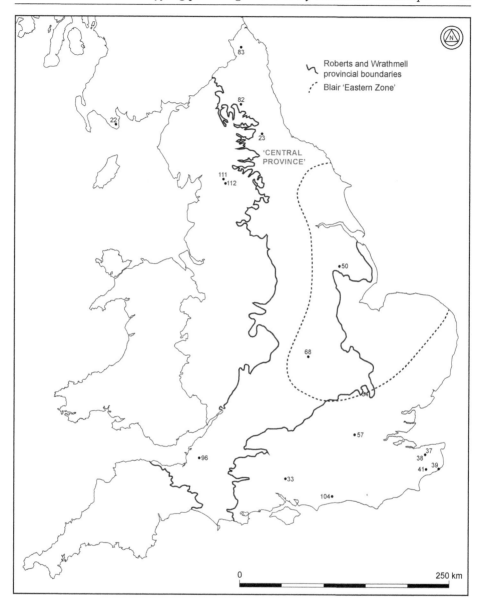

Figure 3.15. Distribution map of all places where grid-planning and/or use of the short or long perch module is evidenced in the laying out of individual buildings (and not the broader settlements that they were once part of).

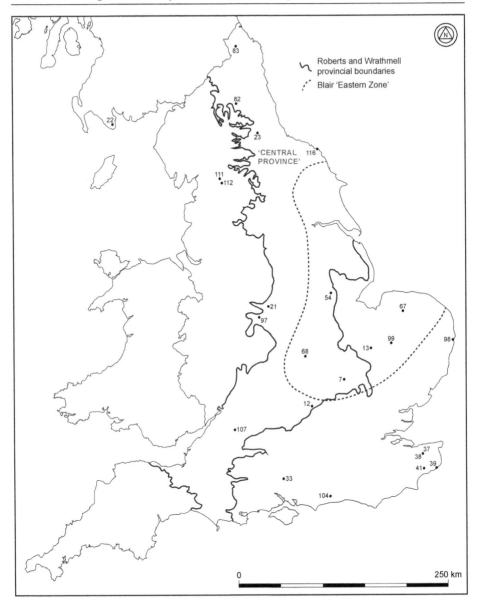

Figure 3.16. Distribution map of all places where grid-planning and/or use of the short or long perch module has been identified in settlements dated by excavation to before AD 850.

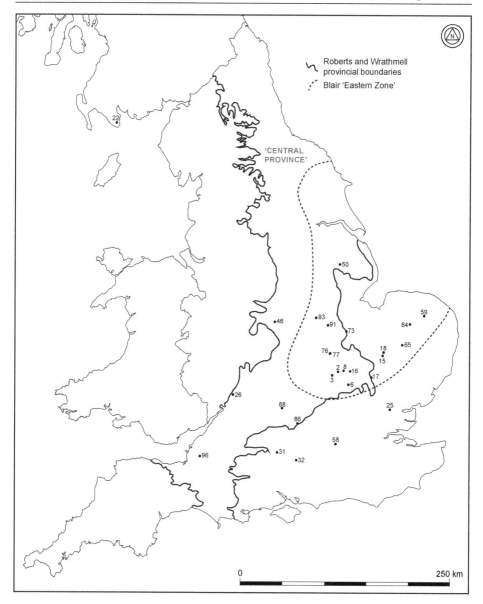

Figure 3.17. Distribution map of all places where grid-planning and/or use of the short or long perch module has been identified in settlements dated by excavation to after AD 850.

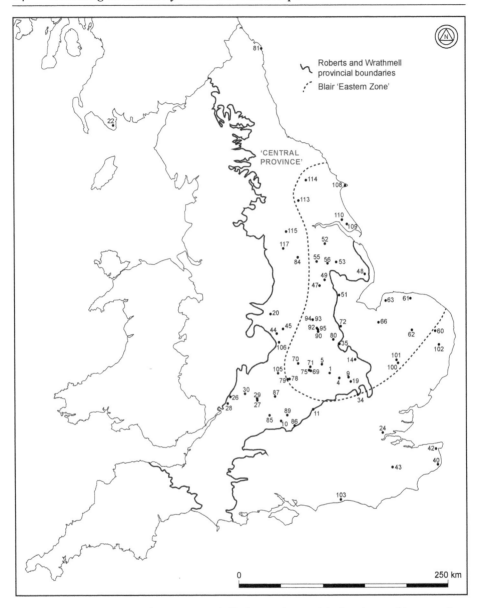

Figure 3.18. Distribution map of all places where grid-planning and/or use of the short or long perch module has been identified on late nineteenth-century village plans or earthwork sites where no additional excavation data is available to help date the planning episode.

The most basic general point concerns distribution. The map evidence allows us to be confident that grid-based planning was not a feature of the landscape in all areas that saw village formation, or at least that it did not survive until the nineteenth century in all areas. When we incorporate the aerial photographs, LiDAR and excavations, they vindicate our early impression that (setting aside some mostly special and isolated cases) grid-planning was indeed limited in its geographical range to central-eastern and eastern England (Figure 3.13).

Moving to a closer level of detail and to comparisons with other phenomena, Figures 3.14 and 3.15 show two sub-sets of these places – those where gridding can be seen across a whole settlement and those where it is apparent only at the level of individual buildings – in relation to Roberts and Wrathmell's 'Central Province' and to John Blair's 'eastern zone'. Turning then to chronology, Figure 3.16 shows the distribution of places where gridding has been identified and dated to before 850, and Figure 3.17 those where gridding has been identified and dated to after 850. Figure 3.18 shows places that are identified only on the basis of nineteenth-century Ordnance Survey mapping, and therefore cannot be dated.

These patterns need to be understood in relation to economic, social and cultural aspects of Anglo-Saxon society, and we return to them later in the book. But they also have a wider context: the planning technologies of the Roman and post-Roman worlds to which the Anglo-Saxons were heirs.

Chapter 4

Planning technologies in post-Roman Europe and their impact on English practice

Tʜᴇ ɪᴅᴇᴀ that technically precise grid-planning was widely used by Anglo-Saxon surveyors, and can still be recognised in the landscape today, may seem a wild one to some readers, as the three authors of this book know only too well from colleagues' reactions. In what way does our argument have more empirical validity than arguments for 'ley-lines' and 'old straight tracks'?

There are two responses to that challenge. The first is that many pre-industrial cultures, including prehistoric communities in the British Isles, have built monuments on a large scale and with geometrical precision: as 'lines in the landscape', none of the grid-systems discussed here compares in scale with the Neolithic cursuses, for instance.[1] The Anglo-Saxons have not usually been conceived as monument-builders, and indeed their surviving buildings (essentially churches) are small and their timber constructions short-lived and fugitive. Yet transience of materials need not imply poverty of conception or planning, as is clearly illustrated by the seventh-century 'great hall complexes' at Yeavering and elsewhere. Increasingly, archaeology shows that the Anglo-Saxons were capable of sophisticated and complex design on a large scale, just as they obviously were on the miniature scale of jewellery and manuscripts.[2] The construction of monuments such as Offa's Dyke, Wansdyke and the Cambridgeshire Dykes, and other civil engineering projects such as watermills, causeways and fishweirs, also points to the ability to plan major projects and command the considerable resources necessary for their execution (see Chapter 2). A culture

[1] Barclay *et al.* 2003.
[2] Blair 2018, 70–1.

of formal and classifiable monument types is no less likely in this period than in the Neolithic and Bronze Age.

More specifically, there is no mystery about the Anglo-Saxons practising grid-planning, since it was regularly practised by their Roman predecessors and continental neighbours. That wider context is important, as it offers an explanatory and interpretative framework for the new English evidence presented here. Accordingly, this chapter will examine the surveying techniques of the Roman Empire, their survival in post-Roman Europe and the ways in which that continuing tradition may have moulded English practice.

The Classical background: Roman land surveyors and their manuals

The profession of land surveyor, which had long existed under the Roman Republic, went from strength to strength from the early first century AD. The Empire needed professionals to survey newly conquered territories, to apportion land, to determine boundaries and to settle countless disputes between neighbours. These *agrimensores* or *gromatici* developed specialised and complex techniques, described in a series of practical manuals that by the fifth century had been gathered into a compendium, the 'Corpus agrimensorum'.[3] It was this 'gromatic' knowledge that the surveyors transmitted to the post-Classical world through their writings and their successors.

Surveying practice varied across the Empire, for reasons that are not immediately obvious from a modern perspective. Since Gunter introduced his chain in 1620, triangulation has been self-evidently the best and most accurate mode of land surveying.[4] In the dry, stable climate of Egypt it was feasible to do this with ropes, allowing the development of triangulation and other geometric techniques, and these in turn formed the basis of Byzantine surveying.[5] But in the West, with its damp and variable climate, the expansion and shrinkage of ropes produced unacceptable inaccuracies.

---

[3] Still the most complete edition, including the post-Classical texts, is Blume *et al.* 1848. A modern edition of the main texts, with translation and commentary, is Campbell 2000. The classic study is Dilke 1971.

[4] When the chain was invented seems curiously difficult to establish. A woodcut showing surveyors using it appears on p. 524 of *Maison Rustique, or the Countrey Farme* (texts edited by Gervase Markham, 3rd English edn, printed by Adam Islip for John Bill, 1616).

[5] Blair 2013, note 28.

Western practice therefore used rods rather than ropes, and was based on the off-setting of right angles by sighting rather than triangulation. When laying out a territory, the main axes (the *decumanus* and *kardo*) were first established in the configuration of a cross, after which the remaining grid-squares were filled in to the desired extent. The prime surveying tool was the *groma*: a staff with a cruciform head fixed horizontally, from the four corners of which hung plumb-bobs. An initial straight line across the landscape was sighted using one opposed pair of plumbs, after which – with the *groma* set up in alignment at the desired junctions – a series of lines at right angles to it could be surveyed with the other pair. Another series of lines, running parallel to the original baseline, would then complete the grid. The superiority of this method over triangulation may seem counter-intuitive to us, but at its best it could achieve virtually perfect accuracy.

The *agrimensores* were employed to set out precise and very extensive grids for the building of towns and forts and for the apportionment (especially to veterans) of tracts of land. Large-scale grid-planning of territories ('centuriation') is widely recognised in the Mediterranean provinces,[6] but a point to be emphasised here is the absence of centuriation from Roman Britain: after so much intensive fieldwork, the failure to find convincing cases is now so striking as to indicate that it never existed (see Chapter 2). Where grids are evidenced in Roman Britain it is in urban street-planning, and the visual impact of these was rapidly eroded as the towns themselves were abandoned. Unlike Mediterranean regions, therefore, Anglo-Saxon England lacked relict Roman grids within which to form its planned landscapes.

The normal products of gromatic surveying were grids of squares. Other forms were possible, however – notably the blocks of strips called *strigae* or *scamna*[7] that also provided potential models for medieval land division. The determination of boundaries – especially to settle disputes – was a major part of surveyors' work, and a high proportion of the gromatic literature deals with types of boundary stone and with methods for ensuring their accurate placement and spacing. That tradition falls outside the present project, but an investigation of its influence on the formulation of boundary clauses in Anglo-Saxon charters might well be productive.[8]

[6] Dilke 1971, 133–87.
[7] Dilke 1971, 94–6.
[8] Crawford 2016 for the continuation of this terminology in Italy up to *c.*900.

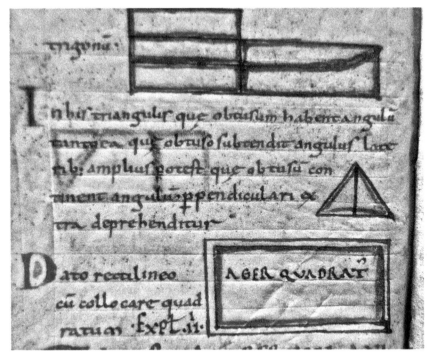

Figure 4.1. Detail of an early tenth-century surveying manual from northern France, illustrating the geometry of a triangle and a rectangle (Cambridge, Trinity College, MS R.15.14, fo.31ᵛ detail. Reproduced by kind permission of the Master and Fellows).

The transmission of surveying technology through the fifth to eighth centuries

Continued interest in the works of the *agrimensores* is demonstrated by their very survival: the 'Corpus', or abridged versions of it, was regularly transcribed through the early Middle Ages (Figures 4.1, 4.2).[9] The two principal surviving manuscripts, Arcerianus A and B, date from the fifth to early sixth centuries, and it has been suggested – though current opinion seems to be against this – that the first belonged to the great scholar Cassiodorus (*c*.485–*c*.585).[10] At all events Cassiodorus had the opportunity to watch an *agrimensor* in action, as he gives an ironic

[9] The standard guide to the manuscript tradition is Toneatto 1994–5. Del Lungo 2004 provides further important data for the early medieval transmission.

[10] Dilke 1971, 127–9; Blair 2013, note 30. Thanks to Michael Crawford for expressing his scepticism about the Cassiodorus attribution.

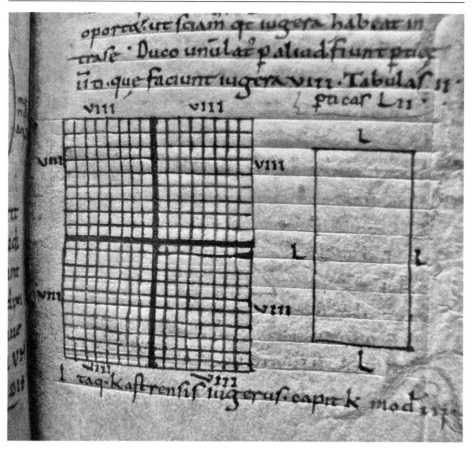

Figure 4.2. Detail of an early tenth-century surveying manual from northern France, showing the measurement of a block of land by means of a surveyed grid (Cambridge, Trinity College, MS R.15.14, fo.68 detail. Reproduced by kind permission of the Master and Fellows).

account of the specialist's odd behaviour: 'His law-court is deserted fields; you might think him crazy, seeing him walk along tortuous paths. If he is looking for evidence among rough woodlands and thickets, he doesn't walk like you or me, he chooses his own way.'[11] In 597 – the very year in which he sent St Augustine to convert the English – Pope Gregory the Great also sent one 'John the *Agrimensor*' to Syracuse to resolve a boundary dispute.[12] There was thus a chronological overlap,

[11] Dilke 1971, 46.
[12] Dilke 1971, 46; Blair 2013, note 32.

however slight, between the continuing profession of land surveyor and the beginnings of Anglo-Saxon Christianity.

It is harder to say how much longer, and how fully, the technical repertoire of the *agrimensores* remained in practical use. Michael H. Crawford has recently traced the continued use of technical gromatic terminology in the land descriptions of Italian documents from the seventh to the late ninth century: 'Had the language of the *agrimensores*', he asks, 'been transmitted in an unbroken line of succession of surveyors?'[13] At some point the *groma* itself was abandoned, and a general simplification – with the passage of time and with distance northwards from the Mediterranean – seems inherently likely.

Nonetheless, the practice of technically precise surveying did not die out. We will see in due course that some strikingly similar methods, including an emphasis on the accurate location of boundary stones, were current in late medieval Provence. In any case, results resembling centuriation are achievable with a very simplified version of the technology. A practical experiment showed that the beginnings of a respectable grid can be laid out – even by a complete novice – by cart-wheeling a 15-foot rod towards a distant landmark, marking the intervals, and setting out right-angled offsets (Figure 4.3). The only faintly challenging task is establishing the right angles. We cannot be confident that the *groma* was regularly used in early medieval Europe (though we will shortly meet startling evidence that it was used on at least one occasion in early seventh-century England). Even without the *groma*, however, it is possible to achieve remarkable accuracy by simple rule-of-thumb methods, such as standing with outstretched arms on a baseline and then clapping the hands together with eyes fixed on a distant landmark. In any case, a prime reason for continuing to put the old techniques into practice may have been their symbolic resonance. By planning out settlements in a rectilinear fashion one could advertise one's Roman (and thus civilised) credentials, even if the procedures used would not have impressed the first-century *agrimensores*.

Early medieval grid-plan and row-plan settlements on the Continent

The survival of large – sometimes very large – areas of centuriation in Italy and southern France has long been recognised. More recently, landscape historians have focused on the development and change of

[13] Crawford 2016.

Figure 4.3. John Blair surveying a line and grid using a wooden pole one short perch in length (photograph by Kanerva Blair-Heikkinen).

those planned landscapes through the intervening two millennia. This work has now shown that areas of up to several square kilometres could be laid out in the Middle Ages on coherent rectilinear plans, closely informed by their Roman predecessors; a block of 'centuriation' at Bagnacavallo near Ravenna, for example, almost exactly resembles the genuine Roman product next to it, but is on a different alignment and respects a church built in the eighth or ninth century.[14] For present purposes, such analogies have two basic limitations: the difficulty of dating these post-Roman schemes (and the relative lateness of those that can be dated) and the extent to which they are simply copies or reworkings of Roman centuriated landscapes, the like of which never existed in Britain.

[14] Franceschelli and Marabini 2007, 74–6, 156–8; Franceschelli 2008; Zadora-Rio 2010a; Commodari 2013. This is now a lively area of study, much of it published in the journal *Agri Centuriati*, and in *Études Rurales*, 167–8 (July–December 2003). We are grateful to Elisabeth Zadora-Rio for her advice in this area.

Figure 4.4. The seventh- to ninth-century settlement at Burgheim, Germany.
    A: Part of the excavated area (after Krämer 1951).
    B: Part of the excavated area overlain with a grid of 3.25m.

More directly relevant, but also less studied, is the phenomenon of rectilinear planning in early medieval settlements of the Merovingian Frankish world and north-western Europe. It is apparently widespread[15]

---

[15] Several of the settlements illustrated by Hamerow 2002, 52–85, would be good candidates for the methodologies of plan-analysis that we use in this book.

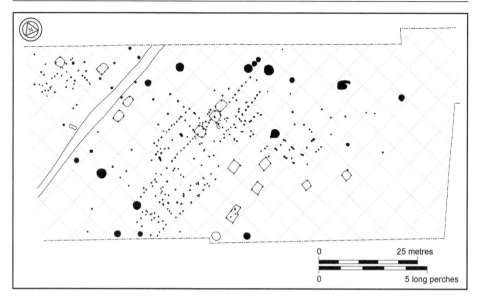

Figure 4.5. Part of the extensively excavated seventh-century settlement at Genlis, France, overlain with a grid of long perches, focusing on the area where planning might have been employed (after Catteddu 1992, fig. 8).

and is well-known to archaeologists, but it has tended to be taken for granted, without much focused attention on the implied background processes. Any comprehensive survey of continental settlements is beyond the scope of this book, although some examples from greater Francia and the Low Countries are relevant, showing as they do that the techniques now identified in Anglo-Saxon England were far from unknown among continental neighbours.

The excavated settlement at Burgheim (Neuburg an der Donau, Bavaria)[16] was on the edge of the Alamannic zone (Figure 4.4). It was apparently laid out in the seventh century, surviving to the late eighth or ninth. Notwithstanding the several superimposed phases, its regularity in both directions (apparently based on a module that equates to 3.25m) is remarkable. Also established in the seventh century, and rather similar in appearance, is a very large and complex settlement at Genlis in Burgundy, France (Figure 4.5).[17] The 'blocky' configuration of these cases points to grids rather than rows; at Genlis a statistical analysis by Clair Barnes has confirmed the existence of an underlying

[16] Krämer 1951.
[17] Catteddu 1992.

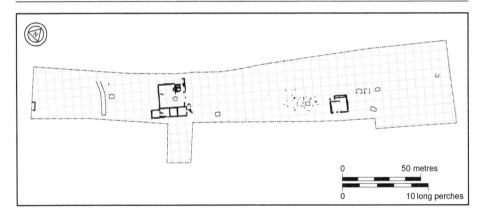

Figure 4.6. Excavated second- to third-century buildings at Pompey, France, overlain with a grid of long perches (after Peytremann 2003, fig. 43).

grid,[18] the module being the 'long perch' – equating to 5.5m – also used in southern England (below, Appendix A).

Burgheim and Genlis were both in territories under Frankish control in the seventh century. The reintroduction of Roman cultural traits through monastic influence, in line with the developments proposed here for England, might be one explanation for these grid-planned settlements. Another possibility, though, is that the grid-planning techniques were assimilated at an earlier date by Frankish elites from the Gallo-Roman aristocracy. In possible support of that conjecture is the group of second- to third-century buildings at Pompey (Lorraine, France: Figure 4.6),[19] the layout of which is consistent with a grid-planned framework – again using the 5.5m module – and which was overlain by a series of seventh-century sunken-featured buildings and a posthole structure in broad conformity to the grid.

Further north, in Flanders and Frisia, a tradition of strongly linear planning in strips – potentially reflective of Roman *strigae* or *scamna* – is apparent in the early Middle Ages. In some cases (as at the late sixth- to seventh-century site of Oegstgeest, Figure 4.7)[20] the configuration of buildings and associated watercourses is notably regular,

---

[18] Barnes 2015.

[19] Peytremann 2003, I, 156, II, 249–50. For another possibly grid-planned Merovingian site – Isles-sur-Suippe (Champagne-Ardenne) – see Peytremann 2003, I, 133, II, 127–9.

[20] Dijkstra 2011, 134–9.

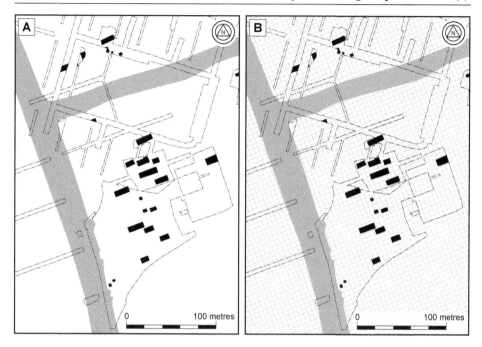

Figure 4.7. Excavated Merovingian-period settlement at Oegstgeest, the Netherlands.
   A: Plan of the excavated buildings (after Dijkstra 2011, fig. 4.15).
   B: Plan of the excavated buildings overlain with a 'best-fit' grid of 4.9m (after Dijkstra 2011, fig. 4.15).

giving the impression that they were framed within strips of equal width. Other influences, though, may be at work here: the indigenous Iron Age tradition of linear planning merging into radial planning (well-illustrated by the sequence at Feddersen Wierde, Figure 4.8), or the alignment of strip-tenements towards jetties at right angles to the shoreline seen at the emporia of Dorestad and Kaupang. Nor have we found evidence in such places for any of the known modules. The relevance of these sites is therefore questionable, though it remains possible that gromatic expertise, spreading northwards beyond the frontiers of the empire in the late Roman period or after, worked on local practice to make indigenous forms more regular.

   The traditions behind these Continental sites are probably complex. The essential point is that formal rectilinear settlements existed over a wide area: the knowledge of Roman surveying technology may never have died out completely in the former Empire, and may even have spread outside it.

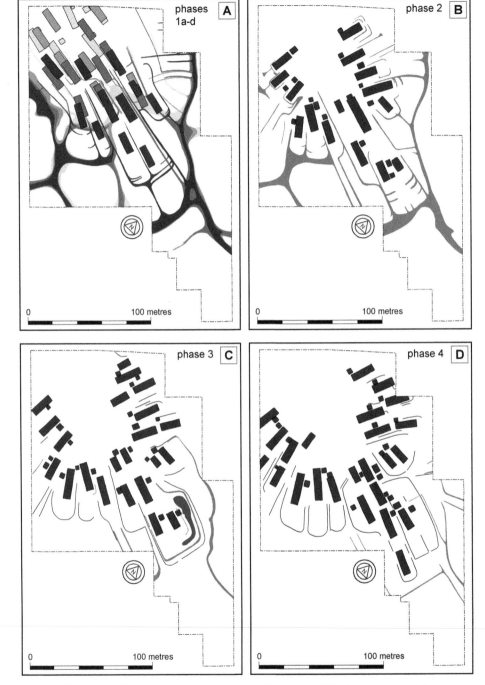

Figure 4.8. The excavated settlement at Feddersen Wierde, Germany (after Haarnagel 1979, figs 21–7).
   A: Phases 1a–d.   **B:** Phase 2.   **C:** Phase 3.   **D:** Phase 4.

The reception of the technology in England, 600–800

One exception, though, was the lost province of Britannia, where centuriation had never existed, and where the remnants of Roman civilisation were effaced with exceptional thoroughness. If the Anglo-Saxons acquired gromatic knowledge it was not from their British neighbours, but as part of the package of Roman cultural traits that started to be reimported from around 600. So far as we can see, that importation happened in two distinct chronological phases.

The first was the original mission from Rome to Kent by St Augustine and his companions. As discussed in Chapter 5,[21] they built at least two grid-planned churches in Kent, using imported technology but an indigenous unit of measurement (Figure 5.1). From Canterbury, the technology seems to have spread through high-level diplomatic channels to Northumbria, where the monumental royal buildings of the early 620s at Yeavering were laid out on an impressively accurate grid (Figure 5.2). An extraordinary aspect of this complex is its integral association with a unique grave, probably of a ritual specialist, containing an object interpreted as no less than a Roman-style *groma* (Figure 4.9).[22] In the present context this is startling indeed, suggesting that English grid-planning, at least in its first phase, employed not just Roman techniques but also Roman instruments.

From the 660s onwards these lines of influence were reinforced by the wealthy English monastic founders – above all Benedict Biscop, Wilfrid and Aldhelm – who visited Rome to acquire equipment, books and knowledge.[23] With the arrival of Theodore of Tarsus as archbishop in 669 there was an unprecedented flow of exotic Mediterranean knowledge to Canterbury. If *agrimensores* were still operating in Italy in the late seventh century it is quite possible that all these people saw them in action. Given Cassiodorus's first-hand knowledge of *agrimensores*, it seems especially relevant that Benedict Biscop is known to have acquired at least one book for Monkwearmouth and Jarrow from Cassiodorus's own library;[24] there could have been others, potentially including gromatic texts. All this provides an eminently plausible context for the seventh- and eighth-century grid-planned settlements discussed later in this book, most if not all of which

[21] Below, pp. 115–18.
[22] Below, pp. 118–23.
[23] Blair 2005, 91–4.
[24] Lapidge 2006, 22–30.

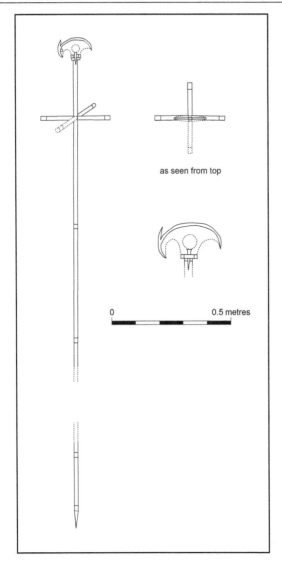

as seen from top

0   0.5 metres

Figure 4.9. The *groma*-like object found in grave AX at Yeavering, Northumberland (after Hope-Taylor 1977, fig. 94).

seem to have been closely associated with this phase of monastic high culture.

The imported technology that underlies the Anglo-Saxon grid-planned settlements involved the laying out of straight, calibrated lines across the landscape and the construction of rectilinear offsets from those lines to form grids. Reference should, however, be made to two other modes of surveying that lie outside the present scope. The first is the construction of broadly circular forms, either (on a small scale) by rotating the end of a rope around a central peg to produce a circle or (on a large scale) by surveying radial lines of equal length from a central point to produce a polygon. These techniques were known to the *agrimensores*, and their impact on the medieval landscape of France has recently been explored.[25] In Anglo-Saxon England there is growing evidence – discussed elsewhere – that some enclosed settlements, compounds and forts were indeed laid out in this fashion, notably by the increasingly ambitious kings of eighth- and ninth-century Mercia and Wessex, though perhaps drawing on earlier Irish concepts of concentric protected space.[26]

More important – and potentially contentious – is the use of triangulation and geometrical ratios, for which architectural historians have made a good case in relation to early medieval churches. In a sense, the tension between grid-planning and geometrical planning lies in the background to the entire argument of this book, especially when it relates to buildings. For the moment we leave this crucial problem to one side, but return to it at the end of the present chapter.

On the whole, it is likely that a wooden rod (a perch in length, whatever the local perch might be) was always the basic tool of Anglo-Saxon surveyors: the *gyrd* or *metegyrd* ('measuring-rod') is mentioned in the few late Anglo-Saxon texts discussing such matters.[27] Around 1000 the German Notker, paraphrasing a biblical description of the apportionment of land by rope, adds that 'nowadays it would be done with a rod (*mit rûuoto*)'.[28] The surveyor's chain, of course, would have been both more convenient and more accurate, but that was a Renaissance-period invention. Notwithstanding references to rope measurement in eleventh-century Normandy (below), such evidence as we have suggests that English surveyors were put off by the inherent inaccuracies of that method and continued to avoid it.

Modules: the short perch, the long perch and other perches

It can be said with confidence that the Classical linear measures used by the Roman *agrimensores* had no significant impact on Anglo-Saxon practice; indeed, it is not clear how far they survived in northern Europe at all. Instead, early medieval surveyors employed the existing

[25] Querrien 2008.
[26] Blair 2018, 143–8.
[27] Blair 2013, 19–20.
[28] Grierson 1972, 20.

customary measures of their own times and cultures, though it is possible that they standardised them to more consistent modules.[29]

For present purposes, the *short perch* of 15 imperial feet (4.57m) is by far the most important and widespread module. A unit of essentially this length (4.65m) was recognised in 1991 by Peter Huggins, who adduced it from the excavated plans of fifth- to seventh-century timber buildings and noted its resemblance to customary perches used in north-western Germany in the early modern era.[30] Independently, John Blair adduced it from the settlement plans illustrated in his 2013 paper, to which Wilfrid Kendall added a statistical appendix supporting the reality of a module of broadly this length.[31] The present project has also found the widespread use of the 15-foot unit in Anglo-Saxon England, and among convincing cases of grid-planning it is overwhelmingly the most common. To some extent, that is a reflection of the fact that our examples concentrate so heavily in the Anglian regions of eastern England and the East Midlands. The short perch evidently derives from the traditional customary measure of the people who settled in those parts, and of their continental homelands; indeed, it might appropriately be called the 'Anglian perch'.

By contrast, the grid-planned sites identified in Wessex – at Winchester (Old Minster), Cheddar and Faccombe Netherton (Figures 1.2, 5.16) – use a *long perch* equivalent to 18 modern feet (5.5m); in the case of Old Minster, in fact, Birthe Kjølbye-Biddle arrived independently at the 18-foot unit (though from a completely different starting point) in 1986.[32] As we saw, this is the module used on some Frankish sites, including a Gallo-Roman one (Figure 4.6). The regional boundary between the 'short-perch' and 'long-perch' zones illustrates a cultural fault-line running through what tends to be conceived as homogeneous 'Anglo-Saxon' territory: broadly 'Anglian' regions using a north-west German module, and broadly 'Saxon' regions using a Frankish one. In the light of that, it seems possible that the dominance of the long perch in the eighth-century emporium of *Lundenwic* – Buildings 6, 11 and 27 excavated at the Royal Opera House appear to have been constructed using this module – reflects

---

[29] See Blair 2013, notes 6–22, for contemporary references to early medieval modules and other research on them: only material directly relevant to this project is repeated here.

[30] Huggins 1991, 22–3.

[31] Blair 2013; Kendall 2013.

[32] Kjølbye-Biddle 1986.

the influence of Frankish merchants trading there (Figure 5.11).[33]
Looking further back, London had been refounded as a bishopric
when it was within the East Saxon kingdom, and the material culture
of the area, in cemeteries such as Mucking and Springfield Lyons, is
Saxon rather than Anglian.[34]

We have found two revealing exceptions to this geographical
boundary. One is mid-Saxon Southampton (*Hamwic*), deep in Wessex,
where the strip-like framework of the Six Dials area, laid out in about
the 670s, used the short perch (Figure 5.10). Anglian influence on the
cosmopolitan West Saxon court may be the best explanation, through,
for instance, the use of a professional surveyor trained in eastern
England (see below) or even through St Wilfrid himself on one of
his visits there.[35] In the second case the church of St Oswald, built at
Gloucester in the 890s by Æthelflaed, King Alfred's daughter, appears
to be an exact copy of the Old Minster at Winchester (Figure 1.2). As
well as anomalously using the long perch in Mercia, this church was
built at a time when grid-planning seems to have died out in England:
the simplest explanation may be that the dimensions were reproduced
faithfully, but without awareness of the underlying grid.

While the long perch may have been an established customary
measure on the Continent, the analysis of excavated settlement plans
suggests the presence of other units, such as the grid of 3.25m squares
at Burgheim and perhaps of 4.9m squares at Oegstgeest (Figures 4.4,
4.7). These modules have not been recognised in England, and indeed
we have found no convincing English cases of grids that are not based
on either the long or the short perch.[36] Given the normal tendency
in pre-industrial societies for weights and measures to vary widely
according to local usage, that is remarkable. What it suggests, perhaps, is
that grid-planning was a specialised technology in the hands of experts,
whose training taught them to use measurements in a precise and
consistent fashion. If this inference is valid, it reinforces our impression
that the technology was never far separated from literate, essentially
ecclesiastical patrons who had access to the gromatic knowledge
transmitted in manuscripts. It strengthens rather than undermines this
point that English reformers around the year 1000 tried to enforce the

---

[33] Malcolm *et al.* 2003, figs 25, 30, 65; below, p. 134.
[34] Rippon 2018.
[35] Below, pp. 124–5.
[36] A building at Tresmorn (Cornwall) might be based on a five-foot grid, but this
is far from conclusive: Blair 2018, 328.

general use of a standard *metegyrd*:[37] that cultural context was strongly ecclesiastical and theocratic, part of the same thought-world in which the late Anglo-Saxon grid-planners apparently operated.

The literary transmission of surveying technology in the eighth to tenth centuries and its reception in England after 940

This restricted socio-cultural milieu helps to explain a striking gap in our evidence, already noticed in John Blair's 2013 paper and apparently confirmed by our subsequent work. Although we have identified several grid-planned sites from before 800, and many more from after 940, we cannot confidently ascribe a single case (excluding the anomalous one of St Oswald's, Gloucester) to the intervening 150 years. It is hard to avoid associating this gap with the troubles that pressed more and more heavily on monastic communities during the ninth century: royal resentment and hostility, disendowment, appropriation to secular uses and, ultimately, the Viking attacks.[38]

In Carolingian Europe, on the other hand, the tradition was kept alive.[39] The Roman texts on surveying were reworked and abridged in complex ways, in combination with more recent texts such as the Pseudo-Boethius 'Geometria I', to produce a variety of geometrical compendia. The focus of this activity was the monastery of Corbie, in northern France, where books were produced with copious coloured diagrams that accurately reproduced the Roman originals (Figures 4.1, 4.2). If the primary function of these books was academic, to supply texts for the geometrical curriculum, it remains no less true that an intelligent and informed reader could use them to learn about practical surveying. Eric Fernie argues below (Appendix B) that the St Gall plan of the 820s embodies a limited grid in the area of the church, though combined with geometrically constructed proportions. In the region around Tours the vocabulary and concepts of academic land surveying derived ultimately from the *agrimensores* had a visible impact on descriptions of territory in the charters of the major monasteries.[40]

It is therefore certain that books containing gromatic learning would have been within reach when, in the 940s, English monastic proponents such as Dunstan and Æthelwold were training in the

---

[37] Blair 2013, 19–20.
[38] Below, pp. 140–3.
[39] Blair 2013, notes 33–6 for the evidence on which this paragraph is based.
[40] Zadora-Rio 2010b, 273–8, 286.

religious communities of Lotharingia and Flanders. The reign of Eadgar (959–75) saw a famous and much-celebrated revival of strict monasticism, centralised and authoritarian in tone and strongly sponsored by the court. Its leaders were idealistic and cosmopolitan: enthusiasts both for the English monastic golden age, as celebrated by Bede, and for contemporary continental religious culture.[41] This combination of ideology with wealth stimulated a flood of books and other ecclesiastical artefacts from the continent to England: a repetition, in fact, of the culture-tourism that had accompanied the first monastic golden age of *c.*660–730. Did that include gromatic texts? At least four of the surviving compendia were certainly or probably in England by the Conquest,[42] and it is hard to believe that members of the English high-monastic milieu of *c.*950–1000 did not acquire material that was so widely available. At any rate that would help to explain the sudden reappearance in England, at around that point, of grid-planning on excavated sites, and on the many village sites that may have been laid out in those decades.

Whether or not academically-derived surveying remained a monastic monopoly in England, it seems to have done so in at least one part of tenth-century France. In the Touraine, Elisabeth Zadora-Rio observes that technical vocabulary, including elaborate modes of calculation and use of the square perch as an areal measure, occurs only in charters from Saint-Martin and Saint-Julien in Tours. As she says, 'the place of mathematics in the cultural makeup of local elites ... might be elucidated by a better knowledge of the patterns of dissemination of geometrical treatises and manuscripts of the *agrimensores*'.[43] The conservative and formulaic style of Anglo-Saxon charters does not allow this kind of analysis, but it is possible that our field evidence tells the same story of a technical expertise that remained quite restricted and elite.

In turn, one obvious explanation for the eventual disappearance of grid-planning in England might be the decline of support for the reformed monasteries after 1000, and the stagnation of their culture between then and the Norman Conquest. At present it is hard to date many convincing cases to the eleventh century, though the association of some of the grid-planned villages with Edward the Confessor's

[41] Blair 2005, 350–1, for a guide to the huge bibliography; Wormald 1988 for the retrospective tone.

[42] Blair 2013, note 34.

[43] Zadora-Rio 2010b, 278, 286 (translation).

earls in Domesday Book might indicate the survival or revival of the techniques in court circles of the 1050s.[44]

Surveying technology on the Continent and in England after 1050

Most of the recent work on the afterlife of centuriated systems in Italy and France has focused on the perpetuation, extension, modification and effacement of Roman-period schemes. Given how strongly an accurately grid-planned framework is likely to have influenced the form of later developments within or near it, the extent to which technically precise grid-planning continued to be executed is hard to elucidate from this field evidence. Charters provide some clues – notably in Languedoc, where indications of an orthogonal system based on a module of around 6m have been noted[45] – but that kind of evidence is difficult to translate into spatial reality.

Great monasteries such as Ghent are likely have had texts of the kind produced in Corbie. Given that the technical challenges of reclaiming and draining low-lying land must have created powerful stimuli for systematic planning, one might well expect to find some practical application of the revived techniques in the Low Countries. Whether that was indeed the case is, however, rather unclear. For example, extensive investigations of the village and community of Assendelft, in the low-lying western Netherlands, have identified extensive reclamation spanning the tenth to twelfth centuries, achieved by means of more or less parallel drainage ditches at varying spacings between c.50m and c.100m.[46] Although this looks essentially pragmatic, with little obvious sign of geometrical regularity, the evidence presented in this book for sophisticated planning technology in early medieval England suggests that a fresh approach to modes of land division in north-western Europe may be timely.

In France, on the other hand, the case for a continuous tradition of professional land surveying – perhaps extending from the immediate heirs of the *agrimesores* to the late Middle Ages – has been argued energetically in recent years. An article by Pierre Portet is the most solid and convincing statement,[47] but the theme has also been developed – sometimes more controversially – by a group of scholars under the

---

[44] Below, pp. 149–54.
[45] Bourin 1995.
[46] Besteman and Guiran 1987.
[47] Portet 1998.

leadership of Gérard Chouquer.[48] That debate (which certainly has some lessons for the present project) has veered between enthusiastic identifications of planned landscapes, complaints about insufficiently rigorous methodology and counter-assertions of the inherent likelihood of professional planning.[49] This is not the place to take it further, but it seems fair to observe that, while not all the identifications may be correct, some of them do look persuasive and valid. The balance of probability seems to be that land surveyors were operating in France – perhaps continuously and at least intermittently – through the central Middle Ages.

There is, moreover, one unique and extraordinary survival proving that sophisticated land measurement, including complex expertise in boundary stones and boundary setting of the kind beloved by the *agrimensores*, was being practised in the region around Arles during the 1390s. This is the 'Book of Bertrand Boysset', a technical manual written in Provençal, which contains nearly 200 naïve but wonderfully graphic coloured drawings of surveyors at work and diagrams of land division (e.g. Figures 4.10–4.11).[50] Boysset did not use the *groma* (his rather implausible instrument for establishing right angles was a giant set-square), but in other respects the similarity of his methods to those of the *agrimensores* is striking, vastly different though his world was from that of the Roman imperial surveyors. Certainly his book leaves no doubt that the technical capacity for setting out precisely measured settlements and field systems existed in fourteenth-century Provence.

The problem is knowing to what extent Boysset was the exponent of a larger and older tradition. His own somewhat bizarre account of his debt to the writings of the alchemist Arnold of Villanova (*c.*1240–1311) and of Arnold's instruction in land surveying by the learned King Robert of Naples (1277–1343) has been dismissed as fantasy by French scholars.[51] It does, however, seem possible that a lost tradition of illustrated Italian surveying manuals underlies his text and pictures. Here an unexpected – and decidedly enigmatic – clue is that three of

[48] See his 'Archéogéographie' website http://www.archeogeographie.org/.

[49] See especially Cédric Lavigne's argument for precise planning in twelfth- and thirteenth-century Gascony (Lavigne 2002), a severely critical review (Zadora-Rio 2003), and a counter-defence (Watteau 2011, 53–5 and note 26). In all of this we are most grateful to Elisabeth Zadora-Rio and Chris Wickham for their guidance.

[50] Portet 2004; Guerreau 1995. The images are accessible on-line at http://lamop. univ-paris1.fr/sites/arpenteur/.

[51] Guerreau 1995, 89–90.

Figure 4.10. Illustration in the Bertrand Boysset manuscript showing surveying with a rod and boundary markers (Carpentras, Bibl. Mun. MS 327 fo.28; reproduced by kind permission of the Bibliothèque-musée Inguimbertine).

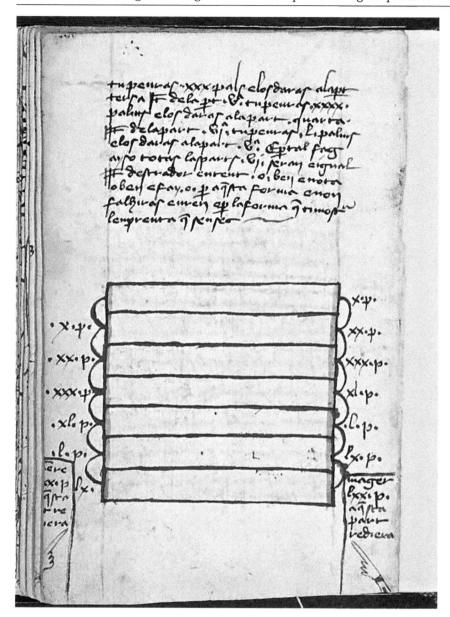

Figure 4.11. Illustration in the Bertrand Boysset manuscript, showing division of a square block of land into measured strips (Carpentras, Bibl. Mun. MS 327 fo.53ᵛ; reproduced by kind permission of the Bibliothèque-musée Inguimbertine).

his drawings appear to share models with illuminations in the 'Codex Aboensis', a legal compendium written in south-western Finland in the 1430s.[52] The solution to this mystery almost certainly lies with the patron of the manuscript, the wealthy and cultivated bishop Magnus Tavast (1357–1452), who studied in Paris, Rome and Prague and was a munificent patron of the arts.[53] Did Magnus acquire a copy of Boysset's source in Italy, which his scribes then used as a model for their drawings in the 'Aboensis'?

Unravelling this tangled web lies far beyond the present project: suffice it to say that English land surveyors up to the late Middle Ages could – if they had wished to do so – have acquired sophisticated expertise in Mediterranean Europe. It is therefore all the more odd that English land surveying of the twelfth to fifteenth centuries looks so amateurish. The supposedly 'grid-planned' towns of Norman and Angevin England were in fact nothing of the kind, but irregularly rectilinear parallelograms.[54] That is in stark contrast to the practice of bastide-builders in south-western France, or *locatores* in east-central Europe, whose new towns of *c.*1150–1300 were often laid out on precise orthogonal plans embodying sophisticated proportional systems.[55]

English town-builders evidently forgot the long-standing warnings – reiterated by Boysset, for instance[56] – against relying on unstable ropes and strings, and sacrificed the high standards of the ancient gromatic technique to convenience and speed. This fundamental change in practice may well have come with the Normans: a partition of land in Normandy in 1017 × 26 is said to have been made 'by a rope, that is by a cord (*funiculo hoc est corda*)', which suggests a context for Orderic Vitalis's famous and enigmatic comment that in the 1080s Ranulf Flambard measured the land of England 'with a rope'.[57] At all events it

---

[52] Huitu and Riska 1977: in the Aboensis facsimile, compare the drawings of a man holding a measuring-rod (p. 18), a man setting a boundary-mark (p. 128) and people in a ship (p. 242) with the equivalent drawings in the Boysset MS, fos 29r, 157v and 52r. Our thanks to Kanerva Blair-Heikkinen for drawing attention to this very unexpected link.

[53] The fullest account of Magnus Tavast is Palola 1997 (which is in Finnish but has a German summary on pp. 490–504).

[54] See the many plans in Beresford 1967.

[55] Beresford 1967; Lilley 2009, 41–73.

[56] Portet 2004, I, 137–8.

[57] Fauroux 1961, 153, No. 46; Orderic Vitalis 1969–80, iv, 172. Dudo of Saint-Quentin (ii, 31) uses a similar expression for the sharing out of land by the Duke of Normandy to his followers: 'illam terram suis fidelibus funiculo divisit'.

seems that rope-based surveying became normal: in 1329, for instance, a tenant commuted his service 'of carrying a rope around the wall of Hereford castle while it is being measured'.[58]

A final point concerns the ultimate fate of the two basic Anglo-Saxon modules, the short and long perches. Neither of them ever appears as an official measure in post-Conquest documentary sources,[59] though there is one explicit if strangely isolated reference to the continued use of the short perch: a survey of the Lincoln bishopric manors, compiled in 1349, states that the lands, meadows and pastures are 'measured by the royal perch of 15 feet' *(mensurat(e) per pertic(am) xv pedum regal(em))*.[60] These manors lay in the East Midlands, where the short perch had been the normal Anglo-Saxon measure, and the text suggests the survival of archaic local practices that some surveyor imagined to be a national standard.

Otherwise, the standard though not quite universal perch in late and post-medieval England had the awkward length of 16½ imperial feet (5.03m).[61] How such an ungainly number was arrived at has been the subject of speculation, most presciently by F.W. Maitland in 1897:

> It is when we ask for the number of feet in a perch that we begin to get various answers, and very various they are. The statutory number, the ugly 16.5, looks like a compromise between 15 and 18, both of which numbers seem to have been common in England and elsewhere. This is the royal equation in the thirteenth century; it has been found in the middle of the twelfth; more at present we cannot say.[62]

Christiansen 1998 (pp. 196–7 note 217) points out that this – and similar phrases in other texts – repeat a formulaic Old Testament expression, but his further conclusion that they tell us nothing about early medieval practice seems to be contradicted by the 1017 × 26 charter. Our grateful thanks to Lesley Abrams, Rosamond Faith and Letty Ten Harkel for their help with this difficult problem.

[58] Richard Freman had held *Fromynton* (Heref.) 'per seruitium portandi unam cordam citra murum castri Hereford dum mensurat(um) fuerit': Blount 1815, 305.

[59] Blair 2013, notes 20–3, for some ambiguous and ultimately insubstantial possibilities. We are grateful to Paul Brand for pointing out that the apparent reference to a 15-foot perch in a late medieval English text (British Library, MS Cotton Cleop. A XVI f.46) is a mistranscription (omitting *e demi* from the phrase *quinz ulne e demi facit j perticam*) from the material of c.1305 printed *Statutes of the Realm*, I, 204–5, 206–7.

[60] Oxford, The Queen's College, MS 366 fo.46.

[61] Grierson 1972, 13–14, 20–1.

[62] Maitland 1897, 374.

Given our demonstration that the established Anglo-Saxon perches did indeed measure 15 and 18 feet, it is hard to resist Maitland's inspired conjecture of a compromise, splitting the difference between the two regional modules to establish a national standard.

But when did that compromise happen? Our project has failed to recognise the 5.03m perch on grid-planned sites, and calculations of Anglo-Saxon linear measurements that have assumed its existence – most notably the various attempts to convert assessments in the Burghal Hidage into the physical lengths of perimeter defences[63] – are thereby thrown into some doubt. One of those, however, cannot be dismissed: the assessment of Winchester at 2,400 hides. Following the calculation (attached to the document) that equates four hides with one perch length of rampart, that implies a wall length of 600 perches, or just over 3,000m if the 5.03m perch is assumed – which corresponds perfectly with the actual circuit of the walls of Winchester.[64] On that evidence, it seems that the standard late and post-medieval perch was already known to King Alfred or his immediate circle. It is tempting to wonder whether Alfred's concern to reconcile differences between the West Saxons and the (Anglian) Mercians under his rule – most strikingly in the clumsy but inclusive compound 'Anglo-Saxon' that is still with us[65] – extended to reconciling their divergent linear measures. If so, it was to be two centuries or more before the new unit gained wide currency.

Two professions, two techniques? Land surveyors, architects and the places where they met

Finally, we must address the vexed question of architects, and the procedures – different from those discussed in this book – that architectural historians regularly ascribe to them. The most discussed practice is the use of geometrical proportions based on the relationship between the side of a square and its diagonal (in other words, one to the square root of two). This has been explored in a series of publications by

---

[63]   Hill and Rumble 1996.

[64]   Hill and Rumble 1996, 94–5, 225–6.

[65]   Keynes 1998, 25–6, proposing that Alfred had a vision of vision of Englishness conceived in the 'overtly political context of a wish to bring the "Mercians" and the "Saxons" together'. It is perhaps not a huge step beyond that to suggest that the 'compromise perch' of 16½ feet had political overtones comparable to those of the metre today.

the architectural historian Eric Fernie,[66] who kindly contributes some comments to this book (Appendix B).

Fernie's conclusion – very helpful in the present context – is that grid-based and geometrically based systems are not mutually exclusive, but could have been used on the same project in successive stages by different groups of people. As he observes, it makes best sense to suppose that the grid was normally established first, and proportional systems then used within its controlling framework. This is most clearly illustrated by Westminster Abbey, laid out by Edward the Confessor in the 1050s, where the architectural proportions of the apse, the west end and the arcade bay-spacings diverge from the otherwise very clear long-perch grid (Figure 5.18). It is also possible, however, that architects did sometimes grid their own building plots, but in ways different from those of the land surveyors, setting out small grids building by building rather than large grids into which multiple buildings and boundaries fitted. The almost complete lack of correspondence between the geographical distributions of settlement grids and of single-building grids (Figures 3.14, 3.15) might tend to support this hypothesis.[67]

At all events it is entirely reasonable and unproblematic to suppose that land surveyors, high-grade architects, and vernacular builders were different kinds of people and that they had different modes of professional expertise. The job of the grid-planners – whose expertise was derived from a literate, monastically transmitted tradition – was to survey their grids accurately, to mark them out on the ground by some such means as strings, pegs or furrows, and then to leave them for others to work on. The architects operated in a different tradition – transmitted orally through their craft – of geometrical construction using ropes;[68] they made use of the grids provided for their convenience, but were not constrained by them when proportional setting-out dictated minor modifications. The various modes of construction carried out on gridded sites by builders in timber will appear many times in this book, and varied greatly, from high-grade, architecturally sophisticated groups of halls to farmsteads surrounded by irregular clusters of enclosures. The separation of functions is crucial: a full appreciation of it removes some of the more obvious superficial objections to the main hypothesis of this book.

[66] For instance Fernie 1990; 2002.
[67] Below, p. 156.
[68] Cf. Richard Gem's comments cited in Blair 2013, note 39.

Conclusion

No text survives in which an Anglo-Saxon surveyor describes his working methods: archaeological and topographical data are all we have, and that fact imposes permanent limitations. We can see the grids, and occasional component features such as roads, but the physical evidence gives no clue to other procedures that are strongly emphasised in the gromatic texts, such as those for partitioning irregular plots and establishing boundaries. It is impossible – so far at least – to decode the sequence of steps employed in laying out a grid; even the base-line can only occasionally be guessed at. There is thus a point beyond which we simply cannot recover the precise ways in which English surveyors interpreted the versions of the Classical gromatic tradition to which they had access.

The general conclusion, however, is more important. Anglo-Saxon grid-planning was not some strange anomaly that developed in isolation, but a well-established European tradition in which the educated elements of English society naturally participated. If there is a mystery, it is why the technology seems to have died out after the Conquest. Given what we know about the culture of seventh- to tenth-century England, and in particular about the monastic role in moulding and disseminating that culture, the indications of planning in the early medieval landscape that the present project has revealed are entirely plausible and predictable.

Chapter 5

Higher-status settlements in England, c.600–1050

B Y ITS NATURE, formal grid-planning was an outcome of literate
learning derived from Mediterranean Europe, not of folk
technology. It would therefore be very surprising to find evidence
for it in fifth- or sixth-century England, and indeed we have no such
evidence. Gromatic surveying can be recognised from the early seventh
century onwards, when Anglo-Saxon elites opened up to cultural
influences from the continent; the people who put it into practice must
have been familiar at some level (whether through training or through
books) with the techniques of the *agrimensores*.

Thereafter, there is no inherent reason why those techniques should
not have been taught to new generations of surveyors at a vernacular
level. Nonetheless, monasteries and royal residences are very prominent
in our corpus of sites, whereas the apparent ninth- to tenth-century
hiatus – coinciding as it does with the general collapse of monastic
culture – tends to suggest that the craft was not easily sustained
without educated teachers and access to libraries. Although, therefore,
the majority of grid-planned sites by *c.*1000 were probably villages, it
looks as though educated (and especially monastic) initiatives were a
necessary context for their proliferation.

The Augustinian mission

The two earliest grid-planned structures that we have recognised in
England are also the two earliest masonry churches with substantial
surviving remains. The mission from Rome to Kent, sent by Pope
Gregory and headed by the monk–bishop Augustine, arrived in 597.
King Æthelberht gave the missionaries a site outside the walls of
Canterbury, on which they started to build a monastic complex with

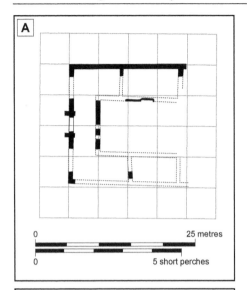

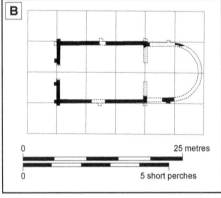

Figure 5.1. Early churches laid out using a grid.

A: The known remains of SS Peter and Paul's church in the monastic complex at Canterbury, dating to *c.*597–618, overlain with a grid of short perches (after Gem 1992, fig. 4).

B: St Pancras's church in the monastic complex at Canterbury, overlain with a grid of short perches (after Cambridge 1999, fig. 10.5).

aligned churches (Figure 5.1).[1] The main church of SS Peter and Paul – datable *c.*597–618 – survives in fragments, but there is enough to show that at least the nave, west end and lateral *porticus* were laid out (with less than perfect accuracy) on a square of 4 × 4 short-perch modules. More complete, and more compelling in its conformity, is the eastern church of St Pancras. Here, the whole building is framed very accurately within a 5 × 2 short-perch grid, comprising six squares for the nave and four for the markedly stilted apse (the geometry of which is clarified by observing that the medial grid-line of this eastern block is the chord of the apse proper).

---

[1] Cambridge 1999.

These buildings are of crucial importance in demonstrating that surveyors were laying out grids, and were using the short-perch module, from the very beginnings of the continental ecclesiastical presence in southern England. We should also, however, recognise the important limitation that the grids were specific to individual buildings: St Augustine's monastery was not laid out as an overall grid into which the churches were fitted. A strong case has been made that the missionaries had direct access to architects from north Italy,[2] and it may well have been they who gridded the building plots as a first step. It is nonetheless interesting that they used the short perch – presumably indigenous to Kent – rather than either a Roman module or the long perch that would have been familiar to Æthelberht's Frankish relatives.

The other early churches from the Kentish mission, including Canterbury cathedral itself, are too fragmentary for useful analysis. But another missing piece of the Canterbury jigsaw may have been equally important: Æthelberht's own residence. In the overblown language that Bede picked up from his informants there, Canterbury was the *metropolis* of Æthelberht's *imperium*.[3] Whether he defined his own rule in such explicitly imperial terms is uncertain. Nonetheless, the Christian rulers of south-east England certainly did share with their continental teachers a strong enthusiasm for *Romanitas*. Just as walled ex-cities were quickly chosen as diocesan seats for eastern Kent (Canterbury, 597), western Kent (Rochester, 604), and the East Saxons (London, 604), so the cosmopolitan standing of the potentates buried in princely style at Prittlewell and Sutton Hoo was celebrated by their treasures from Byzantium and Italy. It is therefore entirely plausible that, in reclaiming Canterbury, Æthelberht built one of the 'great hall complexes' that were becoming fashionable among ambitious English rulers.[4] If so, it has not been found, and obviously we cannot know whether it was grid-planned. That hypothetical possibility is, however, raised by some remarkable if indirect parallel evidence.

[2] Cambridge 1999, 205–9, 224–7.

[3] Bede, *Hist. Eccl.* i.25–6 (ed. Colgrave and Mynors 1969, 72–9); cf. Blair 2005, 272.

[4] Blair 2018, chapter 4, for the general context. If Æthelberht did have a hall, it could well have lain east of St Augustine's monastery, near St Martin's church, which was used by his Frankish queen: Bede, *Hist. Eccl.* i.26 (ed. Colgrave and Mynors 1969, 76–7).

From Canterbury to Yeavering: the secular adoption of grid-planning in a courtly milieu

Probably in the early 620s, King Æthelberht's daughter Æthelburh was married to King Eadwine of Northumbria, the rapidly ascendant power in northern England.[5] The princess made the 300-mile journey in the company of Paulinus, a member of the Italian mission in Kent who was charged with protecting her freedom to practise Christianity at Eadwine's still-pagan court. Although this condition of the marriage negotiations was observed scrupulously, Eadwine himself did not convert at once – unsurprisingly, given that there were still no English Christian kings outside Kent. Indeed, Eadwine's readiness to think seriously about the new faith is a measure of his closeness to the Canterbury court and the Roman world that it represented, a point emphasised by the papal letters and gifts bestowed on the pagan king and Christian queen.[6] In 627–8 Eadwine and his court did at length convert, destroying (according to Bede's highly coloured and perhaps dramatised account) their pagan cult site at Goodmanham (Yorks.).[7]

The point of repeating this well-known story is that it identifies a window of some three to six years when the Northumbrian court was still pagan, but was in regular contact with the Christian and Romanised court of Canterbury: this was therefore a fleeting and unusual phase when paganism and *Romanitas* could have gone hand-in-hand. Moreover, we have a remarkable opportunity to explore that phase in the elaborate architectural development of Eadwine's 'great hall complex' at Yeavering, where (again according to Bede) Paulinus preached and baptised for 30 days in the 620s.[8]

Excavated in the 1950s, Yeavering is both the best-known and the most highly structured of Anglo-Saxon residential sites.[9] It is often cited as a striking case of symmetrical architectural planning, but the rapid sequence of complex phases makes it hard to decode, so that the

---

[5] Bede, *Hist. Eccl.* ii.9 (ed. Colgrave and Mynors 1969, 162–5); Kirby 1991, 32, 38–42, 62–3, for the chronological difficulties of Eadwine's marriage and conversion.

[6] Bede, *Hist. Eccl.* ii.10–11 (ed. Colgrave and Mynors 1969, 166–75); Kirby 1991, 79.

[7] Bede, *Hist. Eccl.* ii.12–13 (ed. Colgrave and Mynors 1969, 174–87).

[8] Bede, *Hist. Eccl.* ii.14 (ed. Colgrave and Mynors 1969, 186–9).

[9] Hope-Taylor 1977.

existence of an underlying grid was only recognised at a late stage in the present project.[10] The grid becomes very clear, however, when the pair of structures identified by the excavator as the first phase built on a grand scale – a gigantic hall (building A2) and an even larger palisaded enclosure (palisade 3) – are isolated from later additions and replacements.[11] Although dating at Yeavering poses many problems, there is broad agreement that this phase probably belongs to the reign of Eadwine or just before, but pre-dates any Christian attack on pagan cult monuments.[12] There is therefore a good chance that it was created at precisely the point when Eadwine was pondering whether to accept his wife's faith along with her Roman culture.

This monumentally formal complex (Figure 5.2) was laid out on a grid of 15 × 5 short-perch squares, the enclosure (8 × 5) occupying the easternmost eight rows at full-width, the hall (7 × 3) occupying the central three rows of the westernmost seven. An internal division within the enclosure falls exactly on a grid-line. Where the wall-lines depart from the grid they may do so for subtle visual effect: to make the hall slightly angle-sided,[13] and the enclosure taper from west to east. Otherwise, the conformity leaves little room for doubt that this was a professionally gridded layout, executed with considerable care and skill.

Although this perception is new, another symmetrical aspect of the complex has long been recognised. Immediately east of the enclosure, two graves (AX and BX), each with a posthole at its foot, were placed precisely on the central axis of the hall complex (Figure 5.2).[14] Because of its extraordinary contents, grave AX is one of the most famous of Anglo-Saxon burials. Its occupant (gender unknown) lay in a slightly flexed posture, with a goat's head at the feet and a broken spear laid diagonally across the torso. Placed last in the grave, precisely on the central axis and with its head pointing eastwards, was a unique object (Figure 4.9). It comprised a roundwood staff with a bird-like wooden feature 'bound by a curve of bronze wire' at the head, bronze bindings on the shaft and an iron spike at the bottom;

---

[10] Thus Blair 2013, 22–3, wrongly defined Yeavering as axial but not gridded.

[11] Hope-Taylor 1977, 51–3, 65–6, 127.

[12] This is 'Post-Roman Phase III AB', which the excavator placed in the 610s: Hope-Taylor 1977, 158–61, 276.

[13] For this kind of visual illusionism (though mainly in a later Anglo-Saxon context) see Gardiner 2013, 70.

[14] Hope-Taylor 1977, 67–9, 73, 131.

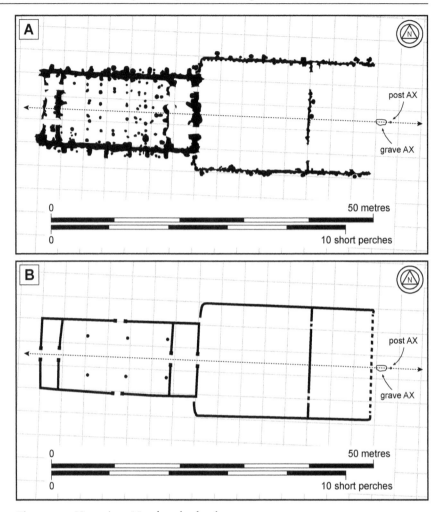

Figure 5.2. Yeavering, Northumberland.
   A: The post-trenches and post-holes of Hall A2, palisade 3, grave AX and
   post AX, overlain with a grid of short perches (after Hope-Taylor 1977,
   fig. 13).
   B: An interpretation drawing of the structural phases depicted in A,
   demonstrating the precise accuracy with which the complex was set out.
   C: Detail of Grave AX and post AX in relation to the eastern end of
   palisade 3 and the axial alignment that passes through Grave BX and post
   BX (after Hope-Taylor 1977, figs 17, 23, 24, 25, 76).

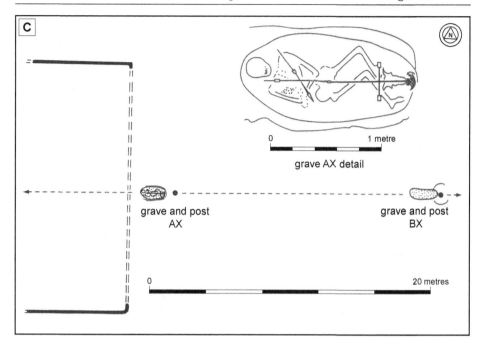

0   1 metre

grave AX detail

grave and post
AX

grave and post
BX

0   20 metres

towards the top, four 'arms' with bronze-bound tips projected in cross formation.[15]

As the excavator realised,[16] this object seems to be a kind of *groma*, the surveying tool used by Roman *agrimensores* to establish right-angled offsets.[17] It differs from the one surviving true *groma* (from Pompeii) in lacking the cranked section between the cross and the shaft that allowed a direct view between the opposed pairs of plumb-lines.[18] On the other hand, a *groma*-like object from Bavaria also had a straight shaft, as does the one represented on the tombstone of Lucius Aebutius Faustus, *mensor*, from north Italy.[19] Lucius's *groma*, unlike the two

[15] Hope-Taylor 1977, 67–9, 200–2. In interpreting the feature at the top, Hope-Taylor vacillated between a stag and a boar, but concluded that 'it would seem more closely to have resembled a sheep or a goat, or a crested bird'. This is clearly very uncertain, and another possibility is that the crest was useful in some way for taking sight-lines.

[16] Hope-Taylor 1977, 202, suggesting that 'one could perhaps see in the whole strange pattern of circumstances some reference to the status of the *agrimensores* whose work is displayed at Yeavering'.

[17] Above, pp. 99–100.

[18] Dilke 1971, 16 and opp. 51.

[19] Dilke 1971, opp. 51, 66.

surviving ones, resembled the Yeavering object in being topped with a decorative crest or panel. A cranked head is not the only possible means of achieving a sight-line: it is possible, for instance, that the Yeavering and Bavarian examples had a narrow slot cut through the shaft. The Yeavering *groma* thus fits convincingly into the Roman technological tradition, even if the decorative crest tends to identify it as a seventh-century insular product.

Earlier accounts have noted the axis running through graves AX and BX, but have associated it with the subsequent timber hall (A4) that was overlaid on the primary palisaded enclosure, adopting its alignment.[20] It is now apparent, however, that the axis of the graves precisely bisected the central row of grid-squares, suggesting that they should be associated with that phase. In the light of that, it is striking that the *groma* was positioned in the grave so as to lie precisely on the axis. This direct spatial association between a continental-style grid-plan and a continental-style instrument designed for use in grid-planning is so extraordinary that it can hardly be other than purposeful.

There are four reasons why the grid-plan and grave AX should be located in a formally pagan context. First, the axis continues westwards to pass through the lateral doorways of building D2, a cult structure containing piles of ox skulls.[21] Secondly, the goat's head in the grave cannot easily be interpreted as a Christian symbol, or as the kind of symbol that was readily transposed to a Christian context. Thirdly, the broken spear across the body has resonances of theatrical pagan rituals recognised in later Scandinavia (most dramatically in a tenth-century chamber-grave at Birka, where a spear was thrown over the corpses to embed itself in the chamber wall) and interpreted there as rites of dedication to Oðinn.[22] Fourthly, the special location of the grave – immediately outside the east end of the enclosure, and therefore liminal as well as axial – combines with its special character to suggest that this was some religious specialist or 'wise-woman/man'. In other circumstances one would be tempted to see the *groma* as an exotic and misunderstood item, recycled as a magic staff, but its direct association with grid-planned structures leads to different conclusions.

Did Queen Æthelburh ask her father to send equipment and specialists from Kent to build a monumental complex, replicating something that he had already built at Canterbury? Did Northumbrian

[20] Hope-Taylor 1977, 131.
[21] Hope-Taylor 1977, figs 12, 43.
[22] Price 2002, 133–9.

religious specialists seize on that technology, in a brief phase of syncretism in the 620s? And was the occupant of the grave an indigenous practitioner of geomancy, whose status and expertise were enhanced by learning the arts of the *agrimensor*? Nowadays, archaeologists are rightly unwilling to interpret excavated evidence in conformity with historical narratives: questions like these would go well beyond acceptable bounds in almost any other Anglo-Saxon context. However, the combination of Bede's narrative with the Yeavering excavation constitutes a uniquely explicit dataset pointing to a specific conclusion. The most plausible explanation for the arrival at Yeavering of a *groma*, and the technology for using it, is that they came from King Eadwine's Kentish in-laws.

How quickly, and how far, that technology spread to other royal residential sites is another question. We can return to it after considering the ecclesiastical institutions that were the main agents for transmitting the inherited Classical learning and putting it into practice.

The era of high monastic culture, c.650–750

The second half of the seventh century saw spectacular, probably unparalleled growth in the English Church, as a missionary phase dominated by continental bishops gave way to one of consolidation and enrichment, in which the protagonists were mostly English and their activities based in a proliferating landscape of monasteries.[23] But the movement remained cosmopolitan, with direct and frequent influences from Rome. In that milieu, grid-planning flourished, as a suitably classicising mode for organising the formal buildings of the new ecclesiastical sites.

The first phase of the Old Minster at Winchester, built c.648 under strong Italian influence, is based on a 4 × 5 grid of long perches (Figure 1.2).[24] This is essentially the system used earlier at Canterbury, and shows the same combination of an imported surveying system with a local module, in this case the northern French/West Saxon perch rather than the Anglian/Kentish one. Once again, this is a single-building grid. When did grid-planning move beyond the scale of individual buildings (or, at Yeavering, one grand building attached to one large

---

[23] Blair 2005, 79–100.
[24] Kjølbye-Biddle 1986 (with calculations that arrive correctly at the long-perch module, but by a very different route); Kjølbye-Biddle 1998 for Italian, probably Milanese influence.

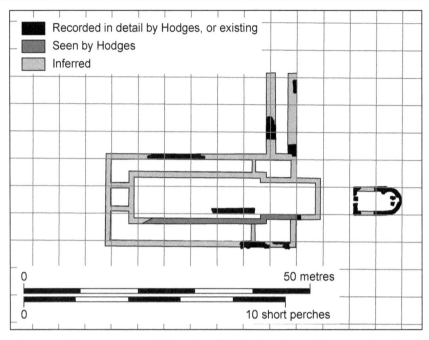

Figure 5.3. The reconstructed plan of Wilfrid's church complex at Hexham in Northumberland, overlain with a grid of short perches (after Cambridge and Williams 1995, fig. 16).

enclosure) to the surveying of large open areas into which several buildings were then fitted?

Possibly the central figure here was St Wilfrid (d. 710), the rich, powerful, combative and cosmopolitan bishop and monastic entrepreneur. His biographer tells us that he studied ecclesiastical computistics while at Rome in the 650s and, given his strong interest in architecture, he could also have studied more practical kinds of technology.[25] The core buildings of his great minster at Hexham, comprising the main church, an axial eastern chapel and a northwards-leading range,[26] were laid out very precisely on a short-perch grid (Figure 5.3).[27] This grid was not necessarily more extensive than the

[25] Stephen of Ripon, *Vita Wilfridi*, cc.5, 17, 22 (ed. Colgrave 1927, 10–13, 34–6, 44–6); Bailey 1991; Blair 2005, 93–6.

[26] Cambridge and Williams 1995, 73–80 and fig. 16.

[27] Blair 2013, 23, 25 and notes 50–1, argues that Wilfrid's crypts at Ripon and Hexham were both planned around a single short-perch square.

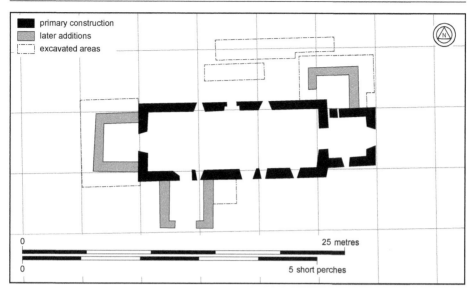

primary construction
later additions
excavated areas

0   25 metres

0   5 short perches

Figure 5.4. Plan of the early church at Escomb, County Durham, overlain with a grid of short perches (after Pocock and Wheeler 1971, fig. 1). Compare figs B.1–3.

Yeavering one, and the buildings were much smaller. Architecturally, however, they were more complex and compartmentalised, with discrete elements tied together by the controlling framework of the grid. Given Wilfrid's cultural links, and his possible connection with a grid-planned site at Polebrook, Northants (Figure 6.2),[28] it is difficult to doubt his formative role in spreading the technology.

Wilfrid's contemporary and rival Benedict Biscop, who (in Bede's words) built 'in the manner of the Romans which he always loved',[29] may have used the same or similar techniques for his monastic complexes at Monkwearmouth (673) and Jarrow (682). These show less conformity to the module, however, and, while their layout is clearly rectilinear, their status as grid-planned sites remains unclear.[30] The plan of the contemporary though undocumented church at Escomb[31] (Figure 5.4) may be based on a row of four short-perch squares, though

[28] Below, p. 159.
[29] Bede, *Historia Abbatum*, c.5 (ed. Grocock and Wood 2013, 32–3).
[30] Blair 2013, 23–6, for references, and for a more optimistic assessment than the present team's considered judgement.
[31] Pocock and Wheeler 1971.

if so the initial grid was slightly modified by the builders as they laid out the foundations (see discussion by Eric Fernie, Appendix B).

Turning from Northumbria's core to its periphery, the western British monastic site of Whithorn experienced a 'colonial' remodelling in the early eighth century after annexation by Northumbria.[32] Excavations have found a pair of apparently ecclesiastical buildings on a terrace, with further lines of timber buildings to the south (Figure 5.5). There is a regular configuration, with some hints of the short-perch module, but the small size of the excavated area makes this an inconclusive case.

Perhaps the largest and most complex of the Northumbrian minsters was the great royal nunnery of Whitby, where the famous synod (at which Wilfrid was a leading protagonist) met in 664. Bede's references suggest a big, rambling settlement, with disparate activities going on in various nooks and corners.[33] Early twentieth-century excavations revealed a dense conglomeration of rubble-footed eighth- to ninth-century structures immediately north of the later abbey church. Unfortunately, these excavations were of poor quality: the available plan shows what is clearly a sequence of superimposed phases, but does not make it possible to distinguish between them.[34] There is, however, a strong impression of rectilinearity, with several individual buildings and pathways conforming to a short-perch grid (Figure 5.6). Some support for that grid is now provided by more recent excavations, up to 200m northwards and 250m north-eastwards, which show groups of ditches and other features in rectilinear configurations conforming to the same alignment.[35] The evidence is frustratingly fragmentary, but it does suggest that the headland occupied by this very wealthy and important community was laid out on a single grid, either at its foundation in the 650s or in the coming decades. In this respect as in others, Whitby could have been a fashion-setter.

On present evidence, grid-planning was recurrently employed for laying out Northumbrian minsters, but is less evident (after the Canterbury episode) in ecclesiastical contexts in central or southern England. This could be a genuine pattern – stemming for instance

---

[32] Hill 1997, 134–82.

[33] Blair 2005, 199.

[34] Cramp 1976, 223–9.

[35] Wilmott, in preparation; many thanks to Tony Wilmott and John Vallender for providing a plan. It seems likely that continuing work on the site will refine these conclusions further.

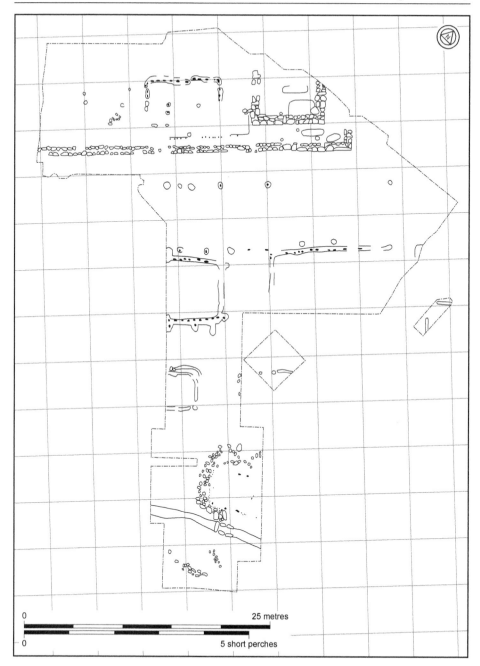

Figure 5.5. Plan of the excavated early medieval structures at Whithorn, Dumfries and Galloway, overlain with a grid of short perches (after Hill 1997, fig. 4.5).

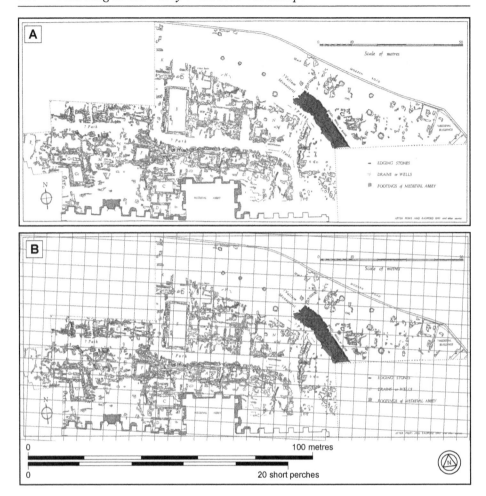

Figure 5.6. Whitby Abbey, North Yorkshire.
　　A: Plan of the excavated early medieval structures recorded on the north side of the extant church (plan drawn by Philip Rahtz, published in Cramp 1976, fig. 5.7, reproduced by permission of Lorna Watts).
　　B: Plan of early medieval structures recorded on the north side of the extant church overlain with a grid of short perches.

from the heavyweight cultural influence of Wilfrid or the Whitby community – or could simply reflect the geography of large research excavations on monastic sites.

High-status secular sites, *c.*640–700

South of the Humber, elite complexes of this period that have been excavated on any scale are mainly secular, and these offer some further evidence for grid-planning. Although none of them quite equals the elaborate formality of Yeavering, several other 'great hall complexes' are now known in Northumbria, the Midlands and southern England.[36] At present it cannot be said for certain how many were grid-planned, since most are known either from cropmarks alone or from cropmarks supplemented by small-scale excavation. In general the individual buildings are precisely rectangular, but it is less clear whether that precision extends to the overall spatial organisation. It could well be that the 'Yeavering mode' was copied more widely – perhaps through the kind of court-to-court exchange proposed above for Yeavering itself – but without professional surveying. Formal gridding is, however, apparent on two hall complexes in the south, and on an anomalous but probably high-status site in the Midlands.

Recent excavations at Lyminge (Kent) have revealed a remarkable sequence of high-status activity.[37] Sixth-century occupation on the edge of a Bronze Age barrow (forming a component of a more extensive settlement) moved southwards during the seventh century and became architecturally more ambitious, culminating in a hall complex in quadrangular configuration based on a short-perch grid (Figure 5.7). This comprised a major west–east hall with external buttresses, a smaller building to its east and a third hall-type building to the south. The major hall was placed centrally within three rows of grid-squares: the medial axis of the central row passed not only through its sequence of internal and end doorways but also through the side doorways of the smaller building, an emphasis on axiality that recalls Yeavering. One of the Lyminge halls of this phase was floored with an imitation of Roman *opus signinum*; this technique, found also in a short-perch-gridded hall at Dover (Figure 5.8), must surely derive from its use to floor the early seventh-century churches at Canterbury.[38] In the light of the present arguments for Yeavering, this fact takes on a special significance: it raises the possibility that at Lyminge, too, the formal layout took its inspiration from classicising architectural display at King Æthelberht's 'metropolis'.

---

[36] Blair 2018, chapter 4, for a review.
[37] Thomas 2017.
[38] Thomas 2017, 107, 111; Philp 2003, 65–7.

Figure 5.7. Plan of the excavated great hall complex at Lyminge, Kent, overlain with a grid of short perches (based on a plan and information supplied by Gabor Thomas).

The cropmark site at Cowage Farm, Bremilham (Wilts.), near the Iron Age hillfort and seventh-century minster of Malmesbury, is well known, but the phases are hard to disentangle (Figure 1.1).[39] A substantial building on its eastern side, in its own ditched enclosure and with an apparent eastern apse, is usually interpreted as a church: a strong possibility is that the complex eventually became some kind of

[39] Hinchcliffe 1986.

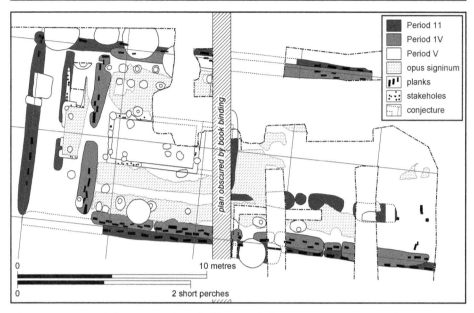

Period 11
Period 1V
Period V
opus signinum
planks
stakeholes
conjecture

0   10 metres
0   2 short perches

Figure 5.8. Plan of the excavated probable great hall at Dover, Kent, overlain with a grid of short perches (after Philp 2003, fig. 4).

dependency or 'grange' of Malmesbury.[40] It seems likely, though, that this post-dates two earlier phases (the sequence of which is undefined), each based on a distinct and differently orientated grid of short perches. One of these comprises rows of small buildings, with little evidence for enclosures, but is dominated by an elaborate hall with detached annexes to north and south. In the other the buildings are fewer, whereas enclosures defined by rectilinear ditch-systems are more prominent; a two-perch by four-perch hall with narrow end bays lies out to the east. An important message of this case is that total clearance, followed by comprehensive regridding with no regard to the earlier layout, was an option on sites of this kind.

The same process is evident at Catholme (Staffs.), beside the river Trent: a site unique not only in its character but also by its location in a part of Midland England where Anglo-Saxon timber buildings are scarcely ever found.[41] The settlement, which apparently spans the sixth to early eighth centuries, faced towards a Bronze Age barrow at its

[40] Blair 2005, 213–14 (alignment of timber 'church' on Bremilham church); Blair 2013, 27–8 (not separating out the two gridded phases proposed here).

[41] Losco-Bradley and Kinsley 2002; Blair 2018, 158–61.

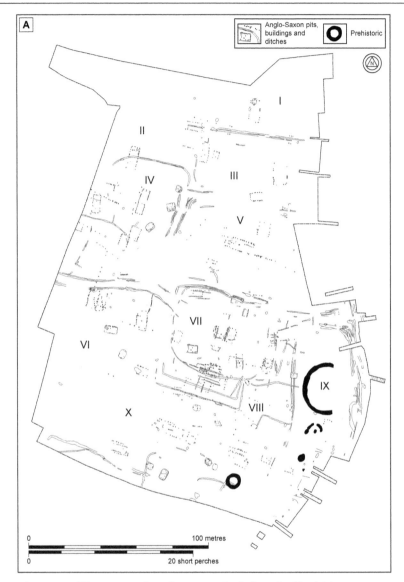

Figure 5.9. The excavated settlement at Catholme, Staffordshire.
    A: Anglo-Saxon pits, buildings and ditches shown in relation to major
    prehistoric monuments (based on raw data provided by Gavin Kinsley
    [formerly of Trent and Peak Archaeological Trust, now SLR Consulting
    Ltd] and published in Losco-Bradley and Kinsley 2002).
    B: The proposed first stage of settlement planning using grids, where
    the laying out of new buildings was still done within the framework of
    pre-existing enclosures and trackways (grid of short perches).
    C: The proposed second stage of settlement planning, based on a
    grid, where only the trackway and the prehistoric barrow survived as
    influential 'legacy' features (grid of short perches).

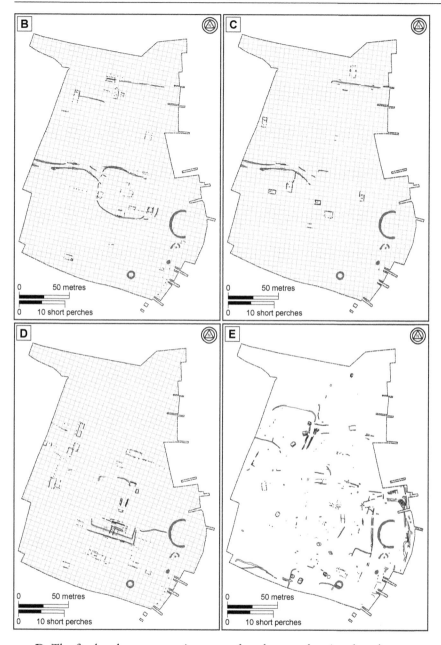

D: The final and most extensive stage of settlement planning, based on a grid, where buildings and new straight-sided enclosures based on ditches and fences were set out (grid of short perches).

E: All other features not fitting into one of the three principal episodes of grid-planning. Note that there are few structures that do not correspond to the proposed gridded phases, and those few are mainly the curvilinear ditches, which we propose to be early in the sequence.

eastern edge, perched on the Trent scarp (Figure 5.9). Phasing of this site is difficult, but the earliest developed stage may be represented by a sub-oval enclosure approached from the west via a ditched trackway. There then appear to be no fewer than three grid-planned phases, each on a slightly different alignment, comprising spaced-out configurations of small timber buildings. The sub-oval enclosure may initially have been retained, but was then replaced by a rectilinear one conforming to one of the grids. This place, whatever it was, is so anomalous regionally that it must have been something special – a conclusion reinforced by its relationship to surviving prehistoric monuments and its focal location next to the Trent crossing of Ryknield Street. The successive grids point to the same clear-and-replace policy observed at Cowage Farm.

One further site of this period is anomalous for a different reason. Although very possibly a product of royal or monastic initiatives, the Six Dials area of *Hamwic* (Southampton) was mercantile in function (Figure 5.10).[42] A west–east street was demarcated by two parallel gullies that may have been the primary setting-out marks, and are one short perch apart. This street kinked in a series of straight sections, one of which was flanked by buildings on both sides. Piecemeal development created a rather heterogeneous townscape, but it is apparent that the plots were set out at right angles to the road and that the short-perch module occurs in several places. A possibly similar configuration to the south, on a different alignment, is represented by one row of buildings and some disjointed fragments. Grid-planning may be at work here, but it is also possible that Six Dials represents a different kind of approach (commercial rather than royal or monastic?) in which streets were established and linear plots then off-set from them, rather in the manner of a high medieval village or town.

Regular planning has not yet been recognised in the contemporary trading settlement of London (*Lundenwic*), but some buildings there were laid out on a module of 1 × 2 long perches (Figure 5.11). To find the short perch at *Hamwic* (in Wessex) but the long perch at *Lundenwic* (at the interface of Essex, Mercia and Kent) is the reverse of what we would have expected. It must tell us something about the origins of the people who established and used these settlements: Mercians (or even possibly Wilfrid's entourage) at the West Saxon court,[43] but Frankish traders at London?

[42] Andrews 1997, 31–2; Blair 2013, 33–6.
[43] Blair 2013, 36.

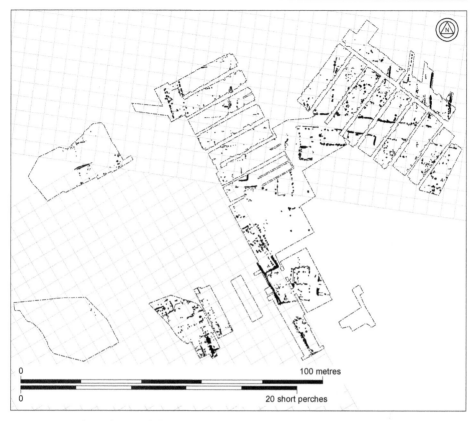

0
100 metres

0
20 short perches

Figure 5.10. Plan of part of the excavated emporium at *Hamwic*, overlain with a grid of short perches (after Andrews 1997, fig. 2). The edges of the trenches are shown in heavy dot-dash line.

In summary, there are strong grounds for thinking that, during *c.*640–700, grid-planning with the short perch became established as a mode of laying out the larger, more elaborate and more important secular settlements. Cowage Farm and Catholme suggest that such settlements could pass through decidedly short-term phases of occupation, readily swept away and replaced. But the owners of these sites, like monastic communities (at least in Northumbria), could call on expert surveyors who would move in and perform their standard grid-planning job in preparation for the next phase of building. We do not know who those people were, but it seems likely that they were still closely tied to the literate high culture of the minsters: as that culture declined in the course of the mid- to late eighth century, they too seem to have faded away.

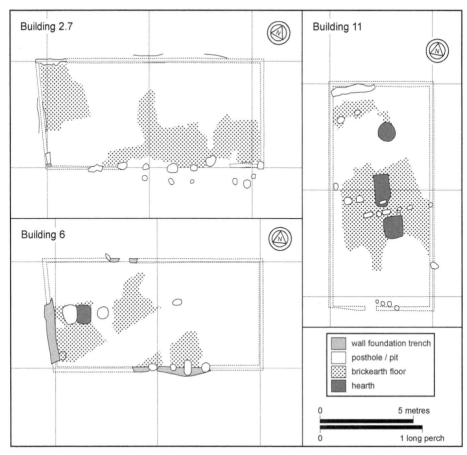

Figure 5.11. Excavated Buildings 2.7, 6 and 11 at the Royal Opera House, London, within Middle Saxon *Lundenwic*, showing evidence for the possible use of the long-perch module in their setting out (after Malcolm *et al.* 2003, figs 25, 30 and 65).

The era of monastic insecurity and stagnation, *c.*750–800

The mid- to late eighth century can be seen as the tail-end of the first phase of grid-planning. Minsters came under political and economic pressure, a sense of insecurity developed, and aspects of their artistic culture became more repetitive and derivative.[44] On the other hand, new injections of creative influence from Francia and Italy were a stimulus for some impressive buildings and some wonderfully innovative

---

[44] Blair 2005, 121–7.

sculpture.[45] The little that we currently know about contemporary grid-planning is consistent with that context: there are only two clear cases, but both are technically of high quality.

The first case is the probably monastic site of Brandon (Suffolk), where material culture of remarkable opulence was associated with a settlement of relatively small-scale timber buildings.[46] 'Phase 2.2' in the excavators' sequence[47] can now be separated into two or more sub-phases by the recognition of two successive gridded layouts (Figure 5.12), the order of which is unclear. One is relatively simple, comprising (within the excavated area) three buildings and a slightly curving ditch. The other is represented by the south-western ends of at least six rows of buildings, some of them very precisely located in relation to the grid. This is clearly just the edge of a substantial and highly structured settlement, most of which remains unexcavated. These episodes of gridding followed the demolition of an elaborate early to mid-eighth-century building interpreted as a church, and were themselves superseded by a different (and somewhat reduced) phase, probably datable to *c*.850. They can therefore plausibly be dated to *c*.770–820, and must have followed each other in relatively quick succession.

One great building can be considered the swan-song of grid-planning in pre-Viking England. The church at Brixworth (Northants) is a unique surviving example of 'Anglo-Carolingian' architecture, built *c*.780–800 out of recycled Roman materials and in the image of the monumental Romanising structures currently going up in Charlemagne's realm.[48] The ground plan (Figure 5.13) is based accurately on a short-perch grid, which determines the shape and size of the nave and lateral *porticus* and the overall length of the choir and apse; a striking but localised distortion at the west end should probably be ascribed to a surveying error. Like Brandon, this shows that high-precision professional grid-planning was still available in England in the years around 800. From that point onwards, however, the metropolitan artistic culture of the Anglo-Saxon monastic Church went into steep, eventually almost terminal, decline.[49] The grid-planning technology seems to have been one of its casualties.

---

[45] See, for instance, the essays in Brown and Farr 2001.

[46] Tester *et al.* 2014.

[47] Tester *et al.* 2014, 18–19, 22–5 (for the radiocarbon dating evidence and the phasing), 63–100 (for the archaeology).

[48] Parsons and Sutherland 2013 for a comprehensive survey and analysis.

[49] Blair 2005, 127–9.

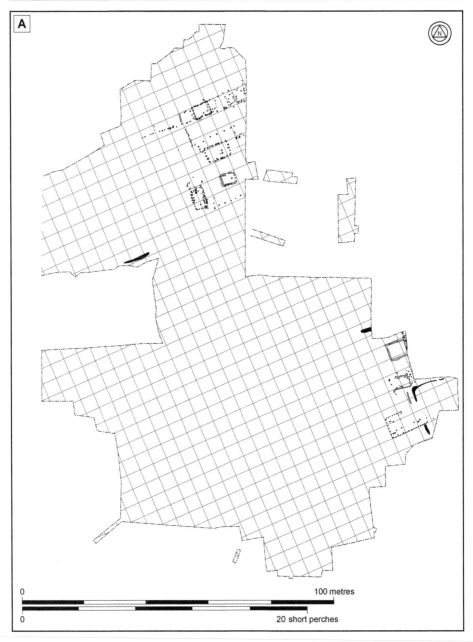

Figure 5.12. The high-status Middle Saxon settlement at Brandon, Suffolk (after Tester *et al.* 2013, fig. 4.23). The chronological order of the two grid-based plans is unclear.

 A: Structures and boundaries of Phase 2.2 which conform to a grid of short perches orientated north-west–south-east.

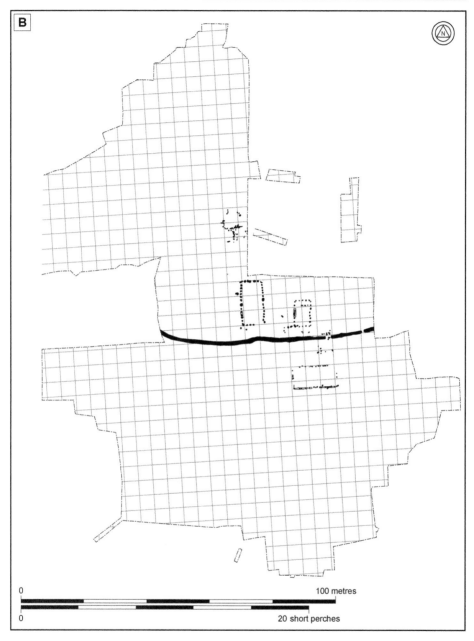

B: Structures and boundaries of Phase 2.2 which conform to a grid of short perches orientated north–south.

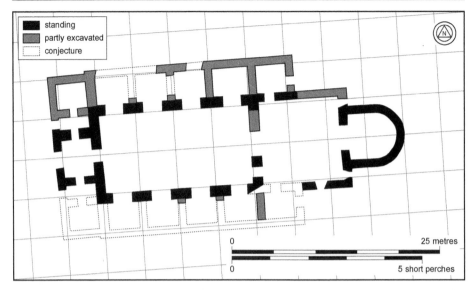

Figure 5.13. Reconstructed plan of the late eighth-century church at Brixworth, Northamptonshire, overlain with a grid of short perches (after Parsons and Sutherland 2013, fig. 12.9).

The interlude

Against the background of so many grid-planned sites identified during this project, a negative result stands out starkly: with one dubious exception, we have been unable to recognise a single new case of grid-planning that can be shown to date from between *c.*800 and *c.*940. Great churches such as those at Cirencester and Deerhurst, built only a little way into the ninth century, show no evidence of the technique. Even if the money to pay for specialists was still there, it was evidently no longer used for that purpose: it seems that either the professional surveyors had disappeared or the patrons were no longer interested in employing them.

The ostensible exception is the minster church of St Oswald at Gloucester, built by Æthelflaed, daughter of King Alfred and 'Lady of the Mercians', in the late ninth century.[50] As Figure 1.2 shows, this building is almost identical in plan (apart from the west-facing apse) to the Old Minster at Winchester. Its layout is therefore based on the long perch – otherwise unknown in central Mercia – and this very surprising

---

[50] Heighway and Bryant 1999.

fact suggests an explanation. In establishing a new central place around which Mercia could regroup after Viking devastation, Æthelflaed may have wished to express symbolic or nostalgic affection for the mother church of Wessex, which she must have known well in her childhood. If she asked her builders to measure and replicate the Old Minster, its ground plan – modular structure and all – would have been carried across automatically. Probably, therefore, this is not a case of deliberate grid-planning, but a grid-plan replicated unconsciously at second-hand.

It is above all at the so-called 'burghal' fortified sites[51] that absence of evidence becomes evidence of absence. The idea that these were 'planned' is so deep-rooted in the consciousness of everyone interested in Anglo-Saxon England that they might seem the first and most obvious places to look for systematic grid-planning. But although we analysed the four conspicuously rectilinear examples – Oxford, Wallingford, Wareham and Cricklade – with great care, and at times thought that we might be detecting fragmentary traces of underlying grids in all of them, we were forced in the end to conclude that such evidence is at best dubious. Only at Cricklade (Figure 5.14) did the rampart approach geometrical regularity, and even that has a kink suggestive of a basic surveying error.

A complexity here is that the origins of these formally rectilinear 'burghal' forts are more uncertain than is usually thought: they may well pre-date Alfred, perhaps by many decades.[52] They could also have developed through several phases (existing settlements being fortified by stronger ramparts, for instance), so it is quite possible that some of them do contain or overlie grid-planned settlements, traces of which show through.[53] But the royal surveyors who built the ramparts and metalled streets in such a consistent and stereotyped fashion were either unable or unwilling to use the technology of the *agrimensores* for laying them out, as the coherent but obviously non-orthogonal street-plan of Winchester illustrates most clearly. They may even have forgotten that the technology had ever existed. Famously, King Alfred recalled that

> before everything was ransacked and burnt, the churches throughout England stood filled with treasures and books. Similarly, there was

[51] Hill and Rumble 1996.
[52] For a comprehensive review, which deconstructs and substantially rejects the 'burh' paradigm, see Blair 2018, 232–46.
[53] A possible instance is the north-western quarter of Oxford, which is notably more regular in its layout than the other three quarters.

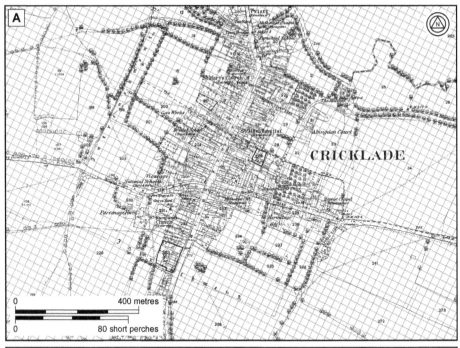

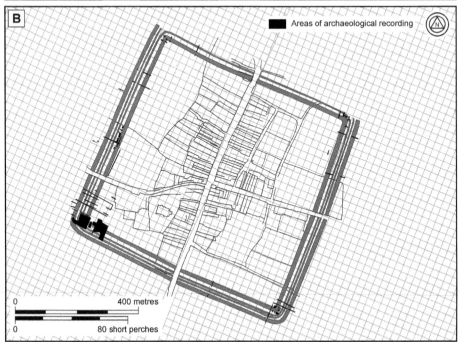

Figure 5.14. *opposite* The Anglo-Saxon fortification at Cricklade, Wiltshire.
  A: The late nineteenth-century plan overlain with a grid of four short perches (first edition OS 25-inch base map: © Crown Copyright and Landmark Information Group Limited (2016), all rights reserved, 1875 and 1877).
  B: The proposed outline of the burghal defences, based on excavated evidence, overlain with a grid of four short perches (based on Haslam 2003, fig. 6).

a great multitude of those serving God. And they derived very little benefit from those books, because they could understand nothing of them, since they were not written in their own language.[54]

Even if some of those churches had owned gromatic texts, they would have found them as incomprehensible as all their other Latin books. The recovery of that technology would have to wait for another great monastic revival.

Monastic sites of the Reform period, *c.*940–1020

As well as regenerating both the wealth and the international culture of the reformed houses, the monastic reform of the mid- to late tenth century prompted an influx of textual material. As we saw, it is likely that this included gromatic manuscripts,[55] and that the monastic context explains the revival of the grid-based surveying technology after 940, even if it was then quickly extended to purely secular sites. Obviously, if this scenario is correct, we should expect the monastic sites themselves to have been grid-planned as a prelude to their remodelling and enlargement to accommodate larger communities, stricter lifestyles and more elaborate liturgical practices.

Does the archaeology support that expectation? There are two reasons why the reformed monastic sites are difficult to interrogate topographically. First, most of them acquired a heavy overlay of high medieval urban topography as they developed into towns during the eleventh to thirteenth centuries. Secondly, the post-Conquest rebuilding of their core premises as formal Romanesque churches and cloisters created layouts that were precisely quadrangular for a different reason, and there is an obvious risk of misinterpreting these as earlier grid-plans. The fact that we can be confident of grid-planning at only

---

[54] Keynes and Lapidge 1983, 125.
[55] Above, pp. 104–5.

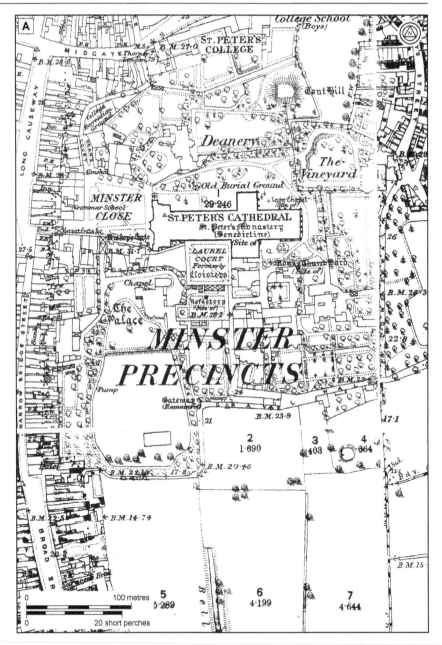

Figure 5.15. The Benedictine monastery at Peterborough, Northamptonshire.
A: The monastery and urban topography in the late nineteenth century
(first edition OS 25-inch base map: © Crown Copyright and Landmark
Information Group Limited (2016), all rights reserved, 1887, 1888 and 1889).

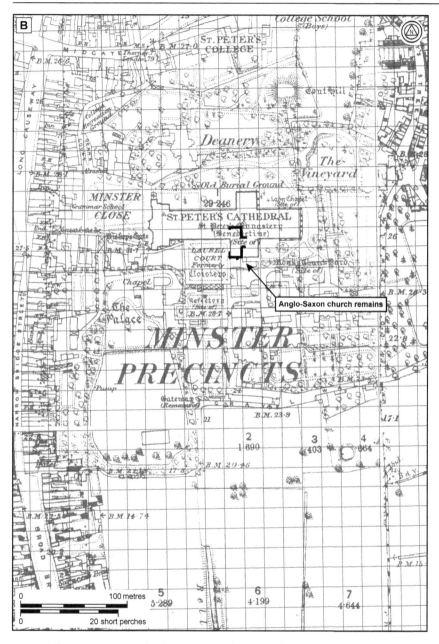

B: The monastery and urban topography in the late nineteenth century, shown with the known footings of the late tenth-century church (after Irvine 1894) and overlain with a grid of four short perches; first edition OS 25-inch base map: © Crown Copyright and Landmark Information Group Limited (2016), all rights reserved, 1887, 1888 and 1889).

two of the major sites may not, therefore, tell us very much: it could easily have been effaced at several of the others.[56]

The first case is Peterborough, a previously rich and important minster that was refounded as a Benedictine house c.970. Here the quadrangular configuration of the church and cloister extends further outwards in all directions, covering an area of more than 300m × 300m, and conforms in several places to a grid of four short perches (Figure 5.15). This in itself might not be strong evidence for a pre-Conquest date, but fortunately the lateral *porticus* of the late tenth-century church are known from excavation, and these conform to both the alignment and the grid.[57] This can therefore be accepted as a reform-period layout, presumably the work of Bishop Æthelwold of Winchester (d. 984), the proprietor and refounder.

Eynsham (Oxon), refounded in 1005, was one of the latest products of the movement. This is another case where the excavated remains of the original core complex are decisive. The later town has the layout of a typical high medieval urban development, grouped around a marketplace at the abbey gate. In its streets and plot boundaries it is possible to pick out elements on both axes that appear to respect a grid of four short perches. On its own, this would be an unconvincing case. However, excavations on the site of the later abbey have located stone-built ranges that formed part of the 1005 buildings, and these conform closely to the same grid.[58] Together, Peterborough and Eynsham show that grid-planning was at least one possible response to the updating of an old monastic site during c.960–1010, even if not necessarily the only one.

The great majority of the many pre-Viking minsters that survived into the tenth and eleventh centuries were never reformed as Benedictine houses. There is, on the other hand, no reason why some or many of them should not have been replanned on grids in this period. The smaller unreformed minsters raise a problem of definition: although probably numerous, they are especially poorly documented in the eastern regions where grid-planned settlements concentrate. An illustration is Whissonsett (Norfolk), which has excavated features from both the pre-800 and post-900 phases in conformity with the grid (Figure 3.11).

[56] At an earlier stage of the project we considered the possibility of a grid at Abingdon. In the end the evidence was considered too insubstantial, though JB still retains some confidence in it.

[57] Irvine 1894. Thanks to Jackie Hall for helpful comments on Peterborough.

[58] Blair 2018, 318–19; Hardy *et al.* 2003.

The large parish church at the heart of the complex – itself aligned on the grid – is now late medieval. However, it contains an impressive and high-quality stone cross-head, probably of *c*.900, while a cruciform mount of similar date was found in a garden to the south.[59] This looks like one case where an early grid was perpetuated into the later period, or at least replanned on the same alignment; the stability afforded by a surviving minster community might help to explain that. How representative this case may be is currently impossible to say.

High-status secular residences, *c*.940–1020

During the two centuries after the disappearance of 'great hall complexes' around 700, Anglo-Saxon settlements and their buildings are remarkably unexpressive of social status or hierarchy. In the course of the tenth century, however, a handful of 'proto-manorial' sites, visibly of higher status than the villages discussed in the next chapter, started to appear on the scene.[60] Their advent was more or less contemporaneous with the revival of grid-planning on ecclesiastical sites, and indeed most of them seem to have been grid-planned. There may therefore be a sense in which the reappearance of hierarchy and display in domestic architecture, and the reappearance of grid-planning, were facets of the same broad socio-cultural change. In the decades after 940 there was more money around, stronger royal government, more peace and stability and a revived interest in modish continental culture that was focused especially on the drive for monastic reform.[61] Given the nostalgia for the 'golden age' of Bede that so strongly tinged the reform movement,[62] it would also be unsurprising if new modes of display were retrospective, reinventing the practices of *c*.650–750.

Two excavated sites, at Cheddar (Somerset) and Faccombe Netherton (Hants), were of elite secular status from the outset and are unique in having contemporary documentation. Both were in Wessex, and both therefore used the long perch for their grid-plans. The royal hunting lodge at Cheddar had two successive gridded phases, of perhaps *c*.950 and *c*.1000, comprising in each case a hall with rather exiguous ancillary buildings.[63] Faccombe (Figure 5.16), where the grid

---

[59]   Blair 2018, 290–1.
[60]   Blair 2018, 362–72.
[61]   Blair 2018, 311–17.
[62]   Wormald 1988.
[63]   Rahtz 1979; reinterpretation in Blair 2018, 362–4.

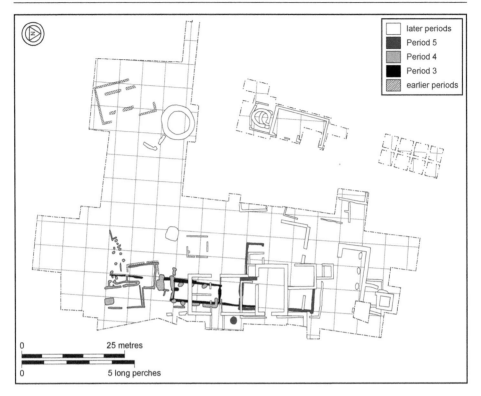

Figure 5.16. Plan of excavated remains of the high-status secular settlement at Faccombe Netherton, Hampshire, overlain with a grid of long perches (after Fairbrother 1990, fig. 1.4).

controls an axially aligned hall and chamber block, was one of various properties bequeathed in the will of the late tenth-century noblewoman Wynflaed.[64] These unambiguously aristocratic residences lie outside the main geographical zone of grid-planning, and may reflect a more hierarchical social structure in Wessex.

In the East Midlands and East Anglia, grid-planned aristocratic residences are less sharply differentiated from grid-planned groups of ordinary farmsteads, and indeed seem often to grow out of them. This category of sites – and the social phenomena that they illustrate – are fully discussed elsewhere, so the present account is a summary.[65] In

---

[64] Fairbrother 1990; Blair 2018, 365–9 (including a slightly more ambitious interpretation than the present one, with two grids proposed).

[65] Blair 2013, 36–45, and Blair 2018, 362–9, where plans and references will be found.

brief, they are all based on short-perch grids, and they tend to begin as one, two or more farmstead units; during *c*.950–1020 a single domestic complex gains topographical and architectural dominance, acquiring more emphatically marked boundaries, more elaborate buildings and sometimes a church. Variants on the theme are illustrated here by Springfield Lyons (Essex), which was probably always a single complex (Figure 1.3), and Raunds (Northants), where we get a clearer picture of an emergent manor house within a larger grid-planned villagescape (Figure 6.11). Other cases are Ketton Quarry (Rutland), West Cotton (Northants), Howbury (Beds.), and Goltho (Lincs.). It is probably wrong to see places like these as different in kind from the semi-nucleated villages to be discussed in Chapter 6: rather, they suggest social competition and change within communities that were subject to the same cultural and technological influences.

Planning in Edward the Confessor's court circle?

One key question that this project has failed to answer with much clarity is when professional grid-planning ceased in England. We have found no compelling evidence that it survived the Norman Conquest – for example, it is not found in the regular row-plan villages of northern England (see Chapter 2) – though that is not something for which we have searched systematically. It seems possible that the practice declined after 1000, very much as it did after 800 and for similar reasons. As the reformed monasteries ran into progressively serious trouble in the years leading up to Cnut's conquest we may well envisage that they would have taken a less dynamic role in land-management technologies. By that point, the majority of grid-planned villages were probably not in monastic hands,[66] although if the technology was now completely freestanding from monastic training or oversight its decline becomes harder to account for.

On the other hand, there are hints – if currently rather inconclusive ones – of a mid-century revival. A possible association between grid-planned (or, by this time, strip-planned) rural estates and Edward the Confessor's earls and their families will be considered later.[67] The case of Stow (Lincs.), which is a plausible if not compelling grid-plan (Figure 3.6), deserves mention here because of its unusual documented context. In the 1050s the bishop of Dorchester collaborated with

[66] Below, pp. 167–71.
[67] Below, p. 171.

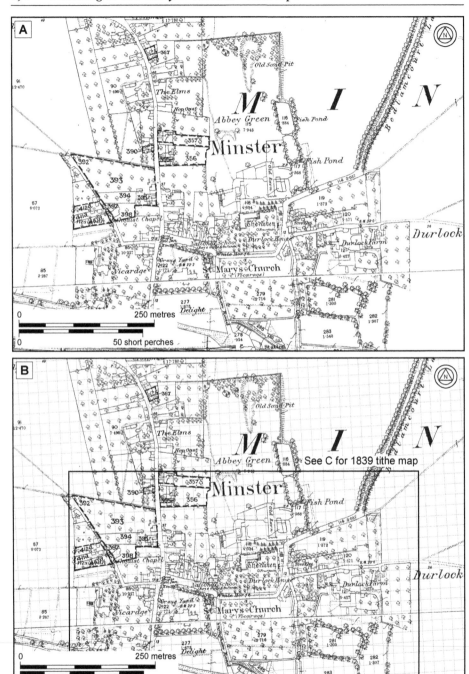

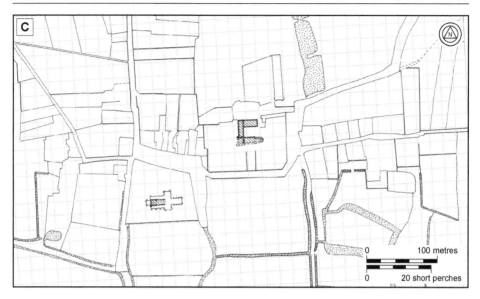

Figure 5.17. The village of Minster-in-Thanet, Kent, and its surrounding fields.
A: The late nineteenth-century landscape (first edition OS 25-inch base map:
© Crown Copyright and Landmark Information Group Limited (2016), all
rights reserved, 1873 and 1877).
B: The late nineteenth-century landscape overlain with a grid of four short
perches.
C: The early nineteenth-century layout, based on a transcription by John
Blair of the 1839 parish tithe map, with key monastic buildings emphasised,
overlain with a grid of four short perches (transcribed from tithe map,
National Archives IR 30/17/254, with additional detail of standing and
excavated Anglo-Norman structures).

Earl Leofric of Mercia and his wife Godgifu to revive this old
minster under an agreement whereby food rents and market dues were
carefully apportioned in one-third and two-thirds fractions.[68] In this
case it is notable that the grid does not align on the (presumably older)
church, and one possibility – it can, of course, be no more than that –
is that the settlement core was regridded at the time of the agreement
and as part of the same negotiations.

Minster-in-Thanet (Kent), one of the richest nunneries of seventh-
century England, retained a community of priests in the mid tenth
century. After disruptions in the early eleventh century the site
was acquired by St Augustine's Abbey at Canterbury, apparently in

[68] Sawyer 1968, S 1478.

the 1030s–1040s.[69] The convincing short-perch grid underlying this settlement could theoretically have been established at any point from the seventh century onwards (Figure 5.17). Its prominence in the post-medieval topography may, on the other hand, suggest a relatively late date, as does the conformity to it of the parish church (late eleventh-century or earlier?) and the late eleventh-century buildings at Minster Court. This is, therefore, a plausible candidate for a grid-plan from the years or decades around 1050.

Cases such as this may simply represent the last gasp of the old tradition. Alternatively, it is not impossible that there was a new injection of continental influence after 1042, when Edward the Confessor returned from his long exile in Normandy and established a court with strong cross-channel links. A dramatic testimony that the technique was alive and well in the 1050s is Edward's greatest architectural project, Westminster Abbey, which is unambiguously laid out on a grid of long perches grouped into 4 × 4 blocks (Figure 5.18). This case – discussed further by Eric Fernie in Appendix B – is important because it implies a pre-surveyed grid within which the builders subsequently laid out the church on the basis of their own different, probably geometrically based, measurements. In a sense, it is a bridge between the last distant echoes of the *agrimensores* and the new world of Romanesque and Gothic architects.

An obvious question raised by Westminster is whether any of the great Romanesque churches of the Anglo-Norman era were also built on pre-gridded sites. That question lies outside our remit, but we hope that architectural historians will now address it in the light of our findings. One case worth mentioning in conclusion, however, is the abbey and town of Bury St Edmunds, since both were laid out by Baldwin, a major figure at King Edward's court, whose career as abbot (1065–97) spanned the Conquest period.[70] The large and complex abbey precinct is clearly rectilinear, and is flanked on its west side by the town, which is laid out on a broadly checkerboard configuration of streets (Figure 5.19).[71] One possibility – considered but not resolved by this project – is that a common grid-plan based on multiples of short perches underlies the

---

[69] Blair 2005, 87–8, 258, 298–9; Kelly 1995, xxviii–xxxi.

[70] See the essays in Licence 2014.

[71] We have used Thomas Warren's plan of 1747, which is redrawn true-to-scale in Fig. 5.19. We could not agree on this case: JB suggests that there is a grid of four short perches underlying the monastic precinct and town, whereas SR and CS were sceptical.

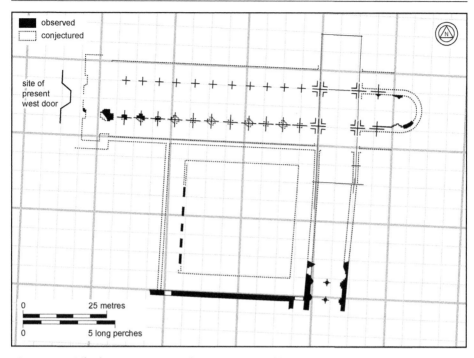

Figure 5.18. The known remains of Westminster Abbey in the mid-eleventh century, overlain with a grid of long perches (after Fernie 1983, fig. 91). Compare Figures Appendix B.8–B.9.

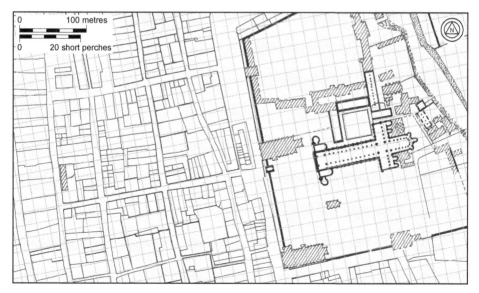

Figure 5.19. Bury St Edmunds: the monastic site and the town, illustrating the possibility of a coherent rectilinear plan (for sources see p. 152 note 71).

precinct and the eastern half of the town. If it does, it must date from early in Baldwin's abbacy: Domesday Book's statement that in 1086 the town 'is now enclosed in a larger circuit of land which [in 1066] used to be ploughed and sown'[72] would then refer to a westwards enlargement in which the primary settlement was remodelled. Even if we discount the hypothesis of a grid, Bury stands as an excellent illustration of the new – twelfth- to fourteenth-century – era of massively constructed but non-geometrical 'planned towns'. That transition takes us into a different world of planned landscapes that is beyond the scope of this book.

Conclusion

This chapter and the previous one have given strong grounds for thinking that grid-planning was in origin an elite and educated practice, not a vernacular one, and that its presence or absence were determined by essentially top-down processes. Of the two periods in which it occurred, the first began with the Italian mission to Kent in 597, which seems to have transmitted the technique to Northumbria as part of a package of religious and cultural innovations. As monasticism spread and flourished during c.660–720, so did grid-planning: this approach to laying out space had resonances with the old Roman world, the source of so much that was both appealing and prestigious, and the same considerations help to explain its adoption on high-status secular sites. During the late eighth and ninth centuries, as the monastic culture declined and ultimately faced ruin, grid-planning seems (so far as our evidence goes) to have disappeared completely, which is hard to explain except on the hypothesis that its intellectual life-blood was cut off. A new era of grid-planning was initiated at the time of the great monastic renewal that occurred in England after 940, perhaps declining in turn as the impetus behind reformed monasticism itself tailed away.

The chronological gaps tend to suggest that the technique was not easily sustained without the back-up provided by educated institutions and their resources. That does not necessarily mean that it was never diffused beyond elite circles. In both periods we have found grid-planned sites that are not self-evidently of high status: they clearly represent a much wider social range that – at least in the later period and in certain regions – extended deep into lay society. It is to the exploration of this wider culture of grid-planning in late Anglo-Saxon England that we now turn.

[72] Little Domesday Book fo.372.

Chapter 6

Rural settlements in England, c.600–1050

AMONG GRID-PLANNED SETTLEMENTS in early medieval England, the distinction between 'high' and 'ordinary' status is sometimes a problematic one. In the period before 800, most excavated grid-planned sites that are not obviously monastic or aristocratic are open to interpretation as monastic offshoots or dependencies. After 940, by contrast, most of the grid-based settlements known from excavations and map evidence underlie developed villages, and their modest status might seem self-evident. The reality may not be quite so straightforward: it is likely that these places have changed radically at some point after the grids were created, constituting 'fossils' of settlements that had originally looked quite different. Nonetheless, there does seem to be a broad trajectory: from the elite and strongly ecclesiastical origins of the technology during the seventh century to a situation by *c.*1000 when – at least in some parts of England – many seemingly 'ordinary' rural settlements had been laid out on grid-plans. The challenge is tracing the social, economic and geographical course of that trajectory.

Grid-planned rural settlements: distributions and regional contexts

In John Blair's 2013 article it was observed that grid-planned settlements seemed to concentrate in certain parts of England.[1] The more thorough survey for the present project – which has greatly enlarged the corpus of sites – supports that conclusion. Since patterns of regional variation may offer important clues to the contexts in which grids were created, this chapter starts with a discussion of them, framed around six distribution maps (Figures 3.13–3.18).

[1] Blair 2013, 49, 54–5.

Based upon the methodology outlined in Chapter 3, Figure 3.13 is a total plot of all the sites and buildings – whether map-based, excavated or architectural – that we accepted by the end of the project as demonstrating grid-planning, in the range of reliability between probable, plausible and possible. Geographical patterning is immediately obvious. The epicentre of the distribution lies in Northamptonshire, Huntingdonshire, Bedfordshire and Cambridgeshire, spreading north-eastwards into western Suffolk and Norfolk and south-westwards into Oxfordshire, Gloucestershire and northern Berkshire. North of the Fens, there is a slightly less dense cluster in western Lincolnshire and Nottinghamshire, becoming more dispersed as it extends northwards into Yorkshire. There are sparse scatters in southern Wessex and Kent, but the whole westernmost third of England provides only very occasional sites.

The next five maps present selections from that total corpus. Figure 3.14 is a plot of cases where gridding is evident across whole settlements, while Figure 3.15 shows the small number of cases where grids appear to be confined to a single building. A striking message of these two maps is that the distributions are almost mutually exclusive: nearly all the isolated buildings – which are also essentially buildings of high status – lie outside the main concentrations of grid-planned settlements. This unexpected result may be showing us a distinction between the practitioners of surveying and of building technologies, as discussed at the end of Chapter 4.[2]

Figures 3.16 and 3.17 plot the datable sites (in other words, those with excavated features or building remains, in several cases with known historical contexts) according to the two chronological phases of grid-planning. The earlier group is too small to be very robust statis-tically, but tends to suggest that the emphasis on the East Midlands and western East Anglia was already apparent by 800. In the more numerous later group that pattern is extremely clear. Finally, Figure 3.18 shows sites that are known only from cartographical and earthwork evidence, and are therefore undated. Here the same pattern stands out very clearly, although it is notable that this group includes most of the sites in Lincolnshire, Yorkshire, Oxfordshire and Gloucestershire. While the heavy concentration of housing and commercial development in the East Midlands since the 1980s has produced a corresponding – and therefore biased – concentration of excavated sites, it nonetheless remains fairly clear that the distribution thins out towards its south-western edge.

[2] Above, pp. 112–14.

In summary, we have good evidence that the grid-planning of settlements concentrated in what may be conceived as a broad, funnel-shaped zone around the Wash, the Humber and their tributary rivers, with the spout of the funnel extending south-westwards into the upper Thames region. There are suggestive signs of this pattern in the early phase (*c.*600–800) and clear evidence for it in the late phase (*c.*940–1050). There is little reason (setting aside the apparently different geography of building-specific grids) to suspect drastic spatial shifts over time, although it does seem possible that use of the technology expanded and intensified within its own heartland in the post-940 period.

It remains to suggest explanations for these phenomena. Figures 3.14–3.18 show the boundaries of two alternative zones that have been proposed, by different recent authors, as defining the socio-economic geography of early medieval England. The first (solid lines) is very well-known: it is the 'Central Province' in the now-classic scheme of English settlement regions proposed by Brian Roberts and Stuart Wrathmell, characterised by nucleated settlements and developed open-field systems.[3] The second (broken line) defines the 'Eastern Zone' that has recently been proposed by John Blair on the basis of excavated settlement archaeology, pottery and metal-detected finds. During 650–850 identified settlements comprising earth-fast timber buildings, and the associated material culture, concentrate overwhelmingly in that region. During *c.*900–1050 the same remains true to a significant extent, although there is a notable spread of visible settlements south-westwards, into Somerset, Wiltshire and the West Midlands, while coins and other metal finds occur much more widely over western England.[4]

It is immediately obvious that the geography of grid-planned settlements bears only a partial relationship to Roberts and Wrathmell's Central Province, whereas it bears quite a striking relationship to Blair's 'Eastern Zone'. The south-westwards expansion after 900 of visible building remains – notably into Somerset – is not matched by a corresponding expansion of grid-planned settlements, which instead continued to cluster within the original zone. It could in theory be argued that different trajectories of later village development in Somerset have masked grids more thoroughly than in the East Midlands, but this seems a weak case in the absence of independent evidence for any such difference.

[3] Roberts and Wrathmell 2000; 2002.
[4] Blair 2018, 32–5, 324–8.

What should we make of these patterns? In the first place it must be emphasised that Blair's dataset is an index of *visible* settlement: in other words, the 'Eastern Zone' was characterised by a cultural package of building technology that can be perceived because foundations penetrated the ground and of material culture including pottery and the small portable items found by metal detectorists. There were plenty of people living further west and north: it is just that their domestic environments were of a kind that eludes archaeological perception.

The basis of the 'eastern-zone' package was partly economic: this was the area of seventh- to ninth-century England where money was widely used, where there was a strong consumer culture and (by inference) where there was high per capita wealth. But cultural factors were also important. The people who lived in the river catchments of the Wash and Humber had direct access to the north-west European sea routes, which were conduits for ideas as well as commodities: there is a case for associating eastern England more with this North Sea socio-economic zone than with regions to its west.[5] It was also the 'Eastern Zone' that contained some of England's richest and most powerful monastic communities, both in the late seventh to eighth centuries and in the Reform period after 940.

There are grounds, therefore, for associating grid-planning with prosperity, material complexity, wide horizons and a cosmopolitan outlook – and perhaps specifically with the great monasteries that embodied all of those things. The western zones into which visible building modes and material culture spread during the tenth century were still – measured by those cultural criteria – slightly peripheral, and it may be that lack of full integration that explains the failure of planning technology to spread correspondingly. Grid-planned settlements were not absent from the western regions, but their occurrence there may have been quite special and specific. We should therefore probably distinguish between areas where grid-planning became firmly rooted in local practice and those where special initiatives by well-connected proprietors were needed to achieve it.

From monastic offshoots to lay settlements, *c.*680–800

A small number of excavated settlements that date from the period 680–800, and are not ostensibly either royal or monastic, are persuasive cases of grid-planning. Compared with the post-940 sites this is quite

---

[5] Blair 2018, 40–6, 276–81.

a select group, sharing in particular a recurrent pattern of proximity to known or possible minsters.

The type-site, because of its unambiguous historical context, is the one excavated at West Fen Road, just outside Ely.[6] It lay on the fringe of one of the greatest royal nunneries of eastern England, and its monastic association – perhaps as a service settlement of estate workers – is beyond question. The first two phases, of *c.*730–50, comprise successive grids of four short perches. In the first phase the boundaries of the grid-squares are marked in several cases with ditches, making this the closest correspondence that we have encountered between the surveyors' grid and the physical structuring of the settlement. Occasional small buildings were fitted within that framework of boundaries.

Four other sites have been excavated on a large enough scale to be intelligible, and suggest a broadly similar pattern. The late seventh-century settlement at Quarrington (Lincs.), near the probable minster of Sleaford, has a configuration of boundaries closely resembling West Fen Road, again on a four-short-perch grid.[7] A large area at Stratton (Beds.), to the south of Biggleswade, includes a late seventh-century phase of boundary ditches that, although defining linear rather than quadrangular enclosures, conform to a four-short-perch grid (Figure 6.1). About a century later the settlement was replanned on a different alignment and perhaps on another four-perch grid.[8] Smaller in excavated area and rougher in layout, but still plausibly gridded, is a group of buildings at Walton (Bucks.), just outside the Iron Age hillfort containing the important minster of Aylesbury.[9] Finally, a seventh-century settlement at Polebrook (Northants), east of the minster at Oundle where St Wilfrid died in 709, comprises buildings and linear ditches conforming to a grid of short perches (Figure 6.2).[10]

All five of these sites were already recognised in time for the 2013 article: the present project has revealed no other comparable cases. So

---

[6] Mortimer *et al.* 2005; Blair 2013, 33–4, for analytical plans and historical context.

[7] Taylor *et al.* 2003; Blair 2013, 33–4, for analytical plan and historical context.

[8] Unpublished data kindly supplied by David Ingham of Albion Archaeology. For a fuller discussion, with analytical plans of both phases, see Blair 2013, 33–5 (where the site is incorrectly called 'Stratford'); JB is still confident of the later grid.

[9] Ford *et al.* 2004; Blair 2013, 27–31, for analytical plan and historical context.

[10] Upex 2003; Blair 2013, 27–30, for historical context.

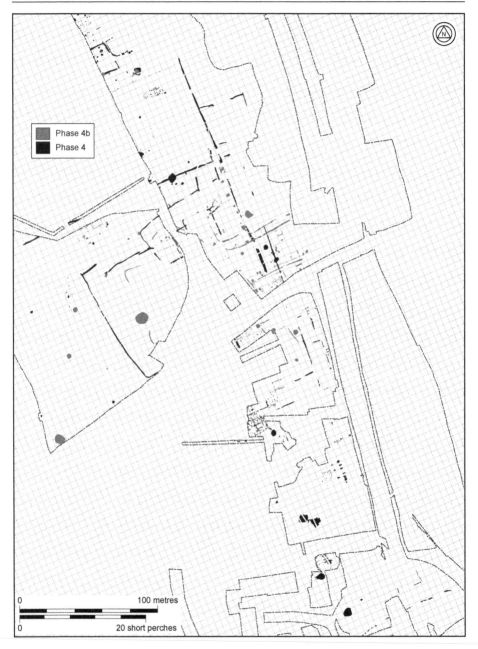

Figure 6.1. Phases 4 and 4b of the extensive excavated seventh- to eighth-century settlement at Stratton, Biggleswade, Bedfordshire, overlain with a grid of short perches (after plans supplied by Drewe Shotliffe, Albion Archaeology).

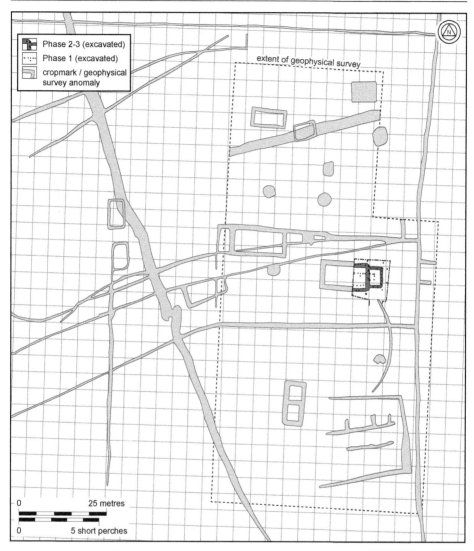

Figure 6.2. Polebrook, Northamptonshire, showing evidence from cropmarks, geophysical survey and excavation overlain with a grid of short perches (after Upex 2003, figs 6 and 8).

– with the reservation that future archaeology may of course change the picture – this looks like a fairly select category. Furthermore, their close proximity to minsters is striking. Minster status is certain in the cases of Ely, Aylesbury and Oundle and highly probable in the case of Sleaford; for Biggleswade no documentation exists, but hints in the post-Conquest sources point in the same direction.[11] Overall, there is a strong case to associate these sites with the monastically-based planning technologies discussed in Chapters 2 and 5, and to envisage them as economically functional satellites, perhaps housing groups of the low-status working 'brethren' mentioned in some contemporary sources.[12]

Apart from this group, identified non-elite cases of grid-planning and the short-perch module from before 800 are on a very small scale, confined to single buildings or groups of two to three: a range at Burpham (Sussex),[13] some farmsteads in north-west Yorkshire on the Pennine slope[14] and a small farmstead at Kentford (Suffolk).[15] In none of these cases is the historical or tenurial context demonstrable; the most they can tell us is that the technologies did perhaps penetrate beyond high-status circles, but only to a limited extent.

One other limitation seems important. With the possible exception of Whissonsett,[16] we have not found a single case of a grid-planned settlement established before 800 where anything of the grid survived to influence the configuration of boundaries, roads or buildings in the tenth century or later. That is in contrast to the period after 940, when – as we shall see shortly – grid-conforming features have been excavated in at least seven villages whose underlying grids can be recognised on the nineteenth-century Ordnance Survey maps, and in many more where the alignments and dimensions of the grids have probably influenced the later topography in less visible ways. There are thus grounds for suspecting that the great majority of grid-planned villages that we have identified from nineteenth-century map evidence were established in the tenth to eleventh centuries, not earlier.

It is tempting to suggest occasional exceptions, where potentially gridded villages – identified only on nineteenth-century maps – are in close proximity to early minsters. For instance, Hartshorn (Derbys.: Figure 6.3), in a region that was a backwater by the tenth century,

---

[11] Biggleswade was a valuable manor of Archbishop Stigand in 1066, later a prebend of Lincoln cathedral; Stratton was a chapelry of Biggleswade parish church. See Blair 2013, note 79.

[12] Blair 2005, 212–15, 254–6.

[13] Blair 2013, 21.

[14] Chapel-le-Dale and Clapham Bottoms: Blair 2018, 159–63.

[15] We are very grateful to Faye Minter for drawing our attention to this unpublished site (excavated by Archaeological Solutions Ltd) just as the project was finishing.

[16] Above, pp. 146–7.

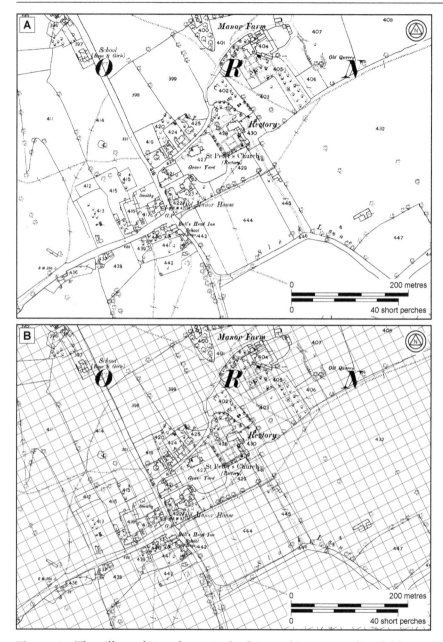

Figure 6.3. The village of Hartshorn, Derbyshire, and its surrounding fields.
A: The late nineteenth-century landscape (first edition OS 25-inch base map: © Crown Copyright and Landmark Information Group Limited (2016), all rights reserved, 1881 and 1882).
B: The late nineteenth-century landscape overlain with a grid of four short perches.

adjoins the great Mercian royal minster of Repton, of great wealth and importance in the seventh to ninth.[17] The late map evidence depicts intriguing clusters of gridded sites around other minsters that were not reformed in the tenth century: Kempston, Howbury and Clapham around Bedford; Stoke Mandeville (and the excavated Walton) around Aylesbury;[18] Great Hale (and the excavated Quarrington) around Sleaford; and Hackleton, Preston Deanery (Figure 3.12), Little Brington and Little Houghton around Northampton. At the important but unreformed minster of Bampton (Oxon) a block of grid-planning lies immediately outside the eastern edge of the ecclesiastical focus.[19]

None of these cases is currently datable (though Kempston has tenth- to eleventh-century features conforming to the grid[20]), and only excavation can show whether any or many of them reflect pre-Viking monastic estate topography. In any case they do not compromise the broader pattern: we can now recognise, in the old 'Eastern Zone' of visible Anglian settlement, a major phase of settlement growth after 940 that for the first time made grid-planning a familiar aspect of ordinary rural communities.

Grid-planned rural settlements, *c.*940–1020: monastic lordship, lay lordship or autonomous choice?

Given the close link between early grid-planned settlements and minster communities, it is reasonable to ask whether similar relationships can be identified between grid-planned villages and reformed monasteries in the post-940 era. To investigate that possibility, we produced maps of all the identifiable properties of three of the wealthiest houses – Bury, Peterborough and Ely – with distinct symbols for the villages that appear to us to show grids (Figure 6.4).[21] In one sense, the result is negative: in all three cases it is only a small minority of these settlements – probably no greater than the overall incidence of visibly gridded villages in Cambridgeshire and Suffolk – that are grid-planned.

---

[17] Biddle and Kjølbye-Biddle 2001.

[18] This is one case where the Domesday entry is helpful: the bishop of Dorchester/Lincoln held Stoke Mandeville, but it 'belongs to the church of Aylesbury'.

[19] Blair 2013, 49, 52.

[20] Below, pp. 246–9.

[21] Bury from data kindly provided by Sarah Foot and Richard Purkiss; Peterborough and Ely selected by JB from Domesday Book in the light of the Peterborough chronicle sources and the *Liber Eliensis*.

Equally, a comparison of the total corpus of grid-planned villages with their entries in Domesday Book does not suggest (even allowing for tenurial change over several decades) that a particularly high proportion of them were in monastic hands. We should therefore probably conclude that in the period *c.*940–1020, unlike the period *c.*650–800, grid-planned settlements were not pre-eminently monastic creations.

In another sense, though, an interesting point emerges from these distribution maps. In at least two of the three cases[22] one potentially grid-planned village stands out as being in close proximity to the parent house, and may have had a special relationship with it. Immediately down-river from Bury was Fornham All Saints (Figure 6.5), where topographical and onomastic hints that this was the early 'central place' of its region[23] offer a context for its continued use by the abbey as an economic focus. And north of Peterborough along the Car Dyke lay Peakirk, an old ecclesiastical site that Peterborough fought energetically to retain in the early eleventh century.[24] In two other cases a comparable relationship can be inferred from topographical proximity to reformed monasteries: Hempsted (Figure 3.4), near Gloucester, and Marcham (Figure 6.6), near Abingdon. A different but comparable scenario is illustrated by the grid-planned village at Church Enstone (Oxon), an outlying but notably valuable property of the reformed monastery of Winchcombe (Figure 6.7). Such cases suggest that the planning techniques used on some of the monastic sites were extended by the religious communities to adjacent or otherwise special estate centres. Even so, it remains uncertain how far these relationships were new creations of the post-940 era, rather than inherited from the pre-Viking past.

It was argued in Chapter 5 that the chronological relationship between periods of monastic wealth and power and periods of grid-planning (*c.*600–800 and *c.*940–1020) is too close for coincidence, suggesting that some kind of educated and literate back-up was necessary to sustain the technology. But alongside that perception must be placed the fact that only a minority of grid-planned villages in the later period seem to have been in monastic hands. The most likely explanation may be that the technology, though provided by the great abbeys, was seized on

[22] In the case of Ely a similar argument might possibly be made in relation to Fordham, but it is considerably further away.

[23] We are grateful to Richard Purkiss, who is currently working on the Bury region, for this suggestion.

[24] Sawyer 1968, S 947; Kelly 2009, 284–7.

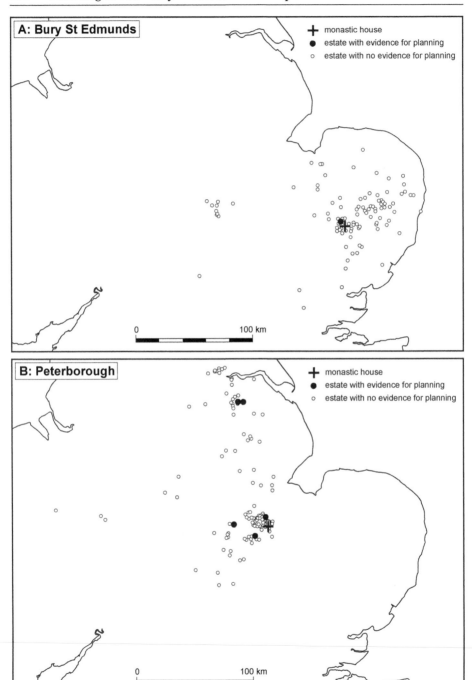

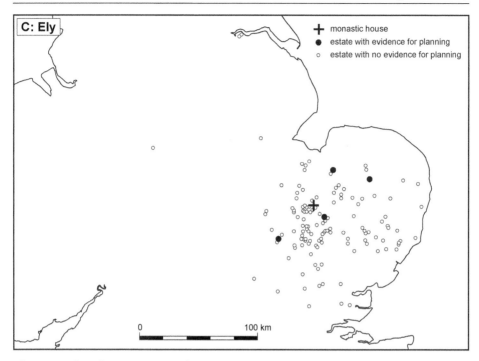

Figure 6.4. Pre-Conquest monastic estates.
    A: Bury St Edmunds, highlighting those estates where the *Planning in the Early Medieval Landscape* project has suggested that grid-planning was employed (based on a list of estates kindly provided by Sarah Foot and Richard Purkiss).
    B: Peterborough, highlighting those estates where the *Planning in the Early Medieval Landscape* project has suggested that grid-planning was employed (based on a list of estates compiled from charters and Domesday Book).
    C: Ely, highlighting those estates where the *Planning in the Early Medieval Landscape* project has suggested that grid-planning was employed (based on a list of estates compiled from charters and Domesday Book).

eagerly by other kinds of landlord, or perhaps by the rural communities themselves.

An obvious line of approach to ownership is through Domesday Book (1086), and we scrutinised carefully the entries for grid-planned places. The results, however, were disappointing. For most (though not all) counties, tenurial information is provided for 'the time of King Edward', notionally January 1066. That was half a century after Cnut's conquest in 1016, which initiated major disruption and change in the landholding classes, including insecurity and loss for several of the

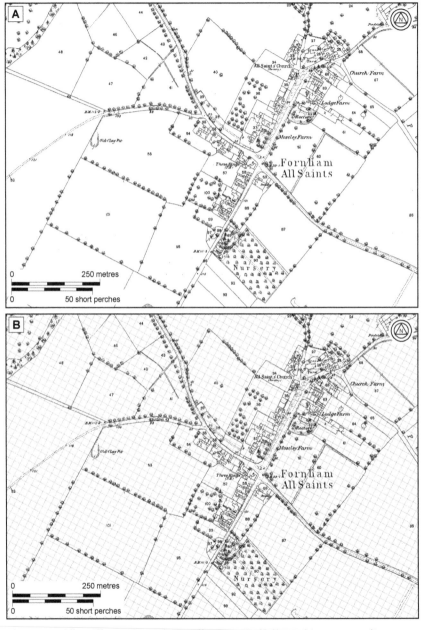

Figure 6.5. The village of Fornham All Saints, Suffolk, and its surrounding fields.

A: The late nineteenth-century landscape (first edition OS 25-inch base map: © Crown Copyright and Landmark Information Group Limited (2016), all rights reserved, 1884).

B: The late nineteenth-century landscape overlain with a grid of four short perches.

Figure 6.6. The village of Marcham, Berkshire, and surrounding fields.
A: The late nineteenth-century landscape (first edition OS 25-inch base map:
© Crown Copyright and Landmark Information Group Limited (2016), all rights
reserved, 1875).
B: The late nineteenth-century landscape, with soil/cropmarks transcribed from a
1947 vertical aerial photograph (RAF/CPE/UK/1953/555/RP/3004/25 MAR 1947),
overlain with a grid of four short perches. Many of the undated soil/cropmarks
conform to the orientation of the proposed grid and the short-perch module.

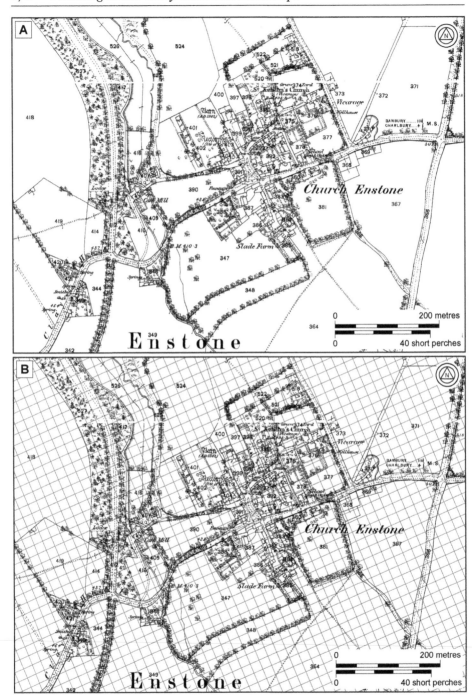

Figure 6.7. The village of Church Enstone, Oxfordshire, and its surrounding fields.

    A: The late nineteenth-century landscape (first edition OS 25-inch base map: © Crown Copyright and Landmark Information Group Limited (2016), all rights reserved, 1881).

    B: The late nineteenth-century landscape overlain with a grid of four short perches.

great monasteries. These changes may have been most marked in the East Midlands and East Anglia, where they were exacerbated by a fluid land market, and it is of course in precisely those regions that most of our grid-plans are located. Domesday Book is thus a poor guide to the kinds of agency that created grid-planned settlements a century or so before its earliest data.

Nonetheless, if the Domesday data are rarely decisive, they can be indicative. One striking and unexpected *absence* is the royal demesne: there is remarkably little correlation between grid-planned settlements and major royal estate centres in King Edward's time. The likely explanation – interesting in the present context, and no less interesting for economic historians – is that the scale and bureaucracy of the central administration encouraged a conservative and undynamic approach to estate management: royal officials had little incentive to embark on the kind of fundamental restructuring that might have employed the revived monastic planning techniques.

There is slightly – *very* slightly – more evidence to suggest that Edward's great earls and their families took an interest. Kempston (Beds.), which (as noted above) adjoins the ancient minster of Bedford but has late grid-conforming features, belonged to Earl Gyrth. Hackleton (Northants) and Whissendene (Rutland) belonged to Earl Waltheof, and Flamborough (Yorks.: Figure 3.10) to Earl Harold. Fordham (Cambs.: Figure 6.8), which has excavated evidence for a relatively late grid, and Fen Drayton (Cambs.) were held by sokemen of Eadgyth the Fair, one of the richest women in England and probably Harold's mistress.[25] If this is a genuine pattern, it is not a very surprising one: the comital families were ambitious, competitive and relatively new, and could well have been more enthusiastic than royal officials about exploring novel modes of estate management and the concomitant topographical forms.

---

[25] Another of Eadgyth's Cambridgeshire properties, Cherry Hinton, is a potentially gridded site that we considered but ultimately excluded from our corpus as too inconclusive.

Figure 6.8. The village of Fordham, Cambridgeshire, and its surrounding fields.
   A: The late nineteenth-century landscape (first edition OS 25-inch base map:
   © Crown Copyright and Landmark Information Group Limited (2016), all
   rights reserved, 1887).
   B: The late nineteenth-century landscape overlain with grids of four short
   perches on two alternative orientations, reflected in both the historic
   landscape and excavated archaeology (see C and D).

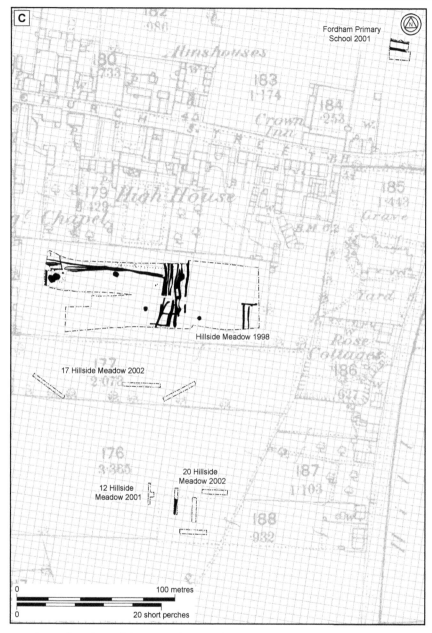

C: Archaeological features of probable Middle Saxon date predominantly sharing the same axis and conforming to one of the proposed grids of short perches (after Connor 2001, fig. 1; A. Hatton 2001, figs 1–2; R.C. Hatton 2001, figs 1–2; O'Brien and Gardner 2002, fig. 2; Patrick and Ràtkai 2011, fig. 3.3).

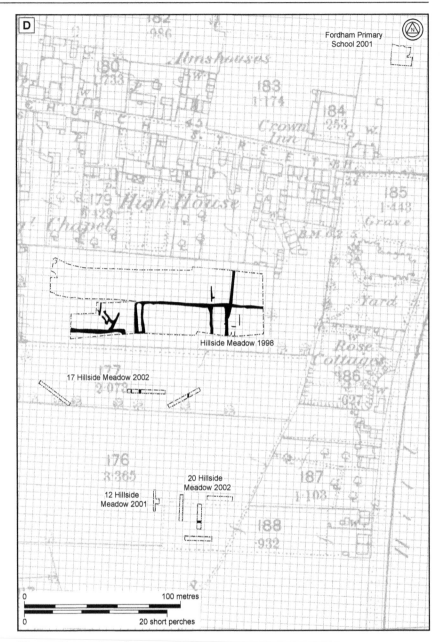

Figure 6.8. *continued*

D: Archaeological features of probable Late Saxon date predominantly sharing the same axis and conforming to the other proposed grid of short perches (sources as for C).

In 1066 the majority of the grid-planned sites in eastern England were held by – or divided between groups of – lesser individuals: sokemen, royal officers and minor thegns. It cannot be assumed that these people, or their immediate ancestors, were responsible for the grids: it is equally possible that they were beneficiaries of the attrition of great estates, both monastic and lay, in Cnut's reign. On the other hand, it could well have been in the ranks of the upwardly mobile, always looking to maximise their profits, that new ways of doing things were explored most energetically. Collective initiatives by groups of sokemen (and indeed by groups of the smaller-scale farmers whom Domesday often ignores) are entirely possible. It is indicative that some of the 'proto-manorial' homesteads on grid-plans can be located in the social range between minor thegns and aspirant ceorls and sokemen.[26]

In fact, the problems of detecting the agency behind grid-planned proto-villages are very similar to those that have always dogged understandings of high medieval village planning: did initiatives for structured topographical change come from above, through the agency of lords, or from below, through the agency of village communities? In general our archaeological evidence is inadequate to address that problem, but there is no obvious reason why we should exclude the purposeful assimilation of the elite technology at a relatively modest social level.

Grid-planned rural settlements, *c.*940–1020: the relationship between village plans and their underlying grids

To reiterate a point made earlier, these potentially gridded villages were not settlements constructed in chequer-board formation: rather, the grid was laid out as a guiding principle to frame whatever kind of settlement was required, whether the high-status ones discussed in Chapter 5 or normal rural communities. As we saw in Chapter 4, the professional surveyors who laid out the grids were probably not the people who built the houses and dug the ditches. The conformity of roads, enclosure boundaries and house sites to the grids was therefore secondary, and often partial.

Furthermore, a second layer of settlement change is usually interposed between the original grid-planners and modern observers. It is now widely agreed that 'classic' high medieval Midland villages, with linear tofts and crofts and houses fronting on the street, were

[26] Blair 2013, 38–41.

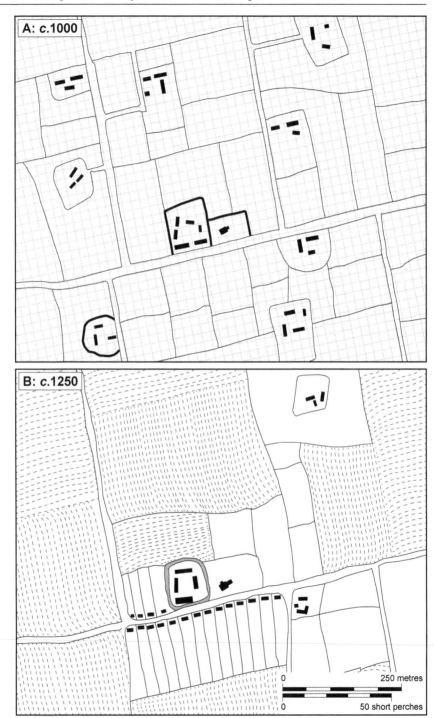

Figure 6.9. Generalised model illustrating how a late Anglo-Saxon grid-planned settlement might have evolved into a typical Midland village of the high Middle Ages. Many of the villages illustrated in this book may be the product of this kind of evolutionary development.

> **A:** A cluster of farmsteads, laid out in partial conformity to the pre-surveyed grid, as they might have looked *c.*1000. Houses, enclosures, and roads tend to follow the grid, but are not bound by it, and sometimes assume less regular configurations that change over time. The central farmstead is starting to display an aristocratic aspect, and has acquired a church and graveyard.
>
> **B:** By *c.*1250 settlement has concentrated inwards to constitute a toft-and-croft village laid out along the main street. Most of the distinct farmsteads have disappeared, but the central one is now a moated manor-house with aristocratic buildings. Open fields have encroached over some of the more peripheral farms and their closes, but the heavily overlaid grid is still sometimes reflected in the alignment of the furlong boundaries.

essentially products of the post-Conquest era.[27] Since most of the rural grids that we have recognised underlie places of this kind, the regularity that shows through must represent the lowest layer of a palimpsest culminating in the developed village. The generalised phase-plan of an imaginary East Midland village (Figure 6.9) is designed to illustrate this developmental sequence: (A) the primary surveyors' grid, *c.*950, and the establishment within that grid of a loose, semi-nucleated settlement landscape of discrete farms, *c.*950–1050; and (B) the concentration of those farm units into a smaller, tighter village nucleus, including the formation of toft-and-croft tenements and the encroachment of open-field furlongs over the former outlying farms, *c.*1050–1250.

The discussion that follows, based on the excavated evidence and on the 'category 1' and 'category 2' map-based cases illustrated in this book and in Blair's 2013 article, is therefore an exercise in 'virtual excavation', seeking to disinter the modes of settlement that the late Anglo-Saxon grids were designed to accommodate. In four villages, significant excavated remains serve both to confirm and to elucidate grids that are independently apparent from the cartographical evidence: Fordham (Cambs.: Figure 6.8), Glaston (Rutland),[28] Shipdham (Norfolk: Figure 3.9) and Tempsford (Beds.: Figure 6.10). More fragmentary cases are Kempston (Beds.), Whissendene (Rutland) and Isleham (Cambs: Figure 1.5). In a dozen or so others, excavated late Anglo-Saxon settlements

[27] Creighton and Rippon 2017; Blair 2018, 408–15.
[28] Blair 2013, fig. 24.

Figure 6.10. The village of Tempsford, Tempsford Hall, and adjacent hamlet of Langford, Bedfordshire, and surrounding fields.

A: The late nineteenth-century landscape (first edition OS 25-inch base map: © Crown Copyright and Landmark Information Group Limited (2016), all rights reserved, 1884).

B: The late nineteenth-century landscape overlain with a grid of 16 short perches.

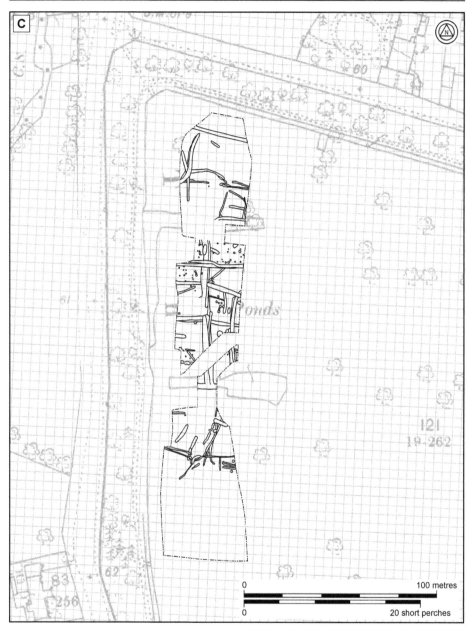

C: Late Saxon features recorded during excavations at Tempsford Park in relation to the historic landscape and overlain with a grid of short perches. The excavated Late Saxon archaeology here appears to be in conformity with the same grid as the historic village topography to the south (after Maull 2000, Figs 1, 2b, 3).

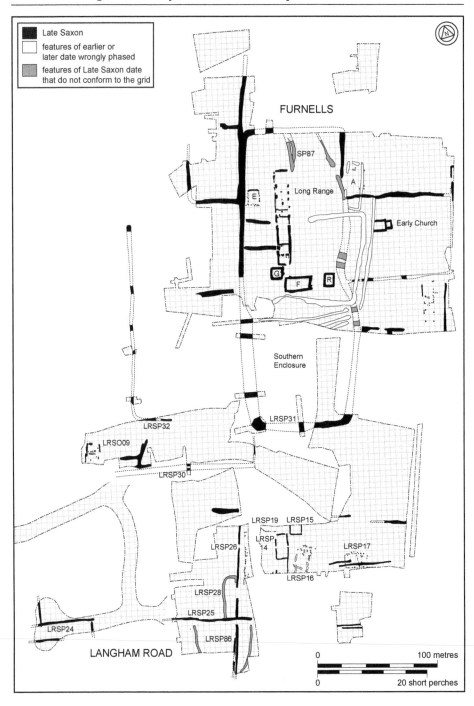

Late Saxon

features of earlier or
later date wrongly phased

features of Late Saxon date
that do not conform to the grid

FURNELLS

SP87

A

Long Range

E

Early Church

G

F   R

Southern
Enclosure

LRSP31

LRSP32

LRSO09

LRSP30

LRSP19   LRSP15

LRSP
14

LRSP17

LRSP26

LRSP16

LRSP28

LRSP25

LRSP24

LRSP86

LANGHAM ROAD

0   100 metres

0   20 short perches

Figure 6.11. The excavated Late Saxon archaeology at Furnells and Langham Road, Raunds, Northamptonshire, offering a revised analysis of the phase-plans presented in Audoy and Chapman 2009, which include features of earlier and later phases on the same plans as that for the Late Saxon period. Our reworked plan is overlain with a grid of short perches (after Audouy and Chapman 2009, figs 5.16, 5.17, 5.27 and 5.57).

that are convincingly grid-planned lie within or under villages that would not feature in our catalogue on the basis of nineteenth-century map evidence alone – although, in several of these cases, as at Raunds (Northants: Figure 6.11) it is fairly clear that the eventual village does take its overall form and alignment from the grid. Among excavated sites, Stotfold (Beds.) (Figure 1.4) is the most useful on account of its exceptional scale. From these scattered fragments we try to reconstruct the planned landscapes of late Anglo-Saxon settlement.

The anatomy of grid-planned settlements, c.940–1020

To describe grid-planned rural settlement zones as 'villages' raises questions of definition. What the surveyors evidently did was not exactly to 'plan villages'; rather, they laid out substantial open areas as grids, within which discrete and perhaps individually constructed farmsteads and their surrounding closes could then be established. To judge from our dataset, the gridded areas were recurrently between 400m and 600m across in either direction. Some, such as Isleham, Flamborough and Tempsford (Figures 1.5, 3.10, 6.10) seem to have been considerably larger, extending up to a kilometre or more, and in the case of Tempsford providing a framework within which two separate villages were eventually formed.

A problem with these large-scale examples is that it can be difficult to distinguish genuinely grid-conforming features from late and peripheral inclosure boundaries that happen to be aligned on the gridded core, but are not contemporary with it. In two cases, however, we are on firmer ground. The grid at Brant Broughton (Lincs.) covers not only the extremely large village but also the surrounding closes and blocks of open-field strips, the precise conformity of which – over an area of more than a square kilometre – is startlingly clear on the LiDAR image (Figure 6.12).[29] And Watlington (Norfolk) provides our best and most extensive physical survival of grid-conforming

[29] See also Blair 2013, 49, 53, for a transcription of a map of 1838.

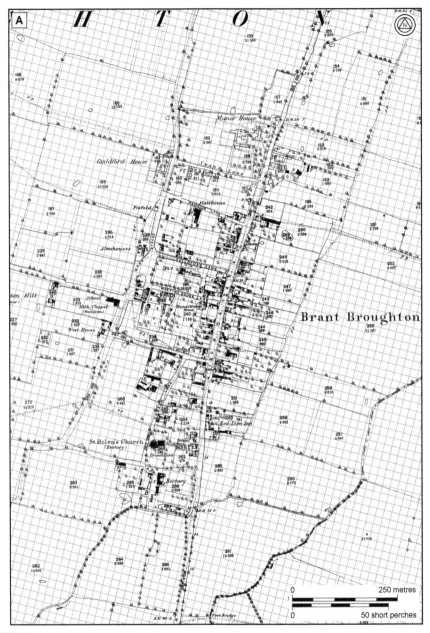

Figure 6.12. The village of Brant Broughton, Lincolnshire, and its surrounding fields.

A: The late nineteenth-century landscape overlain with a grid of four short perches (first edition OS 25-inch base map: © Crown Copyright and Landmark Information Group Limited (2016), all rights reserved, 1887).

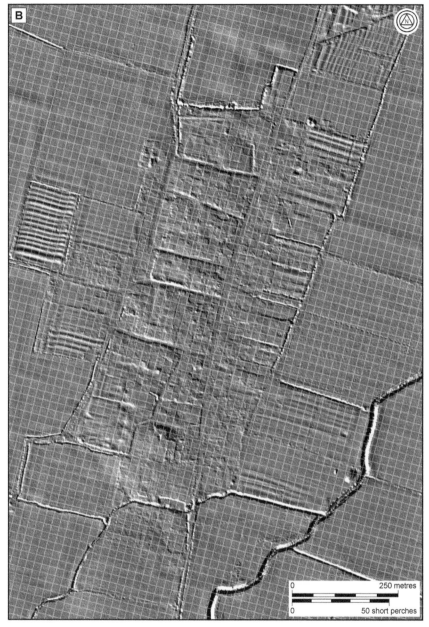

B: A hillshade model of 1 m resolution LiDAR data for the same area as shown in A. Faint earthworks to the west of the parish church (south side of village) and around the manor (north side of village) appear to conform to the proposed grid, as do prominent furlong boundaries on the western side of the village (© Environment Agency copyright and/or database right 2015. All rights reserved).

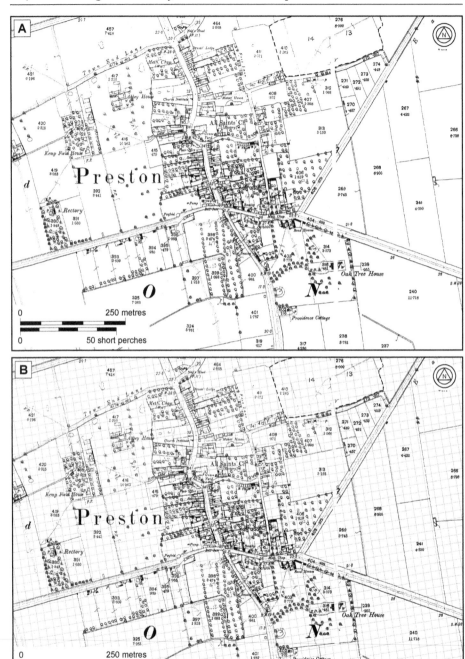

Figure 6.13. The village of Preston, East Riding of Yorkshire, and its surrounding fields.

    A: The late nineteenth-century landscape (first edition OS 25-inch base map: © Crown Copyright and Landmark Information Group Limited (2016), all rights reserved, 1890).

    B: The late nineteenth-century landscape overlain with a grid of four short perches.

boundary features, extending to nearly a square mile (Figure 3.8). Several of these boundaries – low, wide banks and ditches dotted with ancient oak-trees – survive in the modern landscape,[30] and the LiDAR image shows grid-conforming earthworks underlying the parkland around Watlington Hall. Taken together, these cases provide compelling evidence for the impressive scale that grid-planned rural settlement zones could sometimes achieve. This raises confidence in the more numerous but also more ambiguous cases (for instance Preston, Figure 6.13) where a persuasive village grid appears to extend outwards in one or more directions into a landscape of ostensibly late enclosure boundaries. Thus the 'planned landscapes' of the parliamentary commissioners, reflecting as they often do the configuration of open-field furlongs, may sometimes preserve at two removes the planned landscapes of the early Middle Ages.

    Elucidating how grids were actually used faces the challenge of disentangling the 'grid-period' from the 'village-period' features. One phenomenon that does recurrently show through is a distinctive type of major road system, comprising either a single spine road four perches wide or two roads of this width meeting in T-formation. These can be distinguished from later village roads because they conform to the grids, usually running straight along a single row of four-perch squares. This arrangement, which shows up with clarity in the earthworks at Preston Deanery (Figure 3.12), is visible from map evidence at Sulgrave,[31] Hempsted (Figure 3.4), Fornham All Saints (Figure 6.5), Welton (Figure 6.14) and Desford (Figure 6.15) and in more or less plausible fragments at several others. These extremely wide (18.3m) roads should therefore be accepted as characteristic of primary use, the obvious rationale being the need to drive cattle from the new farmsteads to outlying pastures; they were probably laid out as the first stage after establishing the grid.

---

[30] Fieldwork by JB, December 2013.

[31] Blair 2018, 320.

Figure 6.14. The village of Welton, Lincolnshire, and its surrounding fields.
A: The late nineteenth-century landscape (first edition OS 25-inch base map:
© Crown Copyright and Landmark Information Group Limited (2016), all
rights reserved, 1886).
B: The late nineteenth-century landscape overlain with a grid of four
short perches on two alternative orientations, reflected in both the historic
landscape and excavated archaeology (see C).

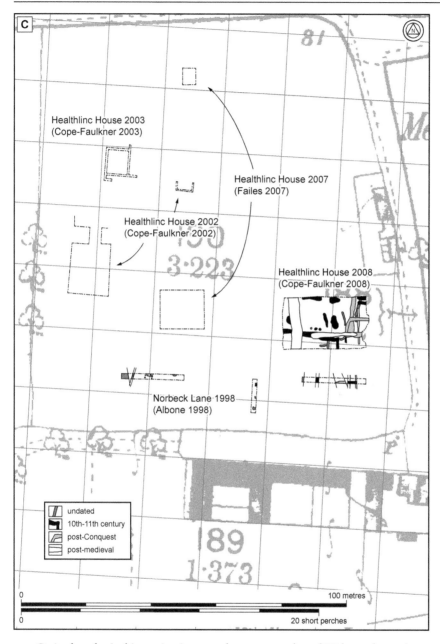

C: Archaeological investigations on the western edge of Welton, shown in the context of the historic landscape. Note how tenth- to eleventh-century and post-Conquest ditches conform to the orientation of the westernmost grid shown on B. There is no archaeological evidence to complement the eastern grid which finds agreement in the historic village topography (after Albone 1998, figs 2–5; Cope-Faulkner 2002, fig. 3; 2003, fig. 3; 2008, figs 3–5; Failes 2007, figs 3–5).

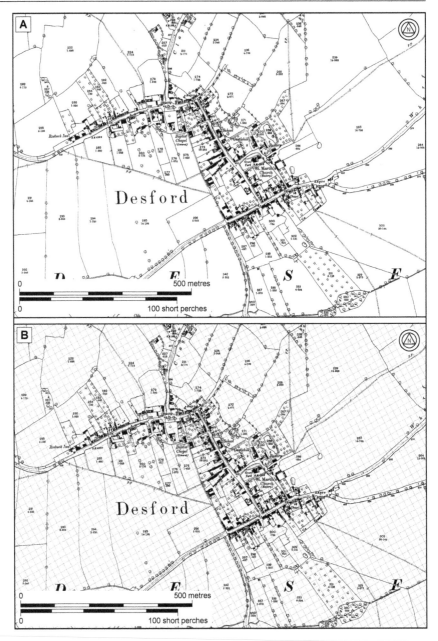

Figure 6.15. The village of Desford, Leicestershire, and its surrounding fields.
A: The late nineteenth-century landscape (first edition OS 25-inch base map:
© Crown Copyright and Landmark Information Group Limited (2016), all
rights reserved, 1886).
B: The late nineteenth-century landscape overlain with a grid of four short
perches.

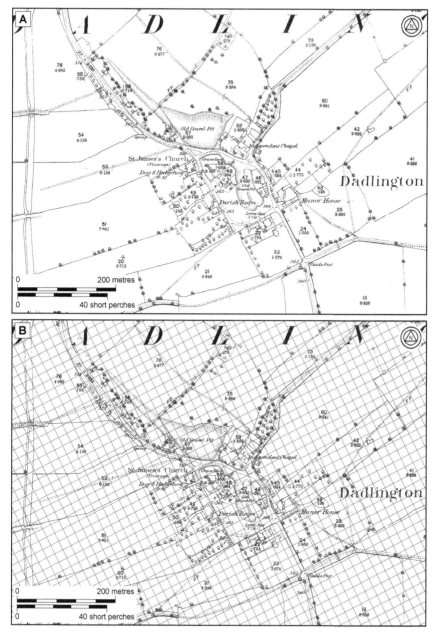

Figure 6.16. The village of Dadlington, Leicestershire, and its surrounding fields.
A: The late nineteenth-century landscape (first edition OS 25-inch base map:
© Crown Copyright and Landmark Information Group Limited (2016), all
rights reserved, 1888).
B: The late nineteenth-century landscape overlain with a grid of four short
perches.

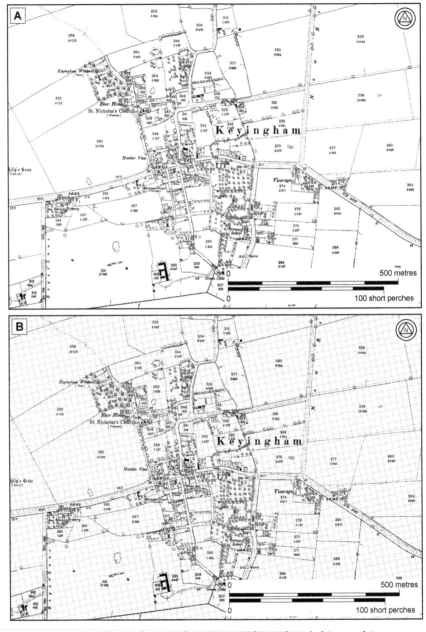

Figure 6.17. The village of Keyingham, East Riding of Yorkshire, and its surrounding fields.

    A: The late nineteenth-century landscape (first edition OS 25-inch base map: © Crown Copyright and Landmark Information Group Limited (2016), all rights reserved, 1890 and 1891).

    B: The late nineteenth-century landscape overlain with a grid of four short perches.

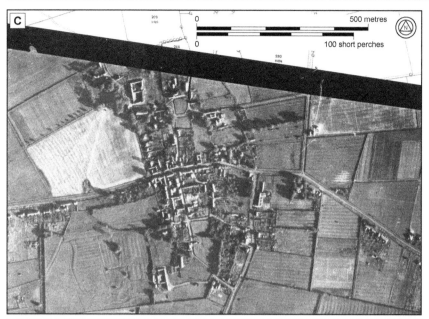

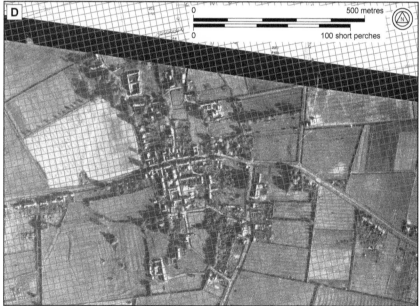

C: A vertical aerial photograph taken in 1946, superimposed upon the late nineteenth-century first edition OS mapping. A complex of earthworks is visible on the south-west side of the village (© Historic England: RAF/ CPE/UK/1748/467/RP/3092/P/TA 244 242/11/21 SEP 1946).

D: The 1946 aerial photograph overlain with a grid of four short perches. The complex of earthworks on the south-west side of the village conform to the proposed grid orientation and seemingly, at least in part, to the short perch module.

Series of narrower grid-conforming roads and lanes, between half a perch and one and a half perches (2.3–6.9m) wide, afforded access to individual plots. These can be seen archaeologically at Stotfold and Raunds (Figures 1.4; 6.11), as earthworks at Preston Deanery (Figure 3.12), and surviving into the modern landscape in several other cases (such as Brant Broughton (Figure 6.12), Dadlington (Figure 6.16), Keyingham (Figure 6.17), and Bampton.[32] They have probably tended to widen over time (the excavated cases are at the narrow end of the range, and scarcely more than footpaths), but even today their presence gives a distinctive, almost maze-like feel to some of the grid-based villages.

A greater variety – indeed, a lack of any clear norms – characterises the house sites and their surrounding closes. The larger excavated cases, Stotfold, Shipdham and Raunds (Figures 1.4, 3.9 and 6.11), illustrate farmsteads spaced at intervals of around 100m, and closes in the general size-range between 8 × 4 and 40 × 20 perches (37m × 18m and 180m × 92m). The map-based cases are compatible so far as they go, though the overlay of nucleated village settlement makes it unprofitable to try to analyse this level of detail. The important point is that the individual farm units, unlike the framing grids, were evidently not constrained by any predetermined spatial modes: so far as the physical evidence goes, they look like the work of free-operating entrepreneurs. This point underlines again the clear difference between grid-creators and grid-users.

Finally, one abnormal case further illustrates the versatility of the technique. The excavated area at Brandon Road in Thetford (Norfolk), laid out *c*.1000 outside the rampart of the late Anglo-Saxon town, is so far unique as a grid-plan in a suburban context.[33] This is the extreme case of a 'latent grid', not archaeologically visible but apparent as the basic structuring principle. Four-short-perch squares articulate the space: some empty, some containing small buildings with pit-groups, and one partitioned by fences into rectilinear enclosures. A metalled road, one perch wide, is aligned on the grid. The squares also seem to control the distribution of pits, which are absent from some of them and in other cases grouped tightly against a grid-boundary or into one corner of a grid-square. Rather than a domestic settlement, this looks like a modern landscape of allotments, with potting sheds, refuse areas, access paths and token marking of boundaries. Indeed, allotments used by urban smallholders growing vegetables for market

---

[32]   Blair 2013, fig. 28.
[33]   Blair 2013, 42, 46.

may be exactly what this site represents. Once again, we can recognise gridding as a mechanical process that had no consistent relationship with function or eventual form.

Towards post-Conquest planning: rows and strips

During the eleventh century nucleated settlement forms in lowland England changed decisively. Although toft-and-croft villages date essentially from after 1050, we can see moves in that direction during the previous decades as plot boundaries started to take on strip- or ladder-like configurations.[34] Some settlements laid out on grid-plans now took this form, most notably West Cotton (Northants).[35] Like earlier cases, such as *Hamwic* and the Low Countries settlements (see Chapter 4) it can be hard to know – especially when excavated areas are small – whether the underlying framework comprised squares or strips: the ditch system at Shepperton (Middlesex: Figure 6.18),[36] which is compatible with a conventional short-perch grid but is strongly linear, illustrates the problem. The sub-manorial complex at Hatch Warren (Hants: Figure 6.19), dating from around or just after the Conquest, displays the accuracy of professional gridding, but not necessarily on more than one axis. It seems likely that these late cases show the technique entering its final phase.

One enigma that we have not wholly resolved is the block of planned landscape around Worthing on the West Sussex coast, comprising Broadwater, Tarring, Goring and Sompting. The boundaries are so obviously rectilinear and planned that they look modern, but the earliest Ordnance Survey maps clearly depict them. In the case of Sompting (Figure 6.20), which we examined in detail, the rectilinear boundaries – shown on estate maps of 1772[37] – conform to the module of four short perches, although the historic boundaries are not in a square-like configuration, but rather in broad rows divided into strips. The exceptional eleventh-century church, with its unique contemporary sculpture,[38] follows the alignment of the grid. There may, therefore, be something to be said for seeing Sompting and its neighbours as mid eleventh-century productions, transitional between late Anglo-Saxon

[34] Blair 2018, 408–11.
[35] Chapman 2010; Blair 2013, 38–40.
[36] Canham 1979.
[37] West Sussex Record Office, Add. MSS 26390, 25797.
[38] Tweddle et al. 1995, 173–84.

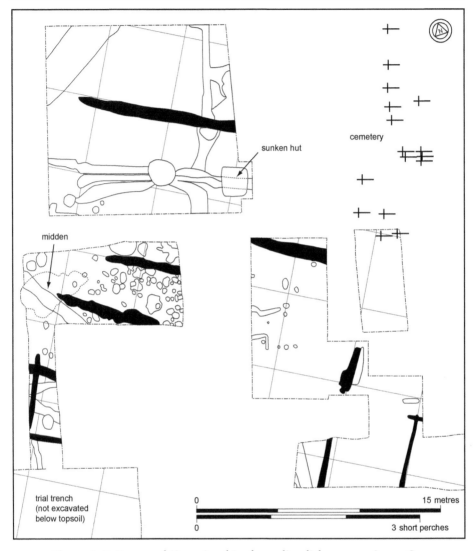

Figure 6.18. Excavated 'Saxon' and 'early medieval' features at Saxon County School, Shepperton, Surrey, overlain with a grid of short perches. Ditches conforming to the orientation of the grid, and/or the short perch module, are filled black (after Poulton 2005, fig. 2).

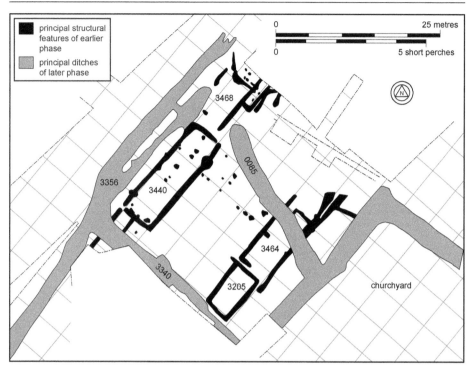

Figure 6.19. The principal excavated mid eleventh- to mid twelfth-century buildings, ditches and pits in one part of the site at Hatch Warren, near Basingstoke, Hampshire, overlain with a grid of short perches. The building ranges appear to predate the ditched phase and might demonstrate the use of grid-planning immediately before the Conquest (after Fasham and Keevill 1995, fig. 44).

grids and Anglo-Norman row-plans. In 1066 Sompting (like nearby Worthing) belonged to one Leofwine: this was a very common late Anglo-Saxon name, but it is tempting to identify him as Earl Leofwine, brother of Harold.[39] If so, Sompting would be one final indication that Anglo-Saxon grid-planning had its swan-song in the aristocratic circles of Edward the Confessor's court.

[39] Stephen Baxter, who has kindly commented in the light of his current work on Domesday Book, thinks that the likelihood of the Sompting man being Earl Leofwine is somewhere around 50 per cent.

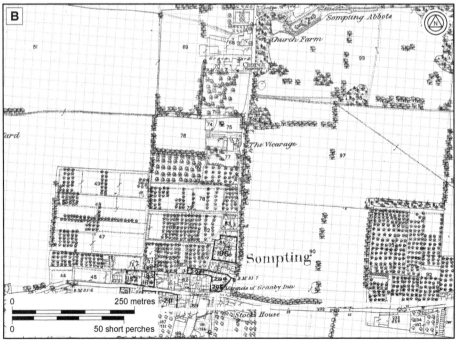

Figure 6.20. The village of Sompting, Sussex, and its surrounding fields.
A: The late nineteenth-century landscape (first edition OS 25-inch base map: © Crown Copyright and Landmark Information Group Limited (2016), all rights reserved, 1875 and 1876).
B: The late nineteenth-century landscape overlain with a grid of four short perches.
C: The late eighteenth-century landscape based on a transcription by John Blair of a 1772 estate map, overlain with a grid of four short perches. The stippled areas reflect the holdings of the manor of Sompting Abbots, while those left blank were held by the manor of Sompting Peverell (transcribed from West Sussex Record Office document Add. MSS 26390 and 25797).

Conclusion

If the technology and practice of grid-planning remained relatively constant, the evidence discussed in this chapter shows that its contexts and functions must have been extended greatly over time. It was introduced into England to provide frameworks within which to construct the display architecture of ecclesiastical and secular elites in the seventh-century 'golden age'. Once familiarised with the technology, those same elites – at least the ecclesiastical ones – applied it to the settlements and buildings of lower-status groups under their control, creating sites such as West Fen Road in Ely and Polebrook. Already in this phase we can recognise an enlargement of the range of contexts: from grids articulating small numbers of grand buildings to grids articulating complex settlements of numerous ordinary buildings that did not necessarily bear a clear architectural relationship to each other. Possibly this reflects a conceptual shift – from a quest for *Romanitas* and architectural grandeur to a pragmatic mode of articulating settlement space and the holdings of multiple occupants – although the former objectives were still expressed in occasional great buildings such as Brixworth.

In the later period the primary uses of grid-planning to facilitate Roman-style grandeur were revived on at least a few of the prestige sites of the tenth-century monastic reform. It was evidently the more pragmatic functions, however, that drove the notable expansion of the technique in the decades after 940. The great majority of identified sites that can be located in that period underlie later medieval villages, and it was almost certainly for the construction and articulation of villages – if of a less nucleated kind – that the grids were originally formed. In a few cases, perhaps originally many more, the grids extended for hundreds of metres beyond the eventual settlement nuclei. Who created these frameworks within which rural communities would live their lives, and why? That is the most important question, but also unfortunately the most obscure.

Some – but probably never more than a minority – were apparently home-farms of important reformed monasteries. A few others – but again probably only a few – may have been established on estates of lay magnates. Many more may have framed the farmsteads of substantial free farmers, on the pattern illustrated most clearly by the Stotfold excavation: it is worth asking whether collective decision-making, based on a consensus of individual free choices, may in fact have been one of the most widespread causes. The gridded places clustered in the East Midlands and East Anglia: an economic zone that, although it eventually morphed into the 'Central Province' of the Roberts and Wrathmell scheme, had a different geographical and ecological weighting, and probably a different social structure. We only have slight evidence for the nature of landlordship in the 'Eastern Zone', and it may have been much less intrusive than is often assumed. We should not underestimate the autonomy, prosperity and initiative of eastern English farming communities: perhaps they combined resources to bring in the experts.

Chapter 7

Conclusions

I N 1913, the historian and archaeologist Francis John Haverfield
published a comment on Roman town planning that makes startling
reading a century later:

> In almost all cases, the frequent establishment of towns has
> been accompanied by the adoption of a definite principle of
> town-planning, and throughout the principle has been essentially
> the same. It has been based on the straight line and the right angle.
> These, indeed, are the marks which sunder even the simplest civili-
> zation from barbarism. The savage, inconsistent in his moral life, is
> equally inconsistent, equally unable to 'keep straight', in his house-
> building and his road-making. ... Whenever ancient remains show
> a long straight line or several correctly drawn right angles, we may
> be sure that they date from a civilized age.[1]

The moral sentiment is not one that would appeal to many archaeologists today. More to the point, though, it would have appealed
powerfully to educated groups among the seventh-century English.
Christianity had come to them as part of a package that was redolent
of Roman civilisation. Their delight not just in the religious doctrines
but also in the material and artistic culture that was their vehicle
shines through the written sources – for instance, in Bede's famous
comment that Benedict Bishop built stone churches 'in the Roman
manner that he always loved'. Given the roots of Anglo-Saxon
grid-planning in the techniques and traditions of the *agrimensores*, it
is clear how attractive those traditions must have looked to seventh-
century monastic pundits and founders, so determined to 'keep
straight' in their doctrine and ecclesiastical discipline. Later, in the
tenth century, the reformers who looked back in horror at Viking
atrocities and inveighed against monastic decadence might have been

[1] Haverfield 1913, 14.

delighted to seize upon anything that would set them apart from 'the savage, inconsistent in his moral life'.

If that was the ideal, it had to reconcile itself to Anglo-Saxon realities. A prime reason why the new planning techniques caught on so quickly after 600 was that so much else was changing at the same time, as the slow build-back from the post-Roman collapse gathered pace. As well as conversion, the seventh century marked the start of linked transformations that included an intensification and expansion of agriculture, the re-emergence of international trade and the focusing of economic and political power. This period of profound change, which continued through to the early ninth century, saw the emergence of new forms of settlement. In order to support the newly successful social groups and the conspicuous consumption of resources with which they were associated, there must have been an increase in food production, and this was itself supported by investment in facilities such as corn-drying ovens, watermills, causeways and fishweirs. It is no coincidence that some of our most impressive and strikingly organised cases of grid-planning date from the first phase of its occurrence, in the seventh to early eighth centuries.

When the technique re-emerged – after a hiatus – around the mid-tenth century, it was in a physical environment that was also changing rapidly, but in different ways. The causes of settlement nucleation and the communalisation of agriculture that villages and open fields represent have been much debated. The recent consensus has been that they resulted from a 'great replanning' of the landscape, whereby a dispersed settlement pattern of isolated farmsteads and small hamlets, each associated with its own fields, was swept away and replaced by nucleated villages surrounded by vast open-field systems (Figure 2.2). The 'great replanning' hypothesis suggested not only that landscapes as a whole were restructured but that many of the individual settlements and field systems so created were laid out in a planned fashion. The evidence for this planning was held to include regularity in the layout of village plans and so-called 'long furlongs' that stretched across the landscape for many hundreds or even thousands of metres.

In 2013–15, however, three studies were published that offered alternative perspectives on this crucial period in landscape history. First, through a detailed study of Northamptonshire, Tom Williamson and his colleagues suggested that the regularity in village plans was actually an effect of the spread of settlement across the strips and furlongs of open fields, and that 'long furlongs' had been created in a piecemeal fashion.[2] Secondly, in *The Fields of Britannia*, Stephen Rippon, Chris Smart and Ben Pears suggested that many Romano-British field systems may have continued in use well into the early medieval period across large parts of lowland England and that it was often from these antecedents that open fields were fashioned (supporting a model of open-field origins, based on gradual evolution, suggested by Joan Thirsk back in the 1960s).[3] The third contribution was John Blair's preliminary assessment of the evidence for technically precise grid-planning in a range of early medieval buildings and settlement plans,[4] which added a new possibility: a great replanning of a different and even more systematic kind that *preceded* nucleated villages and open fields.

In writing the present book, therefore, we have not only faced the challenge of developing a new and still not widely accepted hypothesis but have been compelled to do so against the background of other hypotheses about settlement form and its evolution that are themselves contested, and in no case command universal support. What contribution can grid-planning make to the debate?

The early period (*c.*590–800): royal and ecclesiastical elite sites

Carefully planned landscapes, laid out with sophisticated surveying technology, were not an early medieval innovation. In the Roman period land surveyors were employed to lay out both urban street grids and rural field systems ('centuriation'), although only the former is convincingly evidenced in Britain and none of these Roman street grids survived in use into the medieval period. Across lowland Britain there are extensive areas of countryside that show some regularity in their layout, and have been termed 'co-axial' landscapes. While their origins are still hotly debated,[5] and a Roman date is now clear for several examples,[6] there is still no evidence that they were laid out using grid-based technology. Overall, there are no grounds for thinking that the gridded landscapes created in early medieval England had

---

[2] Williamson *et al.* 2013.

[3] Thirsk 1964; 1966; Rippon *et al.* 2013, but see Rippon *et al.* 2015 for the full report.

[4] Blair 2013.

[5] For the latest discussion see Williamson 2016.

[6] e.g. Hertfordshire (Bryant *et al.* 2005) and southern Essex (Rippon *et al.* 2015, 143–64).

direct Romano-British predecessors or reflect any awareness of Roman surveying techniques inherited from within Roman Britain.

Instead, the practice of using grids to lay out space appears to have been brought across the English Channel as part of a package of Roman cultural traits that became fashionable at the courts of the Anglo-Saxon elites from the very late sixth century.[7] Initially, this appears to have been in the context of the mission by St Augustine and his companions, although it was continued from around the 660s through the work of English monastic founders such as Aldhelm, Benedict Biscop and Wilfrid, who are known to have visited Rome to acquire equipment, books and knowledge. With the arrival of Archbishop Theodore in 669 there was an unprecedented flow of Mediterranean knowledge into Canterbury. These early Christian figures appear to have had access to advanced surveying technology: if *agrimensores* were still operating in Italy at this time then they may have seen them in action, while it is possible that the books known to have been acquired by the likes of Benedict Biscop included gromatic texts.

The symbolic importance of advertising one's Roman – and so civilised – credentials was also a means of asserting one's moral authority, and therefore perhaps one's political power. The imitation *opus signinum* floors in the seventh-century halls at Dover and Lyminge are further illustrations of how *Romanitas* appealed to Anglo-Saxon elites, as is their reuse of Roman building material in some early churches.[8] The appropriation of Roman iconography in their coins reflects both the political appeal of *Romanitas*, the idea that 'real' coins should look like Roman ones, and the Christian significance of Rome.[9] The widespread practice of locating important churches on known Romano-British sites, attested both archaeologically and through documentary sources, surely reflects the perceived link between Britain's Roman heritage and the revival of Christianity led by Augustine, rather than just the use of Roman ruins as a source of building material.[10] Changes in burial practice, the appearance of a new suite of grave-goods and then the cessation of furnished burial can be seen as part of 'a wider cultural re-alignment of England with the Romanised Continent and Mediterranean zone rather than

---

[7] This fashion in grave-goods during the century following the 580s is charted with a new precision by Hines and Bayliss 2013.

[8] Eaton 2000.

[9] Gannon 2003.

[10] Bell 2005; Semple 2013, 132–42.

the Germanic world further north and east in Europe' of which Christianity was just part.[11]

Grid-based surveying in early England must be seen in this broader context. The earliest known cases are on the scale of individual buildings, notably the churches at Canterbury built *c.*597–618 that provide a direct connection with St Augustine (Figure 5.1), and the first large-scale hall and its palisaded enclosure built at Yeavering in the 620s (Figure 5.2). The latter was associated with a grave – in a symbolically important location – that contained an apparent *groma*, illustrating the prestige associated with this newly available Roman technology. It is surely a development of this tradition that we can recognise in the hall complex at Lyminge (Figure 5.7) and on more extensive sites such as Cowage Farm and Catholme (Figures 1.1, 5.9). After 650 the huge expansion in ecclesiastical patronage and monastic foundation shifted the focus back to the Roman and Christian culture through which the techniques had been introduced two generations earlier. In a sense, one might see the era of the 'great halls' as a relatively short-lived aberration,[12] when kings over two or three generations appropriated the newly available surveying techniques in the way that Roman armour styles and other marks of status were appropriated in the Sutton Hoo Mound I burial, or the form of a Roman theatre was appropriated for the assembly structure at Yeavering. With the monastic boom, architecturally monumental symbols of power seem to have become essentially an ecclesiastical monopoly, and indeed there is remarkably little evidence for royal residential buildings of any kind between 700 and 900.

The immediate future for grid-planning therefore lay in the articulation of masonry-built central church complexes such as Hexham (Figure 5.3) or extensive but well-organised monastic settlements such as Whitby (Figure 5.6). Where grids prove to underlie settlements of a seemingly less prestigious character, such as Ely West Fen Road, Quarrington or Stratton, there are usually reasons (sometimes stronger, sometimes weaker) to infer a monastic association or dependency. In any case it cannot be assumed, outside the rather specific milieu of 'great halls', that a high-status settlement would necessarily have included large-scale buildings. Brandon (Figure 5.12) is revealing here,

---

[11] Hines and Bayliss 2013, 549, 553. However, see Blair 2018 for the view that, alongside this enthusiasm for Roman culture, links with northern Europe remained fundamentally important throughout the period.

[12] This outlines the argument of Blair 2018, chapter 4.

because the notably opulent material culture looks so much at variance with the modest-sized timber buildings: what signals the ecclesiastical status of this complex is not grand architecture but the fact that it was laid out on accurately surveyed grids. At present it seems rather dubious whether grid-planning was used in the eighth century for *any* purely secular sites.

While these early grids may well have been laid out using instruments of Roman design (and potentially Roman manufacture), at both Canterbury and Yeavering the modules used were the short perch of 15 imperial feet (4.57m) rather than any Roman metrical unit, suggesting a fusion of Roman and Anglo-Saxon ideas. This study shows that the short perch was the predominant unit used in early medieval England, although the long perch of 18 imperial feet (5.5m) occurs in Wessex. The consistency of these units implies a tradition of systematic training in which surveyors were taught to apply whatever module was in use in a precise and consistent fashion: it is one of several indicators that the phenomena explored in this book were the outcome of professional rather than vernacular practice.

The later period (*c*.940–*c*.1050): reformed monasteries and villages

The period of monastic reform saw a series of important developments, including a nostalgia for the late seventh-century monastic 'golden age', a new influx of textual material in the form of gromatic manuscripts and a large injection of new cash thanks to King Eadgar's enthusiastic support. Grid-based planning appears to have been used in the transformation of some of the refounded monasteries, including Eynsham and Peterborough (Figure 5.15). Edward the Confessor's Westminster Abbey (Figure 5.18) may represent the final grand climax of this culture, while some other potential cases (Bury St Edmunds, Minster-in-Thanet and Stow, Figures 5.19, 5.17, 3.6) can perhaps be associated with members of his immediate social circle.

All this replicated earlier practice. A more novel development seems to have been the application of grid-planning to a wider range of rural settlements that ostensibly – at least in their eventual outcome – were 'ordinary' villages. The production of organised settlement forms that remained sufficiently stable to display their grid-based origins on Ordnance Survey maps seems to be a distinctive outcome of this later phase, and one that sets it apart from the earlier phase. Nonetheless, the settlements initially framed by the grids were decisively different in form from their high medieval successors: not compact toft-and-croft villages but more extensive and spread-out 'semi-nucleations' comprising groups of discrete farms within their own enclosures. The inwards concentration of these clusters of farmsteads brought into being the villages that we know today, but also left their peripheral areas abandoned and available for the encroachment and intensification of open-field furlongs after 1100. It is for that reason that this project has recognised several cases of grids that extend well beyond the villages (as mapped in the nineteenth century) at their cores.

Most of the rural settlements where we have recognised gridding that dates (or is inferred to date) from this later phase lie in central-eastern England, but in a significantly smaller part of it than the zone of villages and open fields characterised by Roberts and Wrathmell as the 'Central Province'. This is corroborative evidence for a new model, recently proposed by John Blair, of a seventh- to ninth-century 'Eastern Zone' that, during *c.*950–1200, expanded to constitute the Central Province as some of its socio-economic and cultural attributes were exported westwards and south-westwards.[13] What complicates matters, however, is that although the second phase of grid-planning fell within that period of expansion the distribution of tenth- to eleventh-century grid-planned settlements remained to a significant extent (and especially if we exclude the undated sites) within the confines of the old 'Eastern Zone'. The patterning of regional variation is complex, and needs a broader-based study in which the grid-planning culture would be one element. Suffice it to say that prosperity, independence, commercial vitality and innovation may have continued to mark the 'Eastern Zone' as they had done in the past, and that this context may have encouraged a dynamic approach to the construction of settlements.

The practicalities of grid-based surveying

There is little direct evidence for how these gridded buildings and settlements were laid out, but the indirect evidence allows some inferences. The potential availability of gromatic texts, and the probable *groma* buried at Yeavering, strengthen the likelihood that the essential similarity of the results to those produced by the *agrimensores* is a consequence of essentially similar techniques.

Any grid must be laid out from a baseline, which is easily produced by sighting along a line of upright poles (Figure 4.3). It is likely that a wooden rod (a perch in length, whatever the local perch might be) was

---

[13] Blair 2018, 324–37.

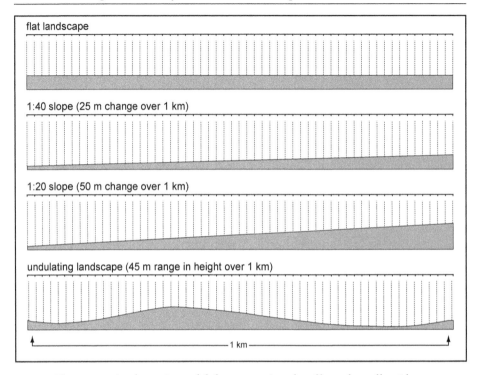

Figure 7.1. A schematic model demonstrating the effect of parallax (slope distortion) when a grid is set out on the ground surface versus how that grid is then perceived from above (as we do when reading maps) in a horizontal plane.

the means of measuring fixed distances. Flipping the rod across sloping ground will result in distances that – when viewed from above as on a map – will be very slightly shorter than if the rod had been held precisely horizontally: in other words, the grid will be foreshortened. However, modelling of the effect shows that this difference is undetectable at the scale of the first edition Ordnance Survey 25-inch maps used in this study (Figure 7.1). There is no evidence for the use of chains during this period, and, while ropes could potentially have been used, their expansion when wet and contraction when dry will have made them unreliable means of measuring out fixed lengths.

Having divided the baseline up into sub-divisions of the required length, right-angled offsets will then have been laid out. That could have been achieved most accurately with a *groma*. After Yeavering we have no evidence that the instrument was used in England, but the point is less significant than it might seem, since rule-of-thumb modes of surveying by eye can produce surprisingly precise right-angles.

Practice makes perfect, and it is reasonable to assume that seasoned Anglo-Saxon surveyors with years of experience behind them will have achieved more accurate results than modern re-enactors. Nonetheless, there are occasional startling deviations in otherwise precise surveys, as in the west end of Brixworth, the rampart of Cricklade and the east cloister range of Westminster (Figures 5.13, 5.14, 5.18). On the whole these suggest simple lapses of attention, though it is always possible that the deviations were deliberate, to accommodate retained structures or obstacles that are no longer apparent.

With the baseline and offsets augmented by a series of equally spaced lines parallel to the base, the grid would be complete. The corners of each square could have been marked by posts, or the lines themselves could have been marked by shallow spade-dug gullies such as the 'marking-out' trenches defining the road at Six Dials, *Hamwic* (Figure 5.10). The initial sets of buildings and linear features would then have been laid out in relation to these grid lines. Nonetheless, it is a recurrent feature of the Anglo-Saxon sites (in contrast to Roman centuriation, for instance) that translation of the marked-out grids into the material permanence of ditches, fences or buildings was not performed in any comprehensive or spatially consistent fashion. Why should that be so? Exploring the dichotomy between surveyed grid and physical settlement may take us closer to the fundamental reasons for Anglo-Saxon grid-planning.

Grids in the mind? Perceptions and realities in the choice of grid-based settlement forms

Why did they bother? That question has been put to us by several sceptics, and at times has made us uneasy. Given that the actual buildings and settlements were not constructed in checkerboard fashion, the rationale for going to the trouble of laying out checkerboard grids is not self-evident.

Before suggesting an answer, we should remember three implications that have emerged at various points: that the grids were not necessarily formed by the same people who then built over them; that their functions were primarily practical and instrumental; and that they could be constructed with relatively short-term aims in mind. The first point is well illustrated by Brandon (Figure 5.12), where the grids are precise and govern the locations of many buildings, but the buildings themselves are of various shapes and sizes (including angle-sided halls) and do not conform consistently to modular lengths or widths: the builders used the grids, but in designing individual structures they were not constrained by them. At Westminster (Figure 5.18) the large scale and formal layout of the church and cloister mean that grid-conformity is more overt; even so – as Eric Fernie shows in Appendix B – the architects who determined the proportions of the west and east ends, and the bay spacings of the nave, used different methods that, again, were unconstrained by the grids. Seemingly there were specialised teams of grid-planners, who did their job and then moved on to the next, leaving architects and builders to take over. That leads to the second point: it is as though – in the quite specific cultural milieux where it occurred at all – the gridding was a basic and almost formulaic initial stage, executed automatically without regard to the character of the stage to follow. The builders of complex settlements – Brandon or Catholme, for instance – would clearly have found the grid-lines very useful for keeping overall control over the project, but perhaps that is all they meant to them. The third point is that on several sites (including again those two) the entire layout was replanned on two or more occasions, at intervals of relatively few decades or even years, with the new grids on different orientations and taking no account of their predecessors.

Nonetheless, it seems unlikely that grids were *purely* instrumental in their implications. The association of the technique with high-status and educated milieux is strong, and the very fact that it expressed order rather than randomness would almost inevitably have given it cultural resonances. A grid offers a good mnemonic technique for conceiving space, even among people without maps. Thinking in straight lines and squares is not inevitable or universal. As Richard Bradley shows, the 'circular archetype' has been the norm in many world cultures, gradually giving way in the face of various socio-cultural pressures but surviving latest in Atlantic Britain, Ireland and Iberia.[14] The practical advantages of square and rectangular forms become more evident in complex and high-density settlements, since rectangular extensions, annexes and close-spaced ranges can be juxtaposed more conveniently than round ones.[15] The Anglo-Saxons had always inhabited a rectangular built environment,[16] and the seventh-century transformations reinforced that inheritance in two ways. The new religion came from the Roman world of square and rectangular forms; its spiritual goal was the Heavenly

[14] Bradley 2012, especially 25–45, 213–16.
[15] Cf. Bradley 2012, 28–32.
[16] Bradley 2012, fig. 4.

Jerusalem, which according to Revelation was built as a square, and was as wide as it was long.[17] More practically, economic intensification stimulated the emergence of settlements that were more intensive, and therefore tended to become more organised. This coalescence of tradition with innovation, and of practice with symbolism, may have given formal rectilinear configurations an inherent naturalness: neither simply pragmatic, nor necessarily ideological in a precise sense, but at some level 'the right thing to do'.

It is nonetheless possible that the gromatic techniques, overtly classical as they were, gained resonance by assimilation to established ideas (whether Christian or pre-Christian) about performing the correct rituals before building. Documented expectations that the site of an early English monastery would be cleansed and purified from lingering evil forces recall geomantic rituals – designed to determine propitious sites or alignments and avoid unlucky ones – that have been practised world-wide.[18] Apparent support for this possibility comes from Burial AX at Yeavering, with its manifestations of pagan cult combined with a Roman surveying rod. That is not to suggest that founders such as Wilfrid or Aldhelm perceived themselves to be practising traditional geomancy, but it is entirely feasible that they inherited – and reinvented – concerns about the importance of correct preparation. An outlook that set great store by solemn, mysterious and awe-inspiring rituals would have been transferrable into a Classical and Christian mode and receptive to the arcane procedures of the *agrimensores*. To return to the point made at the start of this chapter: the very act of gridding could have been understood as a commitment to Roman orthodoxy.

More simply, a basic feeling that 'you've got to do a proper job if it's going to turn out well' could be at the root of at least some cases: it may apply especially to the tenth-century East Midland villages, which the tradition may have reached in a rather second-hand form. Anyone who has been involved in a modern construction project will know that engineers and builders are very attached to their own ways of doing things: even when those do in fact make sense, they can be less self-evidently 'right' to outsiders than their practitioners tend to assume. In both the educated and the vernacular mindsets, what mattered was that the right steps should be gone through: no physical outcome need survive.

[17] Blair 2005, 248.
[18] Blair 2005, 191. Chinese *feng-shui* is an obvious case.

A surveyed Anglo-Saxon grid was thus a means to an end, not an end in itself. There was no concern to express it in a visually intelligible form, let alone to perpetuate that form through time. Buildings were replaced, ditches wandered with multiple rediggings, holdings were divided, amalgamated or replanned. The superimposition of new layers took no account of the grid; as settlements evolved over time, the original gridded layouts were increasingly degraded. That applies especially to still-living villages, which have seen more than a thousand years of changing occupation. It is therefore hardly surprising that only faint traces of gridding are evident on so many of the nineteenth-century plans: without the archaeological and architectural evidence, the reality of grid-planning could hardly have been more than a tentative hypothesis. On the other hand, the limited scale of excavation would have put severe constraints on our understanding if map and field evidence had not also been available, and it has only been through the integrated analysis of these different sources that this project has been able to get so far. It is indeed remarkable how extensively the ghosts of the Anglo-Saxon grid-planners' work are still visible in parts of the modern English landscape: one new dimension to our understanding of that complex palimpsest.

Appendix A

Perches, postholes and grids

Clair Barnes and Wilfrid S. Kendall

Introduction

The *Planning in the Early Medieval Landscape* (PEML) project has organised and collated a substantial quantity of images, and has used this as evidence to support the hypothesis that Anglo-Saxon building construction was based on grid-like planning structures based on fixed modules or *quanta* of measurement. In this appendix we report on the development of some statistical contributions to the debate concerning this hypothesis. In practice the PEML images correspond to data arising in a wide variety of different forms (postholes, actual walls, indications of linear structure arising from hedge and road lines, etc.). Ideally one would wish accurately to reduce each image to a measurement-based dataset that could be analysed statistically to bear on the historical debate. In practice it does not seem feasible to produce a single automatic method that can be applied uniformly to all such images; even the initial chore of cleaning up an image (removing extraneous material such as legends and physical features that do not bear on the planning hypothesis) typically presents a separate and demanding challenge for each different image. Moreover, care must be taken, even in the relatively straightforward cases of clearly defined ground-plans (for example, for large ecclesiastical buildings of the period), to consider exactly what measurements might be relevant. In this appendix we report on pilot statistical analyses concerning three different situations. These not only establish the presence of underlying structure (which indeed is often visually obvious) but also provide an account of the numerical evidence supporting the deduction that such structure is present. Moreover, this approach allows us to map out the range of variation of possible structures suggested by the visual evidence. We contend that statistical methodology thus contributes to the larger historical debate and provides useful input to the wide and varied range of evidence that has to be debated.

Before turning to actual statistical analyses, we note that useful statistics require a sufficient supply of data (and preferably the data should be in reasonably homogeneous form). The following table illustrates this point by comparing sizes of previous datasets used in comparable investigations, drawing in part from the useful survey of past applications of the quantogram technique to be found in the excellent MSc dissertation of Cox (2009).

Reference	Dataset	No. of measurements
Kendall, D.G. 1974	Diameters of megalithic stone circles in Scotland, England and Wales ('primary' dataset SEW_2)	169
Hewson 1980	Ashanti goldweights (geometric *versus* figurative design)	1208+1651
Pakkanen 2004a	Measurements taken from Temple of Zeus at Stratos (tables 1, 2)	17+20
Pakkanen 2004b	Measurements taken from Toumba building at Lefkandi (column 1 of table 1)	27
Cox 2009	Measurements taken from Sanctuary of Great Gods, Samothrace (table 5)	113
Kendall, W.S. 2013	Ground plans of large Anglo-Saxon ecclesiastical buildings	79

Datasets lead to clearer conclusions if they are composed of larger numbers of measurements, though the measurements do need to come from sources that are not too inhomogeneous. As can be seen from the table, the dataset discussed in W.S. Kendall (2013) is relatively small (though large enough that one can still detect a clear signal of an underlying quantum). In the next section we revisit the analysis of this dataset, and supplement it with a separate analysis of 110 measurements drawn from the tables of Huggins *et al.* (1982) concerning smaller Anglo-Saxon buildings.

1. Anglo-Saxon perches

W.S. Kendall (2013) provides a preliminary analysis of measurements taken from five ground plans of large Anglo-Saxon ecclesiastical buildings. D.G. Kendall's (1974) quantogram technique was modified and applied to determine whether there was evidence for a module or quantum q of measurement underlying the ground plans, in the sense that appropriately chosen measurements X_i (for i running from 1 to N) are approximately divisible by q. As noted in these references, the quantogram graphs the formula

$$\sqrt{\frac{2}{N}} \Sigma_i \cos\left(\frac{2\pi X_i}{q}\right)$$

as a function of the frequency $\omega = 1 / q$ corresponding to the possible quantum q. High peaks of the graph in suitable regions can be interpreted as evidence that q might be a quantum. 'High' here is measured in comparison with matched simulations, using random perturbations of the data X_i to generate simulated comparison boundaries.

The first step in applying this technique is to determine the measurements that will constitute the data X_i. The Kendall (2013) analysis was based on 79 measurements taken from ground plans, obtained from 13 lines of measurement derived from faces of walls taken from plans of five sites (Canterbury SS Peter and Paul, Canterbury St Pancras, Hexham, Escomb, Brixworth). The actual data X_i were derived from all possible differences of measurements in each of the 13 measurement lines. The resulting quantogram led to an estimate of $q = 4.75$m (hence frequency $\omega = 0.21$m^{-1}) with a range of error given by ±0.26m.

An alternative approach, espoused by Huggins (1991), is to use not the faces of walls but the centre-lines, where a centre-line is defined as the mid-line running between the two measured faces of the wall. A simple graph suggests this is probably a better choice: compare the following two plots of measurements for each measurement line. Figure A.1 presents measurements of inside and outside faces; Figure A.2 presents centre-line averages (noting that measurements have been duplicated where they correspond not to inside and outside wall faces but to boundaries of large objects). Individual measurements are more clearly aligned across separate measurement lines in Figure A.2, so for our purposes the centre-line measurements in Figure A.2 exhibit a clearer picture and are therefore to be preferred. The averaging process

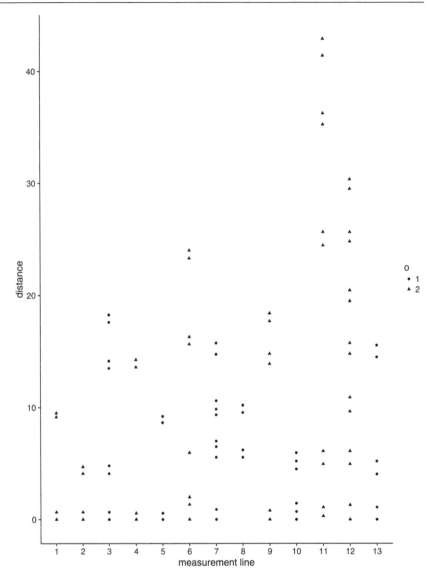

Figures A.1 and A.2. Distances in metres based on measurements of wall faces. Shapes indicate wall orientation (east–west or north–south). Figure A.1 presents locations of faces of walls; Figure A.2 presents centre-lines of walls (duplicating measurements corresponding to internal objects).

effectively halves the number of distinct measurements, but eliminates non-quantum effects arising from half-widths of walls, if indeed the underlying designs are based on centre-lines.

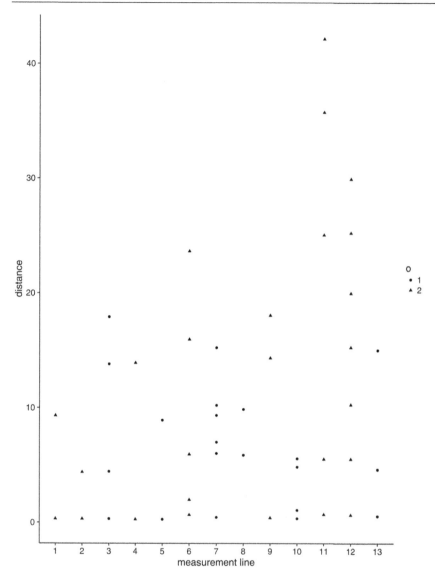

The resulting quantogram, with simulated comparison boundary, is presented in Figure A.3. The comparison boundary is obtained by generating 499 simulated quantograms using suitable random perturbations of the data, and then graphing the 5th highest quantogram height at each frequency. This allows us to assess quantogram peaks: a peak that rises well above the simulated comparison boundary is evidence for a genuine underlying quantum. (Determination of the

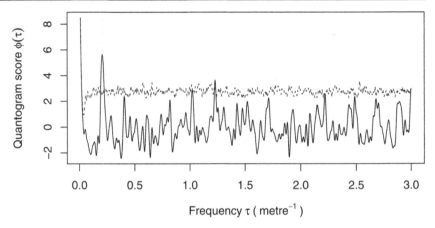

Figure A.3. Quantogram (solid graph) with simulated comparison boundary (irregular dotted graph) for large Anglo-Saxon ecclesiastical buildings (based on all possible pairs of centre-lines).

comparison boundary as the 5th highest level of 550=499+1 quantogram levels allows one to interpret this in terms of a statistical test at the 1% level of significance.) Realistic quantum values are expected to lie in the region of 3m to 6.5m (this corresponds to a frequency range of between 0.15m⁻¹ and 0.33m⁻¹), and in this region the quantogram provides a single well-defined peak at a frequency corresponding to a quantum length of 4.82m, rising clearly above the simulated comparison boundary. Further statistical analysis suggests that a suitable range of error is ±0.26m. Thus this analysis is compatible with the Kendall (2013) analysis (based on facing-wall measurements rather than centre-lines), resulting in a quantum length of 4.75m with error range of ±0.26 m.

Huggins *et al.* (1982) provide a similar dataset relating to smaller buildings: four separate tables containing a total of 110 measurements. These measurements mostly arise as width and depth of separate buildings, rather than as consecutive measurements along selected measurement lines. The resulting quantogram, with simulated comparison boundary, is presented in Figure A.4. There are two major peaks, both falling outside the region of interest. However, the dominant peak is located at a frequency $\omega = 0.59$ m⁻¹, which corresponds to a quantum level of 1.68 m. This is close to one-third of the quantum level of 5.05m proposed by Huggins (1991). Bearing in mind that the buildings of this dataset are of smaller size, and that Huggins *et al.* (1982) suggest that building designs could be based on ratios such as 2:3, it is not unreasonable to take this quantogram analysis as lending

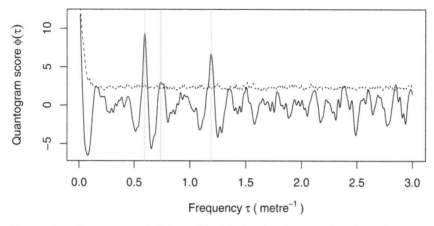

Figure A.4. Quantogram (solid graph) with simulated comparison boundary (irregular dotted graph) for measurements taken from Huggins *et al.* (1982), based on width and depth of separate buildings.

support to a quantum of 5.05m. Further statistical analysis suggests that a suitable range of error is ±0.25 m. Encouragingly, the intervals 4.82±0.26 and 5.05±0.25 overlap.

Evidently it is feasible to produce statistical evaluations of the existence of a quantum or module of measurement, given sufficient data in a suitable form.

2. Postholes and perpendicularity

Much of the PEML data available for analysis does not come in the form of well-defined measurements of distance, but arises indirectly from images of various ground-plans. One seeks to use these images to infer latent linear structure, so obtaining measurements and thus evidence for or against the presence of underlying structure of design. The simplest question of this kind concerns whether or not there is evidence for an underlying design involving organisation along perpendicular lines. A good example is provided by the map of Genlis presented in Figure A.5.

Here interest lies in the information supplied by the postholes recorded on the map. Visually it appears that many of the postholes are lined up in a grid-like pattern. The challenge is to connect this visual impression to a statistical and quantitative approach.

The first step is to 'data-clean' the image by removing components not related to the postholes and then to derive relevant information

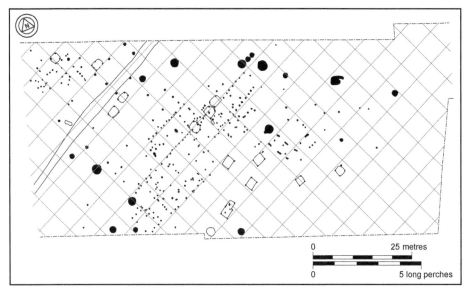

Figure A.5. Genlis map in original form (© Isabelle Catteddu).

from the point pattern given by posthole locations. It is evident that the Genlis image will provide relatively few measurements of distance between walls, and therefore we should not expect this image on its own to supply useful information about quanta. Instead we focus on the question of identifying the walls themselves and then testing whether these walls are organised along perpendicular lines.

Barnes (2015) developed largely automatic methods of image analysis to clean up the Genlis image. These methods involved identification of a list of clumps of connected black pixels, and then removal of those clumps clearly deviating from what one would expect of posthole images (in other words, removing clumps that were too long and thin or which otherwise deviated from circularity, removing clumps that lay on lines determined by long thin clumps and removing very isolated clumps). The remaining clumps could be represented as points in a point pattern (Figure A.6), and were deemed to represent postholes.

To each such point was assigned a direction, being the direction towards its nearest neighbour. It was then possible to use these directions to assess evidence for latent perpendicular structure. The initial step of the procedure is to reduce the angles (measured in degrees) modulo 90 degrees so as to produce grid orientations lying in the range 0–90 degrees. In the presence of perpendicular structure, a histogram of the resulting values should then be strongly peaked.

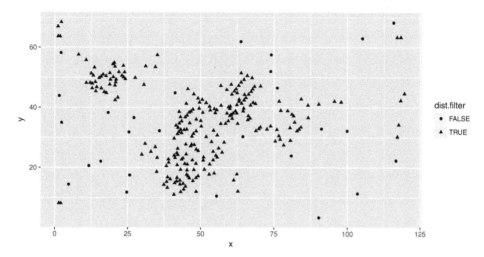

Figure A.6. Post-holes identified from Genlis image after cleaning.
Shape indicates whether post-hole is rejected as being too distant from other
post-holes (round = rejected; triangle = accepted).

The resulting histogram is presented in Figure A.7. It is indeed
strongly peaked, though this is supplemented by a uniform spread
of some grid orientations across the whole range. It is possible
to assess this statistically by estimating the extent to which this
collection of grid orientations is obtained by a mixture of (a) a certain
proportion that are spread uniformly across the range (one might
suppose these to correspond to rather random postholes, not aligned
to any underlying perpendicular structure) and (b) the remainder being
distributed according to some convenient peaked distribution. In this
case the convenient peaked distribution turns out to be the von Mises
distribution, introduced by Richard von Mises (1918) to assess the
fundamental issue in physics of whether atomic weights were multiples
of a given unit. (In fact the von Mises distribution also plays a crucial
theoretical role in justifying the quantogram formula in Section 1, and
will again be central to the issue of fitting grids in Section 3. Its role
in the study of directions and modulus is as fundamental as that of the
Normal distribution to the study of location.)

Having obtained such a mixture it is necessary to check that
the peak genuinely represents perpendicularity (nearest-neighbour
directions clustering in all four directions reducing to the peak
modulo 90 degrees), rather than collinearity (nearest-neighbour
directions clustering in only two opposite directions). Individual

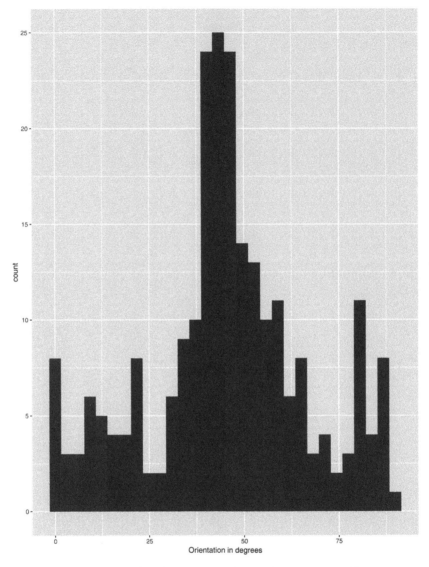

Figure A.7. Histogram of grid orientations for Genlis nearest-neighbour directions.

posthole locations can then be judged to be produced by gridding, or not, depending on a likelihood calculation constructed using the uniform and von Mises distributions estimated for the mixture. Supplemented by a calculation using a spatial clustering algorithm, the result is displayed in Figure A.8: posthole locations are divided into

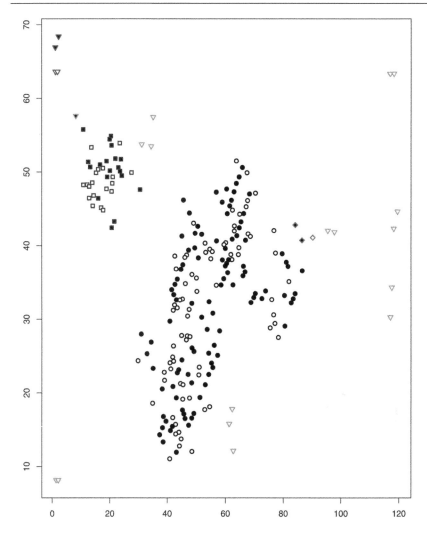

Figure A.8. Black dots indicate postholes which appear to be part of aligned grid structure. Shapes encode spatial clustering.

two potentially grid-like and spatially distinct structures together with a substantial number of locations that are not assigned to either structure.

Note that this analysis depends on there being a single underlying grid orientation holding across the image. The task of dealing with an image that contains two overlapping grids would be much more demanding. We have some ideas on how to approach such a task, but have not yet carried these ideas through to the point of being able to evaluate their practicability. However, in some instances it is already possible to make progress, as is illustrated in the next section.

3. Postholes and grids

We now seek to address the more ambitious challenge of deriving estimates of both quantum length and grid structure from a single image. We consider an image of Brandon (Figure A.9), paying particular attention to the posthole locations. Inspection of the image reveals some issues. There are many postholes, typically organised into segments that are nearly straight but nevertheless can possess some systematic curvature. Rather than devise a statistical technique to deal with this curvature, it was decided to identify corners of buildings manually where possible, and to work with the resulting corner posthole points. In Figure A.9 the corners are highlighted as large black dots: note that in one case the fourth corner of the building is missing.

It then becomes a routine computational task to read in the corner posthole coordinates and to group the coordinates (manually again) according to the buildings to which the corresponding corner postholes belong. The next step is statistical: namely, to undertake a quantogram analysis based on individual building widths and depths after the manner of the investigation of the Huggins *et al.* (1982) data in Section 1 above. This analysis showed no evidence for a significant peak at all (not entirely a surprise: the 17 Brandon buildings are mostly rather small). In order to find structure, it is necessary to consider the buildings in relation to each other. However, as is clear from Figure A.9, there appear to be two distinct grid patterns (compare Figure 5.12). To have any chance of success it is necessary to determine which buildings correspond to which grids.

The methods of Section 2 suggest an effective approach. Consider the directions given by each of the building edges. Reducing angles modulo 90 degrees as before, we obtain the following histogram of grid orientations (Figure A.10: note that the data here are rotated through 45 degrees to avoid splitting a cluster of orientations between the right- and left-hand sides of the histogram).

Figure A.9. *opposite* Plan of the excavated settlement at Brandon, Suffolk. Manually identified corner postholes are indicated here as enlarged dots (© Suffolk County Council).

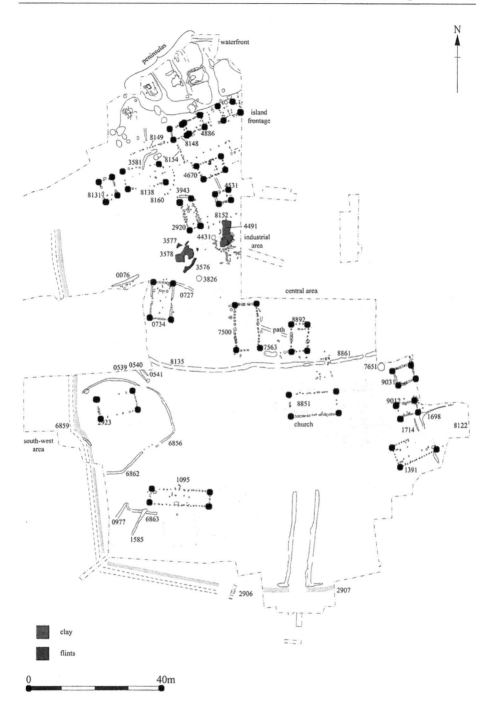

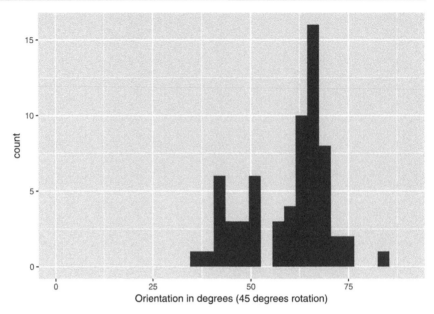

Figure A.10. Histogram of grid orientations for building sides at Brandon: there is clear evidence of two different overlapping clusters.

The histogram suggests the existence of two overlapping clusters. Again, it is possible to assess this statistically, this time by estimating the extent to which this collection of grid orientations is obtained by a mixture of two different von Mises distributions. The best-fitting mixture provides a reasonable statistical fit, making it possible to assign each of the buildings to one of the two grid orientations represented by the mode of the von Mises distributions, depending on whether all edges of the building in question are assigned to one or to the other grid orientation (Figure A.11). Note that one of the buildings is left unassigned, as its edges were not all assigned to the same grid orientation; this building is omitted from the subsequent analysis.

For each grid orientation one can now calculate two perpendicular axes of measurement; we will refer to these as x and y axes. Effectively each posthole belonging to each of these buildings provides an x coordinate and a y coordinate determined by the corresponding grid system. The quantogram technique can now be applied to the compendium dataset obtained as the union of the four sets of all possible differences between coordinates; one set of all possible differences being constructed for each of the four measurement axes arising from

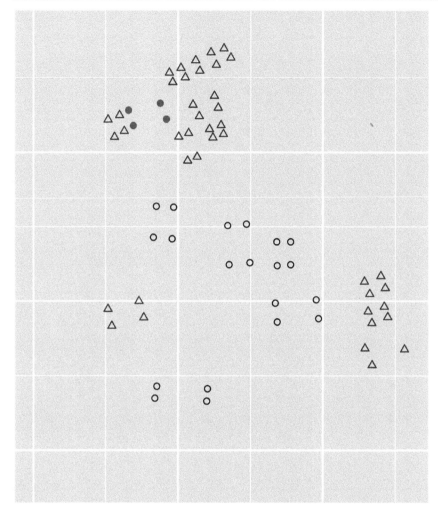

Figure A.11. The two different clusters of buildings at Brandon (corners indicated respectively by open circles and triangles) and the unassigned building (corners indicated by solid circles).

the two grids. The resulting quantogram, with simulated comparison boundary, is presented in Figure A.12.

Here the dominant peak in the region of interest corresponds to a quantum of 4.32 m. However, there are a number of neighbouring peaks, not quite so high. A vertical dashed line indicates a smaller peak located at the frequency corresponding to the quantum of 4.75m used elsewhere in this monograph, and it is reasonable to take the view that the quantogram provides evidence for a quantum in this

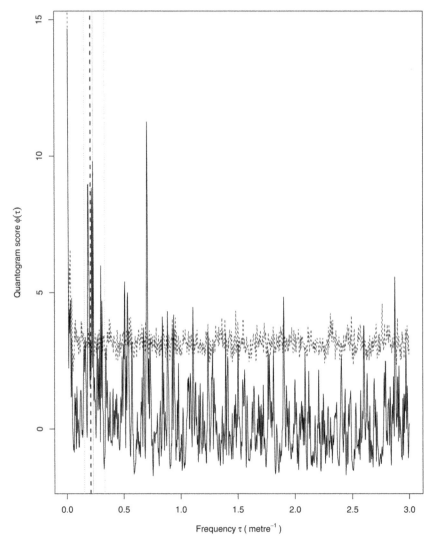

Figure A.12. Quantogram (solid graph) with simulation comparison boundary (irregular dotted graph) using compendium of all distances from Brandon data. The solid vertical line indicates the frequency yielding highest level within region of interest delimited by thin vertical dotted lines). The dashed vertical line indicates the frequency corresponding to 4.75m.

range but without distinguishing (for example) between these two quanta. There is a very large peak outside the region of interest, located at one-third of the quantum of 4.32m and thus possibly related to systematic construction based on a quantum of 4.32m. Bearing in mind the number of closely neighbouring peaks and the chain of statistical procedures required to reach our conclusions, we omit the analysis of range of error and instead simply note that the estimates of quantum size based on this quantogram should be viewed as indicative only.

It should be noted that quantograms were also constructed for each of the four separate measurement lines. For example, taken separately the smaller cluster provides rather weak evidence for a larger quantum of 6.38m. However, the corresponding peak disappears in the compendium analysis of both clusters taken together. Subsequent calculations are based on use of the quantum obtained by the compendium analysis and compared with corresponding calculations using the quantum of 4.75m.

Given a quantum and a grid orientation, one has of course to select from a range of possible grids depending on choice of x and y offset. However, here again the von Mises distribution finds employment: for each cluster we can compute the x and y offsets of each posthole from the grid, fit von Mises distributions to the cluster population of x offsets and separately the population of y offsets, and use the modes of the two von Mises distributions to determine the offsets for the actual grid to be fitted to the cluster. (In fact, the theory of the von Mises distribution shows that this procedure, shorn of its statistical context, corresponds to a natural circular averaging process.) Figures A.13 and A.14 respectively illustrate the grids fitted on the basis of a quantum of 4.32m and a quantum of 4.75m. Visually the difference is not large. On closer inspection, the quantum of 4.32m does appear to provide a better fit. In both cases, the fit to the larger and more spread-out cluster (indicated by open circles, and with grid more at a slant) appears to be better than the fit to the smaller and more compact cluster. Note that in both cases the fit might be improved by excluding a couple of less-well-aligned buildings.

Conclusion

The work above demonstrates that it is possible to produce estimates of quanta and fitted grids for suitable images and data sources, and that the resulting fit can be explored statistically. These statistical treatments supplement, but do not replace, the informed manual analyses discussed in the remainder of this monograph. As noted above, the variety of images means that each separate image requires its own data-cleaning approach, and will typically present further challenges arising from the different sources of data present in the image. We have shown

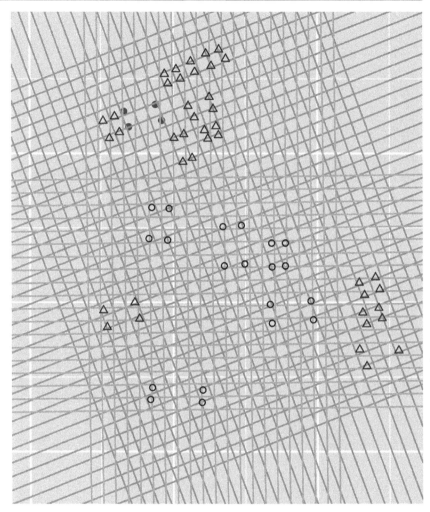

Figure A.13. Fitted grids for the plot of corners using quantum (4.32m) obtained from Brandon data: cluster 1 uses triangles and cluster 2 uses open circles.

how relevant information can be extracted statistically from some well-behaved images and data-sources: this contributes to the debate and particularly emphasises the extent to which estimates (whether of quanta or of grids) should be accompanied by ranges of accuracy.

The statistical approach given here is still only a preliminary approach: the pervasive presence of the von Mises distribution suggests the possibility of assimilating the present layered statistical approach (determine grid orientations, if satisfactory then fit quanta, if satisfactory,

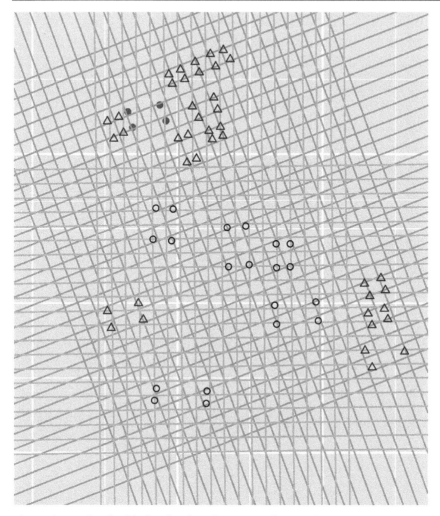

Figure A.14. Fitted grids for the plot of corners using previous quantum (4.75m) obtained from large Anglo-Saxon ecclesiastical buildings: cluster 1 uses triangles and cluster 2 uses open circles.

then choose grids) into a more unified treatment. However, a more pressing question is: how can one deal with grids that are not as well separated as in the Brandon example? This is a substantial question, and it may well be that overlaid grids simply present too great a challenge. We hope to explore the issue in future work.

Appendix B

The combined use of grids and the square root of two

Eric Fernie

THE EVIDENCE presented in this book establishes beyond doubt the widespread use of grids in the planning of Anglo-Saxon settlements. This raises the question as to whether designers also used geometrical proportions. There are arguments against their combination, such as the fundamental difference between the regularity of the grid and the more open-ended processes of geometry, but the case in favour of at least one geometrical proportion is stronger. The combination of a grid with the proportion between the side of a square and its diagonal, or one to the square root of two (1:1.4142 etc.), is plausible, not least because both systems are based on a square.

To test whether grids were used in conjunction with root-two in the relevant centuries I have selected three examples, namely St John at Escomb of the seventh or eighth century, the Carolingian St Gall Plan of the early ninth and Edward the Confessor's Westminster Abbey of the mid-eleventh. Given the more straightforward character of the grid it makes sense to assume (though it may be wrong to do so) that, where there were the two systems, the grid was established first and the proportions applied to it, for a whole building or part of a building. The evidence for each of the three examples is presented in this order, grid followed by geometry. In the cases of Escomb and the St Gall Plan the problem of apparent inaccuracy of execution is also considered.

Escomb

The church of St John of *c.*700 consists of a rectangular nave and a square chancel (Figure 5.4).[1] There are two chief contenders for the unit of length used in the design, namely the short perch of 4.6m and a module of 735mm. The dimensions of the nave can be related to the 4.6m unit, as its length from the interior of the east wall to the exterior of the west one is 13.83m, or three times 4.61m, and its internal width is 4.42/4.43m (Figure B.1). This suggestion is supported by the widespread use of the 4.6m perch in the period, but the discrepancy between the width and the perch raises doubts about its relevance. This is that the 4.42/43m width is 170 or 180mm or 3.7 per cent less than the size of the short perch. That may not seem like a great difference, one that could be explained by the builders erring in the digging of the foundation trenches, but there are two arguments against this. First, the digging of the foundation trenches should have nothing to do with the establishing of the thickness of the walls, other than being of a greater width. This assumption is supported by the second consideration, which is that the north and south walls of the nave have been laid out with exceptional accuracy. This is evident in the internal width, which varies by a centimetre between the east end at 4.43m and the west at 4.42m, and the walls themselves, which are consistently of an even thickness of 735mm (excepting the oddity of the west wall which, at 620mm, is not an inaccuracy but something which requires another explanation).

The observations concerning the short perch need to be compared with the other possible unit, suggested by Jim Addiss and based on the 735mm thickness of the walls. The correlations are as follows (Figures B.2–B.3). The 4.42/4.43m internal width of the nave equates to six units of 735mm ($0.735 \times 6 = 4.41$m, or 0.2 per cent short), and the walls are exactly one unit thick. (That is, as the nave is externally between 5.88 and 5.92m wide the walls are 5.90 minus 4.42m equals 1.48m, which divided by two equals 740mm, and minus 4.43m equals 1.47m, which divided by two equals 735mm.) The interior length of the nave is 13.24m on the north wall and 13.21m on the south, or 18 units of 736 and 734mm respectively, and the east wall, measured at the chancel arch, is 735m thick. In the elevation, the north wall of the nave is *c.*7.4m or ten units high.

This unit coincides so closely with the dimensions of the nave (the thickness of the west wall excepted) that it is difficult to doubt

[1] Taylor and Taylor 1965, 234–8; Fernie 1983, 54–9.

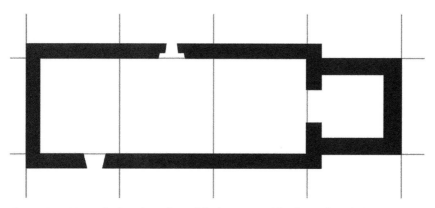

Figure B.1. Escomb, St John: plan with the 4.6m grid (after John Blair).

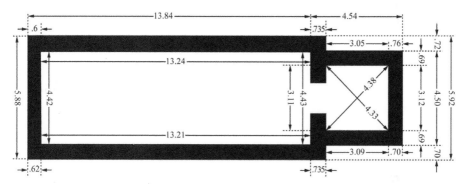

Figure B.2. Escomb, St John: plan, with dimensions provided by J. Addiss.

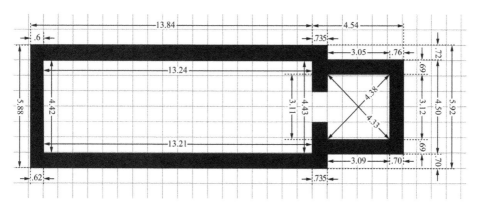

Figure B.3. Escomb, St John: plan with a grid of 735mm squares, based on an original by J. Addiss.

its relevance. There is, however, one apparent substantial weakness in comparison with the perch proposal – namely that, while the short perch is widely attested as a unit used in the period, there is no record of any other building using a unit of 735mm. This should make it inadmissible, but there is a possible explanation. The church contains a large number of reused blocks of Roman stone. These are particularly common in the chancel arch, to the extent that it has been seen as a Roman arch dismantled at its original site and reassembled at Escomb, rather than simply built using recut blocks.[2] The 735mm thickness of the chancel arch could therefore have supplied the unit used to design the church, a one-off or *ad hoc* unit, as it were, derived from the architectural feature which was made into the most significant in the church.[3]

While the dimensions of the nave relate closely to the 735mm unit, the chancel is different. It accords with the grid in that the exteriors of its north and south walls continue the interior faces of the nave walls. Thereafter, however, it departs, as the internal width of 3.11/3.12m divided into four produces units of 780mm, rather than being 2.94m or four units of 735mm, a difference of 6 per cent. The same applies on the east–west axis, where the length is 3.05/3.09m instead of the 2.94m of the grid, and thus four units of 70mm rather than 735mm each. Given the closeness of the grid lines to the walls in the nave it seems unlikely that these differences can be explained by careless laying out, which suggests that the chancel was designed using a different system.

It may therefore be relevant that the diagonals of the chancel square approach the width of the nave, with margins of error smaller than is the case with the 735mm grid applied to the eastern room, as above. That is, the diagonals of the chancel are 4.33 and 4.38m long and the nave 4.43m wide, differences of between 1 and 2 per cent. Also, the average of the four internal sides is 3.09m, and the diagonal of a square with a side of 3.09m will be 4.37m long, a difference of 1.6 per cent from 4.43m, while the longest side, of 3.12m, would form a square with a

---

[2] Taylor and Taylor 1965, 236–7.

[3] 73.5cm equals two and a half feet of 29.4cm, which could therefore have been the unit used by the proposed original Roman designers of the arch. As it is not clear that the Anglo-Saxons had adopted the Roman foot, it is safer to assume that the masons at Escomb used the 73.5cm unit as found. On the relationship between Roman and Anglo-Saxon units of length see Kidson 1990, and Fernie 1985 and 1991 (these two also available in Fernie 1995, 383–91 and 392–7).

diagonal of 4.41m. If the nave's dimensions were established first, then the size of the chancel square could have been determined by using the internal width of the nave as its diagonal.[4]

The St Gall Plan

The St Gall Plan, produced in Reichenau in the 820s and sent to Abbot Gozbert of St Gall, is both a goldmine and a minefield (Figures B.4– B.7). In order to keep matters as straightforward as possible, in what follows I have presented my proposals in the text and discussed differences of opinion in the footnotes.

A limited grid of contiguous squares with sides of between 66 and 68mm defines the church, providing the crossing, the south arm of the transept (the north arm is discussed below) and four double bays of the nave, with a half square for the ninth bay (Figure B.6). These units, especially those of the crossing and transept arm, are so prominent and regular it is hard to believe they were not intended to be square, or that they were not meant to play a prominent part in the design.[5]

---

[4] It is a pleasure to record my thanks to Jim Addiss for his generosity in sharing his unpublished analysis of Escomb (including the dimensions from his survey). When we started corresponding over the subject he had assumed that the 73.5cm grid explained the whole plan and I had assumed that the geometry did. After discussion I agreed with the relevance of his grid to the nave and he agreed that the side-to-diagonal proportion explained the chancel better than the grid. He points out that it would not have been necessary for the builders to lay out a grid for the nave, as the building lines could have been established using the grid unit as a module. The diagonals of the nave are 13.92m north-west to south-east and 13.95m south-west to north-east, establishing the form as a rectangle and not a parallelogram. The likelihood that the side-to-diagonal proportion was intended and is not a coincidence is supported by the occurrences of the same proportional relationship between a square and a rectangle in building A1b in the seventh-century timber palace at Yeavering in Northumberland (Hope-Taylor 1977, 164 and 237–9, figs 13 and 22).

[5] Horn 1966; Horn and Born 1979, I, 82–91. Horn's grid includes the squares of the church referred to here, which are indisputable (Horn and Born 1979, I, fig. 61 and p. 82), but he extends it to the whole parchment (Horn 1966, fig. 14 and p. 303, and Horn and Born, 1979, I, fig. 62 and pp. 90–91). This does not work as, beyond the church and the width of the claustral ranges, his grid lines bear almost no relationship to any of the buildings or streets on the Plan (it is necessary to stress *any*), or to its overall size (Fernie 1978). On the Plan in context see Jacobsen 1992. Florian Huber (2002) has also proposed a grid, but unlike Horn's it coincides closely with the lines of buildings on the Plan, which in its accuracy helps again to disprove

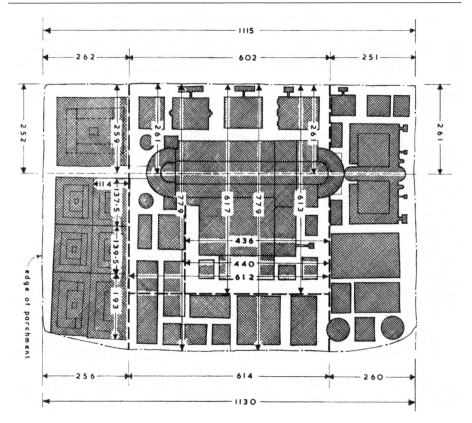

Figure B.4. St Gall Plan: dimensions in millimetres.

The side-to-diagonal proportion can be argued most clearly in three aspects of the church, to do with the location of its axis, the widths of the nave and aisles and the relationship between the overall width of the nave and aisles and the length of the transept.[6]

Horn's grid (see, for example, Huber's figures 1b, 2a, 3, 4, 6, 7, 8, 9, 11, 12 and 13). Norbert Stachura (2004) makes a contribution of basic importance, in establishing, beyond reasonable doubt, the unit of length used in setting out the design, namely one of 25.9mm, or an inch of a foot of 311.4mm. He adds that the use of a unit makes the use of geometry in the setting out unlikely. This claim, however, needs to be proved, as the two processes are not mutually exclusive and occur together in numerous analyses, such as Vitruvius's description of the proportions of the human body (Book III, chapter 1, section 2 – in numbers, and section 3 – in geometrical forms), and specifically of buildings (such as Fernie 1979).

    [6] Fernie 1978. Werner Jacobsen (1992, 330–1, note 26) rejects my 1978 analysis of the plan in terms of root-two on the grounds that the margins of error in what

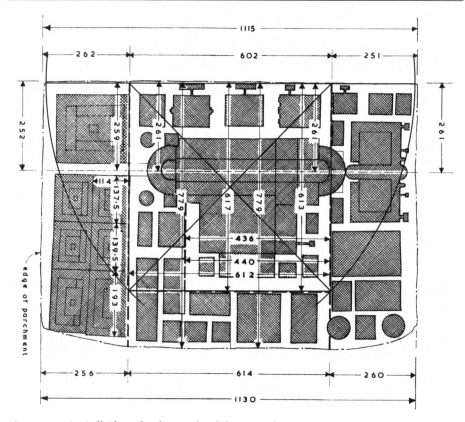

Figure B.5. St Gall Plan: the diagonals of the central square swung out to lie along the north edge of the parchment.

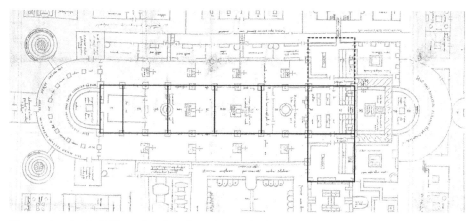

Figure B.6. St Gall Plan: the church with a grid of 67mm squares.

The axis of the church is related to the existence of a basic central square in the design, central because of its position and because it includes both the church and the claustral buildings. One side is marked by the north edge of the parchment and the other three by the outer sides of the east, south and west roads (Figure B.4). The diagonals of this square swung up to right and left to align with the north edge extend to the north-east and north-west corners of the parchment (Figure B.5). The extra length of the diagonal over the side of the square is the same as the distance between the north edge and the axis of the church, so that its position would appear to be determined by the geometry. In terms of measurements, the sides of the basic square are 602, 613, 614 and 617mm respectively, an average of 611.5mm. The diagonal of a 611.5mm square is 253mm longer than the side, while the eastern and western extensions of the central square are 251 and 262mm respectively, and the axis of the church lies 252mm from the north edge of the parchment at the west end and 261mm from it at the east end.

The relationship between the width of the nave and the width of the aisles can be set out in terms of the side-to-diagonal ratio as follows. The lines of the squares in the crossing, south transept and nave described above should represent the centres of the walls, as they bisect the columns and their bases. In the nave it is therefore not unreasonable to take the inner sides of the bases as representing the face of the arcade wall. The width of the nave between these faces in bays 1, 4 and 7 is 57,

I proposed are too great. His argument is, however, very odd, as the examples he gives of such margins are all of small buildings that I do not discuss (and with margins so great that no one would have proposed them), and conversely he does not mention any of the 13 lengths concerning the church, the cloister and the parchment which I do propose. For a statistical analysis and defence of the margins of error in the 1978 article see Fernie and Fearn, in press.

There is one proposition in the 1978 article which needs further examination: that concerning the 301mm nave length multiplied by root-two, which produces 426mm, running from the west end of the nave to the chord of the apse. The chord is normally, and understandably, taken as being in line with the eastern walls of the flanking buildings, which lie 66mm (or a standard square length) east of the crossing, whereas the 426mm length reaches only to 59mm. There are, however, clear spandrel shapes between the flanking buildings and the chancel, indicating that the curve of the apse was assumed to begin a few millimetres to the west – that is, on or near the 59mm line. This suggestion is supported by the form of the western apse, which is also extended, with the geometrical chord lying west of what might be called the functional chord – that is, where the apse meets the western end of the nave.

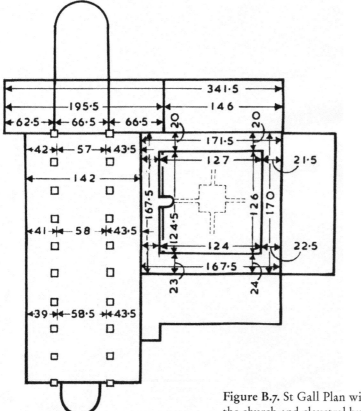

Figure B.7. St Gall Plan with dimensions of the church and claustral buildings.

58 and 58.5mm and the aisles (including the thickness of the nave walls) at these points are 42 and 43.5, 41 and 43.5, and 39 and 43.5mm wide. These produce averages of 42–58–42mm, while a square with a side of 42 units will have a diagonal of 59.

Third and finally, the total width of the nave and aisles relates to the length of the transept as the side of a square to its diagonal. The nave and aisles are an average of 142mm wide (42+58+42), and a square with a side of 142mm has a diagonal of 199.4mm. The crossing and the south arm of the transept are each 66.5mm long. The north arm, however, is only 62.5mm long. If symmetry is invoked and this is assumed to be an error, then it would measure 66.5mm, and the transept would be 66.5 × 3 or 199.5mm long.[7]

---

[7] For possible explanations for the short north arm see Fernie 1978, 587, and Horn and Born 1979, I, 101.

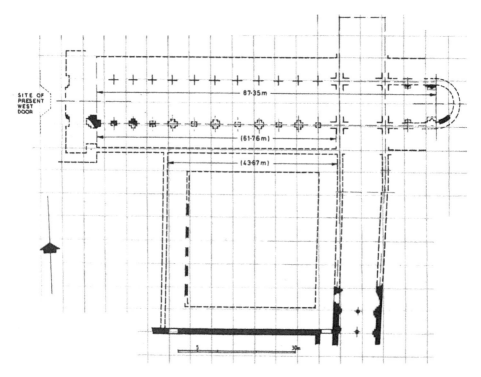

Figure B.8. Westminster Abbey, Edward's church: plan with a grid of 5.5m squares.

Westminster Abbey

A grid of the 'long perch' of 5.5m, when applied to the plan of Edward's church, produces a number of correspondences (Figures 5.18, B.8). The lines of the grid coincide with the centres of the north and south arcade walls of the chancel and nave and the south wall of the cloister (the aisle walls, and hence the north wall of the cloister, are lost), and on the other axis with the east and west walls of the east claustral range and hence by extension with those of the transept and crossing. As these are primary elements there is consequently a strong case for accepting it as the basis of the plan.

There are, however, two important points that do not coincide with the grid, namely the chord of the apse and the west end of the nave, both of which have been established from remains.[8] It is therefore of interest

---

[8] I am very grateful to John Blair for pointing out the correspondences between the plan and the grid and also where they differ from each other.

87.35 m

61.76 m

43.67 m

0   5   10 m

30 ft

N

Figure B.9. Westminster Abbey, Edward's church: plan with root-two dimensions.

that the approximately 61.7m length of the nave relates to the 87.35m length from the west end of the nave to the chord as the side of a square to its diagonal (61.7 × 1.4142 = 87.25). This is a common arrangement in Norman churches in England, where in addition the side of the cloister multiplied by root-two (and, therefore, if it is square, meaning its diagonal) equals the length of the nave (Figure B.9). The west wall of the cloister at Westminster is lost, but the remains of the garth wall indicate that there is a good case for reconstructing the cloister to form a square with walks of a normal width, in which case the west wall will be located as shown on the plan, in the right place for a square cloister with a diagonal as long as the length of the nave.[9]

A third element that does not coincide with the grid is the sizes of the bays, in both the chancel and the nave. They would presumably have been determined by subdividing the lengths of the two parts. It has to be acknowledged that this looks like an odd procedure, as bays

---

[9] Fernie 1987 and 2009. For the proposed location of the west wall of the cloister see 1987, 64.

fit so easily with a grid, but it is supported by the bay lengths being different in the two parts.

Conclusion

These three examples provide evidence for the combined use of grids and the root-two proportion. The two systems are, as noted, close in terms of form and, I would maintain, also in terms of consistency of use over the centuries. While the grid is a well-established feature of architectural and agricultural planning throughout Antiquity and the Middle Ages, it is sometimes argued that the position with the side-to-diagonal proportion was very different. That is, it could not have been used for several centuries after the fall of the Western Roman Empire because the West was then ignorant of the Greek and Roman literature on the relevant geometry, which arrived only via translations of the Arabic intermediaries late in or after the first millennium. This, however, is a misunderstanding: masons did not read texts, they worked in a tradition, and the traditional status of root-two was particularly high, as it floored Pythagoras, helped make Plato's reputation and led to Vitruvius passing it on with the highest praise despite his not understanding why it was so important.[10]

---

[10] On the strength of the tradition and the reputation of the proportion see Fernie 2015, 53–5, and Fernie 2018.

Appendix C

Catalogue of grid-planned sites

THIS CATALOGUE includes all sites and buildings – whether recognised from maps, from excavations or from standing fabric – for which the team (or individual members of it) accept at least a potential case for grid-planning, as described in chapter 3. It does not include the many cases that, after consideration, were rejected by general agreement. Except where otherwise stated, potential grids underlying village plans were identified during the nationwide assessment of the later nineteenth-century first edition Ordnance Survey six- and 25-inch maps. Counties are as before 1974.

At the start of each entry the different categories of evidence are given reliability ratings, in the following order and separated by slashes:

map evidence: 1 (probable), 2 (plausible) or 3 (possible)

excavated evidence: I (probable), II (plausible) or III (possible)

overall assessment: A (probable), B (plausible) or C (possible)

For example:

-/I/A means that, although there is no map evidence, the excavated evidence is enough to constitute a very strong case.

1/-/A means that, although there is no excavated evidence, the map evidence is enough to constitute a very strong case.

2/II/A means that, although neither the map evidence nor the excavated evidence is unambiguous, their independent witnesses to the same grid combine to constitute a very strong case.

3/-/C means that the case rests on rather inconclusive OS map data, uncorroborated by excavation, and therefore ranks only as possible.

Bedfordshire

Clapham (2/-/B)

Nineteenth-century plan: The orientation of the suggested grid is based on the broad road that runs WNW–ESE through the village. The village has a strong linear form, but there are multiple boundaries parallel and at right angles to the road that conform to a four-short-perch grid, particularly in the area of the church (St Thomas Becket) and Church Farm. The historic landscape is characterised by enclosed common-field land, although that nearest the settlement is not obviously the result of parliamentary inclosure.

Excavations:
- Ursula Taylor Lower School 2008: excavation revealed a twelfth- to thirteenth-century ditch (Newboult 2008b), but this does not conform to the suggested grid alignment, or indeed to the layout of the village.
- Ursula Taylor Lower School 2007: evaluation revealed part of three pits, of twelfth- to fourteenth- and fifteenth- to sixteenth-century date (Walker 2008).

LiDAR: Little additional detail shown on 1-m LiDAR corroborates gridding, except that in the field N of the church and E of Church Farm some apparent earthworks conform to the axis of the suggested grid. This area has not been developed and is still agricultural land.

Aerial photographs: Aerial photographs held in the NMR were consulted but no features of relevance were evident.

Historic maps: The 1839 parish tithe map adds no extra useful detail (Clapham, tithe map, 1839: Bedfordshire Archives and Records Service, P117/3/15).

Howbury (Renhold) (–/II/B; Blair 2013, fig. 21)

An excavated tenth- to eleventh-century settlement: two rows of buildings can be ascribed to a short-perch grid with moderate confidence. (Timby *et al.* 2007, 161–77; Blair 2013, 40–5)

Kempston Up End (2/II/B)

Nineteenth-century plan: JB initially recognised evidence for potential gridding in the late nineteenth-century plan. He also identified excavations within the village that potentially revealed ditches conforming to the axis of the purported grid.

The assessment of nineteenth-century settlement plans confirmed the presence of considerable regularity across a wide area; given the distance across which there is a common orientation, it seems unlikely that the pattern can be wholly due to the enclosure of common-field strips. There are numerous examples where field boundaries are spaced exactly two, four or other multiples of four short perches apart. The manorial complex also has the orientation of the proposed grid. There is a strong sense of rectilinearity to the settlement and surrounding areas, even though specific parts of the settlement do not conform.

Excavations:

- The Bury, Cemetery Road 2012: 1km from the village core in fields associated with Bury Farm. Roman ditch and undated ditches. A small number of medieval ditches and pits containing twelfth- to thirteenth-century pottery were also recorded. The evidence suggests agricultural rather than settlement activity and does not support the hypothesis of a manorial complex (Mordue 2012). These features bear no relationship to the orientation of the village grid.
- Outdoor Centre, Hillgrounds Road 2005: 500m N of village core on land adjacent to the River Ouse. No archaeology noted (Pixley and Beswick 2005).
- King William Road 2005: in the historic village core. A series of Late Saxon ditches broadly share the orientation of the proposed village grid, though not exactly. A pair of parallel ditches may mark the outer boundary of a tenement plot. Curiously, a Roman ditch is on a similar orientation and is aligned with a historic boundary (Walker and Maull 2005).
- Kempston Rural Lower School 2009: in Kempston Church End, next to All Saints Church. No relevant features (Luke 2009).
- Kempston Mill Lane 2003: to the SW of the manor house and NW of the village core, adjacent to the river Ouse. Within the area of broad rectilinearity. O'Brien (2003) reports that 'The excavation revealed evidence for Saxo-Norman and medieval farming dating from the ninth to late thirteenth centuries. It revealed linear ditches which were probably part of a system of field boundaries and drainage ditches. Several pits were recorded, including one that appeared to be a pottery dump or rubbish pit, as it contained over 13 kg of ceramics dated to the mid ninth to twelfth century. The limestone foundations of a small medieval or post-medieval structure were also found.' Area 1 is of most interest: ditches of Phase 1 (ninth to eleventh centuries), Phase 2 (tenth to thirteenth centuries) and

Phase 3 (tenth to thirteenth centuries) all conform to the axis of the proposed grid, though none falls directly on grid-lines.

- Kempston Mill Lane 2010: site to the E of Mill Lane 2003. Observation of ground reduction and foundation trenches revealed no archaeological features (Pozorski 2010).

- Grey's Lane 2002: halfway between the village core and the manor house. Single evaluation trench. No archaeological features were recorded. The ground may have been previously truncated during construction of the school (Edmondson and Preece 2002).

- 18 High Street (Fox and Hounds pub) 2012: in the centre of the historic village core. Pits of post-medieval and medieval date (Egan *et al.* 2012). Does not contribute to evidence for gridding.

- 134 High Street 2009: small-scale observations (building footings and cable trenches) on the W edge of Bell End, and on the nineteenth-century periphery of the village. Only a single post-medieval pit recorded (Gregson and Koziminski 2009).

- Cutler Hammer Sports Ground 1999: located to the NW of Bell End, beyond the historic village core but possibly within the area of broader rectilinear morphology. Predominantly Iron Age and Roman features, associated with a settlement at Box End. Numerous furrows, noted in geophysics and evaluation trenching, followed the orientation of the historic fields (Luke *et al.* 1999). Nothing sharing the axis of the proposed village grid.

- Box End 2004: to the N of All Saints Church, Kempston Box End. Part of an extensive Roman settlement. No medieval archaeology (Preece *et al.* 2004). None of the Roman features has the orientation of the proposed village grid.

- Box End 2000: large Roman settlement and enclosure complex (Luke *et al.* 2000). Numerous ditches are on the same axis as the proposed village grid, but as this site is 1.3km NW of the historic village core this might well be coincidence.

LiDAR: Kempston has seen considerable growth in the twentieth century, and much of the open ground surrounding the nineteenth-century settlement has now been built over, concealing any earthworks that may have been present. However, 1-m LiDAR shows a parcel of undeveloped land at Cryselco Sports Field 350m S of the church where remnant ridge and furrow shares the same orientation as the proposed grid.

Aerial photographs: RAF vertical aerial photography shows a series of linear earthworks, to the SW and SE of the manor house, which conform to the orientation of the proposed grid (RAF/CPE/UK/1952 25 MAR 1947 Frame 3357).

Historic maps: The two historic maps examined provide no additional information (Kempston, 1804: Bedfordshire Archives and Records Service, X1/25/1; Kempston, 1870: (Bedfordshire Archives and Records Service, SW 118).

Northill (2/-/B)

Nineteenth-century plan: The rectilinear layout of the roads through Northill gives a strong impression of regularity in the framework of the village. Some approximately N–S-orientated field boundaries conform, particularly to the SE of the village. The rectilinearity is confined to the village and its immediate hinterland: beyond that, roads and fields are less regular. A four-short-perch grid fits fairly well but might not be the best fit.

Excavations: None identified on ADS.

LiDAR: There is full 1-m LiDAR coverage for Northill. The historic core of Northill has seen some development in the twentieth century, particularly on land E of St Mary's church. To the E of the village the pattern of ridge and furrow is evident, some of it broadly aligned on the proposed grid. To the W of the village there are a number of linear earthworks in open fields that conform to the grid orientation and alignment.

Aerial photographs: Aerial photographs held in the NMR were consulted but no features of relevance were evident.

Historic maps: The two historic maps consulted provide no additional information (Northill, 1634: Bedfordshire Archives and Records Service, X1/39; Northill, 1781: Bedfordshire Archives and Records Service, X1/87).

Podington (3/-/C)

Nineteenth-century plan: JB initially recognised potential evidence for gridding in the late nineteenth-century plan. He also identified excavations within the village including ditches in possible conformity with the orientation of the suggested grid.

The proposed grid is orientated SW–NE/NW–SE, and conformity can be seen to the south of St Mary's church along High Street. On the south side of High Street are a series of tenements, with a consistent back boundary, that run perpendicular and parallel to the road. South of these, the boundaries of a large field share the same orientation. There is little else within the wider settlement or surrounding field pattern that conforms, and the village plan north of the High Street does not relate to the proposed grid.

Excavations:
 • Vicarage Lane 2004: various ditches, gullies, pits and postholes in three evaluation trenches, most of them not on the orientation of the proposed grid (Grant and McConnell 2004). The only ditch that has a similar orientation is [1051] in Trench 1, which yielded tenth- to eleventh-century pottery.

LiDAR: The 1-m LiDAR coverage does not add any useful detail.

Aerial photographs: Aerial photographs held in the NMR were consulted but no features of relevance were evident.

Historic maps: The two historic maps examined provide no additional information (Podington, 1765: Bedfordshire Archives and Records Service, OR 917; Podington, 1765: Bedfordshire Archives and Records Service, OR 944/2).

Stotfold (-/I/A; Blair 2013, fig. 17; Blair 2018, figs 112, 117, 140; present Figure 1.4)
The largest Late Anglo-Saxon settlement ever excavated, Stotfold provides a unique overview of that stage in village formation. Post-excavation work is currently in progress; we have access to this material by kind permission of Wesley Keir and Albion Archaeology. John Blair's suggestion of a different grid in another part of the nineteenth-century village plan was not accepted by the whole team.

The settlement is a complex one: the excavated area lies within what may previously have been a circular livestock enclosure, developed for housing around the mid-tenth century. There appear to be two superimposed phases of houses and surrounding enclosures, laid out c.950 and c.1000. The later phase is clearly grid-planned on the short-perch module so, probably, is the earlier one, though the ditches do not confirm so closely to the grid.

It has further been suggested that another area of the village, on the NE edge of the circular enclosure and including the parish church, may be grid-planned (Blair 2018, fig. 117), though the boundaries show conformity with the four-short-perch module in only one dimension. (Blair 2013, 38; Blair 2018, 320–2, 371)

Aerial photographs: Aerial photographs held in the NMR were consulted but no features of relevance were evident.

Historic map: Stotfold (Beds), tithe map, 1849: National Archives IR 30/1/50.

Stratton, near Biggleswade (–/I/A; Blair 2013, fig. 12; present Figure 6.1) A large area excavation of an important seventh- to tenth-century settlement. Post-excavation work is currently in progress; we have access to this material by kind permission of David Ingham and Albion Archaeology.

The early phases are based on two successive short-perch grids, of the late seventh and late eighth centuries respectively, which are on different alignments: the second conforms to a Roman road. Boundaries and buildings fit the grids accurately, despite the fact that they are organised on strip-like rather than box-like configurations. (Blair 2013, 33–5)

Historic maps: The historic map consulted provides no additional information (Biggleswade, 1838: Bedfordshire Archives and Records Service, MAT 5/1).

Tempsford / Tempsford Park (2/I/A; present Figure 6.10)
Nineteenth-century plan: JB initially suggested that there was evidence for gridding in the late nineteenth-century plan. He also identified excavations within the village that included ditches apparently orientated with the purported grid. Tempsford village has a strong linear plan and is orientated N–S with tenements perpendicular to the straight road. There are, in addition, several boundaries spaced far apart which conform to the proposed grid, notably S of Gannock's Castle and N of St Peter's church.

Excavations:
- Tempsford Park 1999: a large open area excavation revealed Early and Middle Saxon enclosures, Late Saxon enclosures and settlement and a medieval moated manor house (Maull 2000). Some rectilinear arrangements within the Late Saxon complex, and a number of ditches in that phase, appear to be broadly orientated with the proposed village grid. The later moat also fits within the proposed grid framework.
- Tempsford Hall, Station Road 2008: a watching brief for a temporary access road, pipeline and compound on the SW side of Tempsford Hall revealed no archaeological remains (Leigh 2008).

LiDAR: There is complete 1-m LiDAR coverage. While it shows the pattern of pre-enclosure ridge and furrow, there are no extant features corresponding to the grid orientation that do not appear already on the 1st edition OS 25-inch map.

Aerial photographs: Aerial photographs held in the NMR were consulted but no features of relevance were evident.

Historic maps: The historic map consulted provides no additional information (Tempsford, n.d.: Bedfordshire Archives and Records Service, X1/41).

Wrestlingworth (3/-/C)

Nineteenth-century plan: The distinguishing feature of Wrestlingworth is the square churchyard, set away from the core of the village. There are a series of lanes that run at right angles to the churchyard, as well as a number of the surrounding field boundaries, and these have a notably different orientation from that of the wider pattern of settlement, roads and fields.

Excavations:
- Home Farm Manor, High Street 2013: observation of a 35 × 20m topsoil strip E of Home Farm revealed no archaeological features (Gregson 2013).
- Home Farm, High Street 2013: evaluation trenching revealed twelfth- to thirteenth-century ditches 200m S of the church (Gregson 2012). Three ditches in Trench 1 are on the same orientation as the proposed grid. Two ditches in Trench 2 are on a different orientation. St Neots Ware regarded as 'residual' in ditches [111] and [205].
- Lower School, Church Lane 2007: observation of excavation of footings for a school extension revealed the 'remains of a possible early medieval post-built structure or fence corner'; only three truncated postholes were seen, and further interpretation is impossible on this limited evidence; one posthole contained a single sherd of twelfth- to thirteenth-century pottery (Newboult 2008a).
- St Peter's church 2007: a service trench to a depth of 0.5m from the N side of the churchyard to the church (Lodoen 2007) was too limited in depth and width to reveal underlying deposits in a graveyard context.

LiDAR: The available 1-m LiDAR ends just S of the historic settlement so provides no useful data, except that the pattern of long furlongs is evident.

Aerial photographs: Aerial photographs held in the NMR were consulted but no features of relevance were evident.

Historic maps: The historic map consulted provides no additional information (Wrestlingworth, 1801:Bedfordshire Archives and Records Service, MA 23).

Berkshire

Abingdon (not classified)
JB has suggested that traces of the same – very large – grid-planned area can be observed in the property boundaries of the town and in the field boundaries of Northcourt, to the N, as shown on nineteenth-century maps. The other members of the team were not persuaded.

Marcham (3/-/B; present Figure 6.6)
Nineteenth-century plan: The proposed grid takes its orientation from the dead-straight Church Street. A series of exactly perpendicular tenements fronting this road are in conformity with the proposed grid, as are a small number of boundaries in the surrounding fields. The case for gridding hinges on whether the Church Street area is the oldest part of the historic settlement, as elsewhere the village is strung out along sinuous roads and has no regular structure. There is, however, a possibility that this part of the village owes its origins to post-medieval estate development associated with Marcham House and Park, though this needs exploring further.

Excavations:
- 3–5 Mill Road 2006: a watching brief during excavation of four house foundations revealed no archaeological features or deposits (Gill 2006).
- Marcham Bypass, 2005: narrow trenches identified probable middle-Saxon enclosures W of the village, but provided inadequate data to determine alignments (Cockin 2005).
- Priory Lane 2012: geophysical survey and evaluation trenching of land to the rear of Priory Lane revealed Saxo-Norman to thirteenth-century remains, principally boundary and enclosure ditches, as well as wall foundations (Holmes and Walker 2012). Anomalies picked up in the geophysical survey, and ditches in the evaluation, are generally orientated with the proposed grid, though some of the anomalies appear to track slightly sinuous courses and are not dead straight.

LiDAR: There is full coverage of 1-m LiDAR, but extensive twentieth-century development within and surrounding the historic core renders much of it useless. There are, however, some long, straight earthworks that are aligned with the grid and might be furlong boundaries (although a complex of rectilinear earthworks 1500m NE of the village, which might be settlement-related, are not). Within the historic core there are few remaining undeveloped areas, but in one, the Cricket Ground, there are two linear earthworks conforming to the proposed grid alignment.

Aerial photographs: RAF vertical aerial photography shows a rectilinear pattern of earthwork ditches to the south-west of the village on land adjacent to a stream. These ditches reflect the orientation and, in some places, the position of the proposed grid. It is evident that the course of the stream has been altered, as it makes a number of 90-degree turns (RAF/106G/UK/1721 06 Sep 1946 Frame 4012; RAF/CPE/UK/1953 25 MAR 1947 Frame 3004).

Historic maps: None consulted.

Buckinghamshire

Stoke Mandeville (2/-/B)

Nineteenth-century plan: The proposed grid orientation is reflected in the main road entering the village from the NE, and that leading NW to the parish church. Furthermore, there are multiple boundaries – both field and tenement – that conform to the same axis. This is particularly evident in the area surrounding St Mary's church and Malthouse Farm. The regularity in this core area contrasts with the curvilinear remnants of former open field on the W periphery of the village and the large-scale rectilinear post-medieval enclosure on the east.

Excavations: None identified on ADS.

LiDAR: 1-m LiDAR data shows that the expansion of Stoke Mandeville in the twentieth century has obscured anything around the historic core.

Aerial photographs: Aerial photographs held in the NMR were consulted but no features of relevance were evident.

Historic maps: None consulted.

Walton, near Aylesbury (–/II/B; Blair 2013, figs 1, 9)
An excavated group of seventh- to eighth-century buildings, possibly on a courtyard layout. There is broad overall conformity to a short-perch grid, even though the individual buildings are not very precisely located. (Ford *et al.* 2004; Blair 2013, 27–31)

Wolverton Mill (not classified)
JB has suggested that the excavated mid-Saxon rectilinear enclosure is in conformity with a short-perch grid, also reflected in the property boundaries of Old Wolverton as shown on nineteenth-century maps. The other members of the team were not persuaded. (Chapman *et al.* 2015)

Cambridgeshire

Cherry Hinton (not classified)
Nineteenth-century plan: JB initially considered that there was evidence for gridding in the late nineteenth-century plan: not in the historic village core itself, but around Church End to the N. Numerous lengths of road and field boundary orientated SW–NE/NW–SE are at right angles to each other and seem to be in broad conformity with a four-short-perch grid. He also identified excavations within the village that may have had ditches conforming to the axis of the purported grid. The team eventually concluded that the regularity of this area reflects the enclosure of open-field strips, not grid-planning.

However, the numerous excavations in the western part of the village do seem to provide quite convincing evidence of grid-planning. The problem is that these are so fragmentary and diverse, and so difficult to correlate on a single map from the data currently available, that we were unable to analyse them coherently. We have therefore reluctantly placed this case in the 'not classified' category, though we believe that it has considerable potential for future work.

Excavations: There have been extensive investigations around Church End in Cherry Hinton. Key reports include:
- New Vicarage, 2 Fulbourn Old Drift: slightly beyond the core area of the proposed grid. Two evaluation trenches dug ahead of the construction of a new vicarage. Nothing of note in Trench 2, but in Trench 1 there were a series of three recut ditches dating to the tenth/eleventh and twelfth/thirteenth centuries. These do not appear to have the same orientation as the proposed grid, although the orientation of these features may not have been recorded very

accurately as the features were only excavated across 50 per cent of the trench width (Fletcher 2004b).

- Neath Farm Industrial Estate 2011: in the area of Church End, excavation of two areas revealed a 'densely packed sequence of linear ditches and gullies of 12th-14th-century date'. The dated features were in Area 1 and the undated features were in Area 2. These all follow the proposed grid orientation (Slater 2011a).

- Neath Farm Business Park 2011: in Church End, in the area of proposed gridding. A single L-shaped evaluation trench revealed a densely packed sequence of ditches and gullies of twelfth- to fourteenth-century date. These ditches conform to the orientation of the proposed grid, and one ditch (F 1000) is aligned exactly with it (Slater 2011b).

- Junior School 2011: away from the area of proposed gridding, showing furrows aligned with the historic landscape, perhaps coincidentally the same as the proposed grid at Church End (Gilmour 2011).

- Coldhams Lane 2007: evaluation trenching revealed multi-period features, including prehistoric burials, an early Roman field system and funerary enclosure, an early Anglo-Saxon cemetery and remnant ridge and furrow. Ditches associated with the early Roman field system appear to conform to the orientation of the proposed grid, as do the later furrows (Mortimer 2007).

- 69–115 Church End 1999: in the area of proposed gridding. Roman cemetery and twelfth- to fourteenth-century ditches. Numerous ditches conform to the orientation of the proposed grid, some precisely aligned with it (Murray and Vaughan 1999).

- 63 Church End 1999: in the area of proposed gridding. Late Anglo-Saxon ditches, pits and postholes containing St Neots and Thetford Ware. Ditch 27 in Trench 5 is on same orientation as suggested grid but others are at different angles to it (Kenney 1999).

- 63 Church End 2003: extensive ninth- to fourteenth-century remains including structures, boundaries and trackways. Some ditches associated with Phase 3 (mid-tenth to eleventh centuries) share a very similar orientation to the proposed grid, although the longest stretches of ditch associated with the trackways are gently curving and not dead straight. Buildings, particularly Structure 1, appear to be orientated on the same axis as the proposed grid (Cessford and Mortimer 2003).

- Rosemary Lane 2003: seven evaluation trenches revealing various ditches, pits and postholes dating from the Roman period, eighth to ninth century, tenth to eleventh century and post-Conquest period (Mortimer 2003). Difficult to georeference precisely because the plan in the report is on such a small scale, but there is a suggested general agreement between the orientation of medieval features and the proposed settlement grid.

LiDAR: No 1-m LiDAR is available.

Aerial photographs: Aerial photographs held in the NMR were consulted but no features of relevance were evident.

Historic maps: The historic map consulted provides no additional information (Cherry Hinton, draft map showing pre-inclosure boundaries, 1806: Cambridgeshire Archives, 152/P7).

Fen Drayton (3/-/C)

Nineteenth-century plan: A relatively weak case on the available evidence. The area of regularity, where a number of boundaries run 90 degrees to one another, is NW of St Mary's church.

Excavations:

- Manor Farm House 2004: two evaluation trenches revealed two undated ditches orientated E–W and modern features (Hickling 2004). Nothing relevant to this study.
- Wilderspin Garage 2003: evaluation trenches revealed part of a Roman field system and a medieval and undated pond (Wills 2003). Nothing relevant to this study.

LiDAR: There is complete coverage of 1-m LiDAR. The village has expanded considerably since the nineteenth century, so that nearly all open spaces within the historic settlement have been filled in. LiDAR is of little use, except that significant surviving furlong boundaries to the NE and SW of the historic core are orientated with the proposed village grid.

Aerial photographs: RAF vertical aerial photography shows three areas on the N and E sides of the village where there are slight earthworks that broadly conform to the orientation and position of the proposed grid (RAF/CPE/UK/1952 25 Mar 1947 Frame 3019).

Historic maps: The historic maps consulted provide no additional information (Fen Drayton, photo of a plan, 1792: Cambridgeshire Archives, TR869/P17; Fen Drayton, inclosure map, 1841: Cambridgeshire Archives, Q/RDc61).

Fordham (2/I/A; Blair 2013, fig. 26; present Figure 6.8)

Nineteenth-century plan: Two distinct (and presumably successive) four-short-perch grids are proposed at Fordham (cf. Blair 2013, 49–50). One is orientated with Church Street, WNW–ESE. While the core of the historic village appears to have a strong linear plan, there are numerous boundaries that run perpendicular to Church Street and others that are exactly parallel, including some at a distance from the road (e.g. N of the village core around Waterside Lodge and Lords Barn). The other grid is represented by an excavated group of rectilinear closes and some adjoining field boundaries.

Excavations (for which also see Patrick and Rátkai 2011):

- Hillside Meadow 1998: excavation revealed a sequence of rectilinear enclosures and settlement in three principal phases: Early–Middle Saxon (500–700/750), Middle–Late Saxon (700/750–850) and Late Saxon (850/900–1100). There is a continuity in the orientation of enclosures, and some continued directly in use between the phases (Mould 1999). Both Middle–Late and Late Saxon systems conform to the proposed grid layouts.
- 12 Hillside Meadow 2001: a single evaluation trench revealed a ditch, gullies and postholes. There was little secure dating evidence, but various features share the same orientation as the second proposed phase of gridding (Casa Hatton 2001). The principal ditch (2), which is orientated with the grid, yielded one sherd each of Iron Age and Roman pottery, but there is a suggestion in the report that all features are of broadly similar date (Middle/Late Saxon).
- Fordham Primary School 2001: excavation revealed a Middle Saxon post-built structure and Late Saxon ditches (Connor 2001). Parallel ditches are spaced one short perch apart and fit well with the later phase of proposed gridding.
- 20 Hillside Meadow 2002: evaluation comprising four trenches revealed two ditches, both containing 'Saxon' pottery (O'Brien and Gardner 2002). Each ditch was aligned with one of the phases of proposed gridding.
- 17 Hillside Meadow 2002: three evaluation trenches revealed five ditches and a gully, all of 'Saxon' date (Sutherland and Wotherspoon 2002). 'Saxon' ditches in Trenches 2 and 3 conform well to the second proposed phase of gridding, while one undated ditch in Trench 1 is also on the same orientation.

LiDAR: The 1-m LiDAR provides little additional information because of twentieth-century development and the ravages of cultivation: there is very little trace of ridge and furrow and only the more significant earthworks associated with the furlongs survive. In the field between Manor Farm and Waterside Lodge, immediately N of Church Street, there may be slight earthworks that appear to conform to the orientation and alignment of the proposed grid, although these features could be a product of the original LiDAR data collection and manipulation.

Aerial photographs: RAF vertical aerial photography shows the same earthworks between Manor Farm and Waterside Lodge that are visible on the LiDAR data (RAF/106G/LA/124 09 Feb 1945 Frame 2054).

Historic maps: The Fordham inclosure map shows additional boundaries to the N and S of Church Street that do not appear on the late nineteenth-century 1st edition OS 25-inch map, and which appear to follow the same orientation of both proposed phases of gridding (Fordham inclosure map, n.d.: Cambridgeshire Archives, Q/RDc33).

Gamlingay (3/III/C)

Nineteenth-century plan: The rather limited evidence for grid-planning centres on the sub-square churchyard, located uncomfortably with the layout of the village (which is strung out along two major roads). St Mary's church is orientated with the proposed grid, WNW–ESE. Church Lane is at right angles to the graveyard, and several other boundaries in the immediate vicinity conform exactly to its alignment. Although the number of elements conforming to the proposed grid are few, there is some general agreement with the four-short-perch multiple.

Excavations:
- St Mary's Field 2013: seven evaluation trenches dug E of the church revealed a fourteenth- to fifteenth-century building and a number of medieval and post-medieval ditches (Atkins 2013). Features in Trenches 1 and 5/6 are not orientated with the proposed grid (about 30 degrees off) but ditches in Trench 5 are. Ditches 11 and 13 both date to the fourteenth century. These ditches do not conform to the wider historic landscape like those in other trenches.
- West Road 2007: there are ditches orientated with the proposed grid 700m SW of St Mary's church, in an area shown as fields on the nineteenth-century map (Doyle and Harris 2007).
- Green End Industrial Estate 2010: three evaluation trenches and four test pits at Green End Industrial Estate, 800m W of St Mary's church, revealed no features or finds. It was suspected that the land had previously been truncated (Collins 2010).

- Station Road 1996 and 1998: excavation 500m SE of the parish church, on the opposite site of Millbridge Brook, revealed fifth- to eighth-century settlement and funerary evidence, including ditches, pits, buildings and a cemetery (Murray 1996; McDonald and Trevarthen 1998). None of the phases conforms to the proposed grid.

LiDAR: The 1-m LiDAR coverage does not add any useful detail.

Aerial photographs: RAF vertical aerial photography shows an earthwork which probably represents a southwards continuation of the E churchyard boundary. This conforms to the position and orientation of the proposed grid (RAF/AC287 08 MAR 1943 Frame 5218).

Historic maps: The historic maps consulted provide no additional information (Gamlingay, plan of manor, 1602: Cambridgeshire Archives, TR274/P1; Gamlingay, inclosure map, 1844: Cambridgeshire Archives, Q/RDc67; Gamlingay, tithe map, 1850: Cambridgeshire Archives, P76/27/1).

Hinxton (3/III/C)

Nineteenth-century plan: JB had suggested that Hinxton might be gridded, and also that excavated ditches might conform to this proposed grid, but after discussion it was concluded that the regularity in the village plan might be derived from the enclosure of former open-field strips. The settlement plan has a distinct linear form, with property boundaries and lanes running at 90 degrees from the main NNE–SSE orientated road, although this regularity might be a product of expansion over former fields. While some boundaries conform to the four-short-perch multiple, there is little agreement over a wider area.

Excavations: There have been extensive investigations around Hinxton, the plans of which are yet to be brought together. Key reports include:
- Wellcome Trust Genome Campus Extension 2002: Iron Age, Roman and Saxon remains across 30+ evaluation trenches (Kemp and Spoery 2002). Previous excavations to the S of Hinxton Hall in 1993–4 and 1994–5 revealed extensive multi-period remains. This area of archaeological features is S of the historic village core, and the dearth of medieval remains perhaps indicates that the settlement shifted northwards. Curiously, the Iron Age phases conform exactly with the proposed grid, the Roman and Anglo-Saxon ones less so.

LiDAR: There has been relatively little twentieth-century expansion across Hinxton, so much of what was open ground in the nineteenth century remains so. There is, however, only one place where the 1-m LiDAR shows earthworks that might relate to the underlying grid: in the fields N of the parish church, where there is a pair of rectilinear enclosures. These do not appear to be related to features on nineteenth- or twentieth-century maps.

Aerial photographs: OS vertical aerial photography shows a single linear earthwork on the W side of the village, on land adjacent to the river Cam, which conforms to the orientation of the proposed grid. (OS/52R57 07 SEP 1952 Frame 10).

Historic maps: The 1833 map depicts some additional conforming boundaries to the S of Hinxton Hall and potentially NW of the main village street (Hinxton inclosure map, 1833: Cambridgeshire Archives, Q/RDc47).

Isleham (1/II/A; present Figures 1.5, 1.6)
Nineteenth-century plan: The framework of roads, property boundaries and fields within the historic village core largely conforms to a rectilinear layout, with many components at exact right angles to each other. A grid using the four-short-perch module appears to fit well across a wide area.

Excavations:
- Fordham Road 2006: open area excavation to the S of Street Farm on the southern side of the village revealed eleventh- to twelfth-century, twelfth- to fourteenth-century, fourteenth- to sixteenth-century, and sixteenth-century and later phases. The later phases appear to relate to the extraction of clunch. The eleventh- to twelfth-century features are largely ditches and pits (Newton 2006): the ditches are orientated with the proposed village grid, and one is in exact conformity. Some Phase 2 ditches also follow the orientation of the grid.
- Isleham Recreation Ground 2012: seven evaluation trenches totalling 147m in a field immediately S of the village centre. As at Fordham Road, there was evidence for medieval clunch extraction and processing, but also early medieval occupation dated to the eleventh to twelfth centuries. This includes a large number of ditches and postholes, indicating two areas of settlement bounded by ditches (Rees 2012). There is good agreement between the orientation of ditches and the proposed grid.
- Beck Road 2009: five evaluation trenches dug to the E of Beck Road, S of the modern cemetery and 270m SE of the parish church,

revealed a scatter of undated pits and one dated to the twelfth to fourteenth centuries. No other features were identified (Ennis 2009).

- 12 West Street 1998: evaluation revealed thirteenth- to fourteenth-century linear features associated with the Benedictine Priory, including the western ditch of the precinct. Other late medieval ditches were interpreted as plots off West Street (Knight 1998). Features correspond to the orientation of the grid, but it is likely that this is a later adherence to established village topography.
- 12 West Street 2000: recording during a watching brief on the same site as the 1998 evaluation confirmed earlier observations (Macaulay 2000). Features correspond to the orientation of the grid, but it is likely that this is a later adherence to established village topography.
- Former Allotments 2004: evaluation trenching and test pits on the S side of the village revealed medieval features including a quarry pit, undated postholes and a twelfth- to fourteenth-century ditch (Kenney 2004). The ditch might be orientated with the proposed grid, but since the evaluation trench cut transversely across its line, and therefore only exposed a short stretch, its exact orientation is not certain.

LiDAR: There is complete 1-m LiDAR available for the village and surrounding countryside. There has been considerable infill development and new housing on the periphery of the historic village core, which negates the value of LiDAR in these areas. There are no earthworks within the remaining open areas that further the argument for or against gridding, although later ploughing might have removed any evidence (there is no evidence for ridge and furrow despite the area clearly once being cultivated as open fields). The most interesting aspect of the LiDAR data is that it shows the pattern of furlong boundaries surrounding Isleham. These are sinuous at a distance from the village, but there is distinct rectilinearity to the S and SW, with long, straight furlongs that are exactly parallel and perpendicular to one another; there is some consistency with multiples of the four-short-perch module, with 10 × 4 short perches being common and a strong sense of gridding over an area of about 1.5km^2.

Aerial photographs: Aerial photographs held in the NMR were consulted but no features of relevance were evident.

Historic maps: A remarkable plan of 1790 shows Isleham before enclosure, including the pattern of strips and furlongs, as well as roads, that enclosure obliterated. While it is not possible to transcribe this map with absolute accuracy it is clear that the pattern of furlongs, strips and older lanes to the S and SW of the church would conform to the orientation of the proposed grid. This is confirmed by cross-referencing with the later 1844 draft inclosure map, which shows some of these older features as well as the layout familiar on the Ordnance Survey 1st edition map (Isleham, manorial plan, 1790: Cambridgeshire Archives, 311/P1; Isleham, draft inclosure map, 1844: Cambridgeshire Archives, 515/P).

Steeple Morden (2/-/B)

Nineteenth-century plan: The distinguishing feature of the proposed grid is that while many of the field boundaries across a distance of about 500m conform to a rectilinear layout, the road pattern is quite different, suggesting that they overlay an earlier framework. There is some agreement with the four-short-perch module. St Peter and St Paul's church is aligned with the proposed grid.

Excavations:

- 15–17 Hay Street 2002: trial trenching N of the parish church revealed extensive evidence for Romano-British occupation, predominantly enclosure ditches, comprising part of a wider cropmark complex. Despite the ascribed 'Roman' date, some features were actually aceramic (Grant and Wilkins 2002). A further evaluation identified a large Roman ditch (Rudge 2002). There is no obvious conformity with the proposed settlement grid.
- The Whitehouse 2007: two trenches totalling 70m in length revealed one undated ditch and one undated posthole (Stocks 2007). There was no similarity between the orientation of the ditch and the proposed settlement grid.
- Steeple Morden Primary School 2001: two evaluation trenches revealed two undated ditches. They were sealed by post-medieval layers and were thought to be no later than late medieval (Kenney 2001). The ditches were not on the orientation of the proposed grid.
- 1 Cheyney Street 2004: excavation of a single evaluation trench revealed a probable late medieval ditch terminus, posthole and pond/quarry pit (Fletcher 2004a). There is insufficient exposure to ascertain whether the ditch accords to the proposed grid.

LiDAR: There is full coverage of 1-m LiDAR, but little to further the argument for or against gridding, as much of the historic settlement has been infilled with modern development. The only earthworks that might be of interest are in the playing field NW of the village, but these could well be recent.

Aerial photographs: RAF vertical aerial photography shows a rectilinear arrangement of earthworks W of the parish church, in the vicinity of the site of Morden House, which conform to the orientation, position and perhaps dimensions of the proposed grid (RAF/CPE/UK/1917 09 JAN 1947 Frame 4020).

Historic maps: The historic maps consulted provide no additional information (Steeple Morden, inclosure map, 1817: Cambridgeshire Archives, Q/RDc28; Steeple Morden, tithe map, 1839: Cambridgeshire Archives, 296/P35).

Trumpington (not classified)
An excavation by Oxford Archaeology East was kindly brought to our attention by Richard Mortimer as this project was concluding. A sequence of mid- to late Anglo-Saxon rectilinear ditched enclosures gives a strong impression of grid-conformity, but further analysis was not possible at that stage.

West Fen Road, Ely (–/I/A); Blair 2013, fig. 11; Blair 2018, fig. 112.)
Two eighth-century phases of an excavated settlement are based closely on successive short-perch grids; the first phase, in particular, has a box-like configuration that conforms unusually closely to the squares of the grid. The gridded aspect of the site faded away during the later Anglo-Saxon period, and it leaves no trace on nineteenth-century maps. (Mortimer *et al.* 2005; Blair 2013, 31–3)

Cornwall

Mawgan Porth (not classified; Blair 2018, fig. 121)
JB has proposed that the buildings of the excavated tenth-century settlement were planned in conformity to a short-perch grid. The other members of the team were divided in opinion. (Bruce-Mitford 1997; Blair 2018, 328–9)

Derbyshire

Hartshorn (1/–/A; present Figure 6.3)
Nineteenth-century plan: There is a strong sense of regularity in the village plan, with roads and boundaries parallel and perpendicular

to each other. Main Street, which enters the village from the NW, is remarkably straight and provides the principal axis of the proposed grid. The regularity around the village core contrasts strongly with the irregularity in the surrounding landscape. St Peter's church is orientated with the proposed grid, on a WSW–ENE axis. There are places where the boundaries are spaced at multiples of the four-short-perch unit.

Excavations:
- Land Adjacent to 6 Main Street 2005: observation of foundation trenches and topsoil stripping in advance of a new building immediately S of the parish church identified no archaeological features (Hunt 2005).

LiDAR: 1-m LiDAR is available for only part of the village, SW of the parish church. It does cover part of the area where gridding is proposed and, although it does not reveal any boundaries in addition to those shown on the 1st edition OS 25-inch mapping, the hillshade models do show distinct shadows alongside some of the conforming landscape components, particularly the roads, perhaps suggesting that these lie on significant earthworks.

Aerial photographs: RAF vertical aerial photography shows a pattern of ridge and furrow and probable furlong boundaries N of the village that conform to the proposed grid (RAF/CPE/B/UK/15 16 APR 1948 Frame 5218; RAF/541/28 17 MAY 1948 Frame 4403).

Historic maps: None consulted.

Repton (–/II/B; Blair 2018, fig. 31)
Excavations under and around the E end of this important Mercian minster located an axial pair of large timber buildings at right angles to the church, which may be part of a great hall complex. The halls and the church appear to conform to the same short-perch grid. (Biddle and Kjølbye-Biddle 2001)

Dumfries and Galloway

Whithorn (-/II/C; present Figure 5.5)
The 'Anglian' phase of the excavated monastic site includes a line of rectilinear buildings that may conform to a short-perch grid, but the visible remains are too simple and restricted to allow a high level of confidence. (Hill 1997)

Durham

***Escomb* church** (–/I/A; Blair 2013, fig. 3; present Figures 5.4, B.1–3)
JB has proposed that this late seventh-century church was laid out on
a short-perch grid. Eric Fernie (Appendix B) proposes a more complex
scenario based on proportional planning, but possibly also involving
gridding. (Pocock and Wheeler 1971; Blair 2013, 25)

Jarrow monastic site (not classified; Blair 2013, fig. 4)
JB proposed that Benedict Biscop's monastic complex at Jarrow was laid
out on a short-perch grid. However, the team concluded that, while this
remains possible, the evidence is inadequate to sustain a useful case.

Essex

Horndon on the Hill (2/–/B)
Nineteenth-century plan: The proposed grid is orientated NNW–SSE/
WSW–ENE, an alignment followed by St Peter's church. The main
road through Horndon is on a similar (N–S) axis but does not conform
to the grid. Much of the settlement layout relates to this road and
does not have a gridded appearance. There are, however, a number of
boundaries, distributed across the settlement and immediate hinterland,
that conform to the proposed grid orientation and which are set out at
right angles to one another.

Excavations: Horndon on the Hill Primary School 2010: no features or
finds were observed (Smith 2010).

LiDAR: No 1-m LiDAR is available.

Aerial photographs: Aerial photographs held in the NMR were consulted
but no features of relevance were evident.

Historic maps: None consulted.

Springfield Lyons (-/I/A ; Blair 2013, figs 1, 18; Blair 2018, fig. 139;
present Figure 1.3)
The excavated late Anglo-Saxon settlement, comprising a minor aristocratic domestic complex, shows convincing conformity to a short-perch
grid. No grid is visible on the nineteenth-century map. (Tyler and
Major 2005)

Gloucestershire

Bishop's Norton (3/-/C)

Nineteenth-century plan: There is some regularity across an area of fields between Bishops Norton and Bishops Court, with general agreement with a four-short-perch grid. There is, however, no conformity to the grid within the settlement plans. The surrounding field pattern is of semi-irregular closes, and it is possible that this area of more rectilinear fields and lanes may be a product of the relatively late enclosure of waste or common between two field systems.

Excavations: None identified on ADS.

LiDAR: No 1-m LiDAR is available.

Aerial photographs: Aerial photographs held in the NMR were consulted but no features of relevance were evident.

Historic maps: None consulted.

Bourton-on-the-Water (2/-/B)

Nineteenth-century plan: At first glance there is little obvious sign of gridding in the nineteenth-century plan of Bourton, as the majority of buildings and tenements are loosely arranged along the main NW–SE aligned road running through the village, or the river Windrush to the S of it. However, a broader view indicates that there may be some regularity in the wider landscape over which the village has developed. The orientation of a NNE–SSW road leading to Salmonsbury Camp is replicated by boundaries on the E edge of Bourton and in a former furlong boundary SW of the village. At 90 degrees to this (so on a WNW–ESE orientation), there are a number of roads and boundaries on the S side of Bourton, notably the lane adjacent to the police station.

Excavations: There have been a large number of investigations around Bourton-on-the-Water, but so far they have not been brought together or coherently plotted in relation to each other.

LiDAR: No 1-m LiDAR is available.

Aerial photographs: Aerial photographs held in the NMR were consulted but no features of relevance were evident.

Historic maps: None consulted.

Gloucester, St Oswald's church (not classified; present Figure 1.2)
The ground-plan of this late ninth-century church appears to show conformity to a long-perch grid. It is suggested above that this simply reflects a mechanical copying of the ground-plan of the long-perch-gridded Old Minster at Winchester. (Heighway and Bryant 1999)

Hempsted (1/-/A; present Figure 3.4)
Nineteenth-century plan: The plan of Hempsted is remarkably regular. The proposed grid, orientated NW–SE, looks a very strong case. A road entering the village from the NE meets the High Street at right angles, defining the axis of the settlement plan. From these two routes others are set at 90 degrees, such as that running SW from the market cross. There is a high degree of conformity to the grid in closes within the village and fields to the NE (this regularity differs markedly from the surrounding fields). St Swithun's church is orientated true W–E rather than on the grid alignment, but nearly all other substantial buildings conform to the grid.

Excavations: None identified on ADS.

LiDAR: The 1-m LiDAR coverage doers not add any useful detail.

Aerial photographs: A single cropmark of a former boundary is visible on RAF aerial photography to the S of the village, and this shares the same orientation and approximate position as the proposed grid (RAF/106G/UK/1283 25 MAR 46 Frame 6048).

Historic maps: None consulted.

Lower Slaughter (3/-/C)
Nineteenth-century plan: The possibility of gridding beneath the nineteenth-century village of Lower Slaughter was recognised by JB during his pilot work. Much of the village S and SW of the church has an irregular plan following the curving main road and adjacent watercourse, in this respect resembling nearby Upper Slaughter. However, the N half of the village, W of St Mary's church, has a stronger rectilinear layout, with a NNE–SSW/WNW–ESE axis. There is some conformity with a four-short-perch grid in this area and, more notably, across fields to the N. Not every boundary is orientated with the proposed grid, but there are conforming boundaries on both axes as far as Kirkham, 1.3km N of the village. Similarly aligned boundaries can be seen NW of Upper Slaughter, near Copse Hill. Given the limited conformity within the settlement core and the patchy agreement in

the wider field pattern it could be that this regularity is a product of the enclosure of common-field furlongs, whose morphology was influenced by topography, or that it relates to a broad framework of gridding that influenced that system. However, it is worth noting that the orientation of the proposed grid here is almost identical to that suggested for Bourton-on-the-Water (just to the SE).

Excavations:
- Copsehill Road 1999: a Middle Saxon enclosure excavated W of the church (Kenyon and Watts 2006) might be superimposed on the underlying grid.

LiDAR: The 1-m LiDAR coverage does not add any useful detail.

Aerial photographs: Aerial photographs held in the NMR were consulted but no features of relevance were evident.

Historic maps: None consulted.

Winchcombe (2/-/B)

Nineteenth-century plan: This example was identified by JB in his preliminary work. The evidence for rectilinear planning is restricted to St Mary's Abbey and its immediate environs; most obvious are four parallel SW–NE-orientated boundaries that are seemingly spaced exactly four short perches apart. A length of Abbey Terrace/High Street on the S side of the monastic precinct also has this orientation and conforms to the four-short-perch module. There is, however, little on the transverse axis. The town of Winchcombe itself is typical of small urban settlements, with long, gently curving tenements fronting onto a series of roads. There is nothing within this town plan to indicate gridding beyond the monastic complex.

Excavations: There are numerous excavation reports for Winchcombe available on the ADS but only one is for an excavation in the area of interest (in the vicinity of the abbey).
- Winchcombe Abbey 2014: trench evaluation surrounding the abbey revealed some Roman activity and medieval and undated features. No early medieval archaeology was noted. The linear features were a possible Roman ditch [605] in Trench 6, which is orientated with the adjacent historic boundary but not the proposed grid; a post-medieval ditch [1003] in Trench 10, which is orientated with the proposed grid; and the N edge of feature 803 in Trench 8, which is orientated with the proposed grid but is of unknown age (Barber

and Riley 2014). Nothing revealed in this evaluation either supports or undermines the case for gridding.

LiDAR: Due to extensive twentieth-century development NW of the historic settlement, the 1-m LiDAR coverage does not add any useful detail.

Aerial photographs: Aerial photographs held in the NMR were consulted but no features of relevance were evident.

Historic maps: None consulted.

Hampshire

Faccombe Netherton (-/II/B; Blair 2018, fig. 139; present Figure 5.16)
The excavated late Anglo-Saxon settlement, comprising an aristo-cratic domestic complex (Fairbrother 1990), shows fairly persuasive conformity to a long-perch grid. JB suggested that the parish boundary to the W might also conform to the grid, but did not persuade the other members of the team.

Hatch Warren (-/II/B; present Figure 6.19)
An excavated eleventh-century sub-aristocratic complex. The width and spacing of the two parallel ranges constitute convincing evidence for use of the short-perch module. However, it remains unclear whether the underlying framework comprised strips or a grid. (Fasham and Keevill 1995)

Southampton, **Hamwic** (unclassified; Blair 2013, fig. 13; Blair 2018, fig. 59; present Figure 5.10)
The major area excavation (Six Dials) within the late seventh-century commercial emporium of *Hamwic* revealed a complex of ranges placed end-on towards a metalled street, with clear and recurrent evidence for the short-perch module. However, it remains unclear whether the underlying framework comprised strips or a grid. (Andrews 1997; Blair 2013, 33–6)

Winchester, Old Minster (–/I/A; present Figure 1.2)
The ground-plan of this mid seventh-century church was laid out accurately on a long-perch grid. (Kjølbye-Biddle 1986)

Hertfordshire

Westmill (2/-/B)

Nineteenth-century plan: In the nineteenth century Westmill had a regular plan, with a broad main street and associated boundaries on a NNW–SSE/WSW–ENE axis. Most boundaries and buildings share this orientation. It is questionable whether the four-short-perch module presents the best fit here. Late enclosure predominates in the surrounding historic field pattern, but there is some evidence to suggest that the village may have expanded over former common fields (e.g. reversed-S boundaries evident within the settlement plan W of St Mary's church). The church itself is aligned E–W, and not with the proposed grid. Another factor that may have influenced the layout of Westmill and the surrounding landscape is Ermine Street, whose alignment is almost exactly that of the proposed grid, and which is located 400m E of the settlement core.

Excavations: None identified on ADS.

LiDAR: No 1-m LiDAR is available.

Aerial photographs: A single cropmark of a former boundary is visible on RAF aerial photography to the SW of the village; this shares the orientation and approximate position of the proposed grid (RAF/58/42 19 MAY 48 Frame 5165).

Historic maps: None consulted.

Huntingdonshire

Glatton (3/-/C)

Nineteenth-century plan: The village plan of Glatton had two distinct areas in the nineteenth century. The S part of the village consisted of buildings within long tenements that appear to have been carved out of enclosed common-field strips. In contrast, the (probably) older part of the settlement, around St Nicholas's church and Manor Farm, has a regular, rectilinear layout. Numerous boundaries, roads and buildings orientated SW–NE/NW–SE, as well as earthworks SW of Manor Farm, show some conformity with a four-short-perch grid. In addition, lines of trees E of Glatton Hall may represent former field boundaries that potentially conformed to the grid. Although multiple features share the proposed grid alignment, they are generally not dead straight.

Excavations: None identified on ADS.

LiDAR: No 1-m LiDAR is available.

Aerial photographs: Aerial photographs held in the NMR were consulted but no features of relevance were evident.

Historic maps: None consulted.

Orton Longueville, Botolph Bridge (-/II/B)

An excavated eleventh-century settlement shows encouraging if partial conformity to a four-short-perch grid, though too small an area is available to permit certainty. (Spoerry and Atkins 2015)

Kent

Canterbury, St Augustine's monastery, church of SS Peter and Paul

(-/II/B; Blair 2013, fig. 2; present Figure 5.1A)

The main church of the first Anglo-Saxon monastery, built *c.*600, is known from excavation. It appears to have been laid out accurately on a short-perch grid, though the fragmentary state of the building prevents complete certainty. (Blair 2013, 23–4)

Canterbury, St Augustine's monastery, church of St. Pancras (-/I/ A;

Blair 2013, fig. 2; present Figure 5.1B)

A subsidiary seventh-century church, located immediately E of the last, still stands in part, and the ground-plan has been clarified by excavation. It conforms accurately to a short-perch grid. (Blair 2013, 23–4)

Dover (-/II/B; Blair 2018, fig. 40; present Figure 5.8)

The excavated area of the Anglo-Saxon monastic complex, within the Roman fort, included a large timber hall that was probably originally secular. It was probably laid out on a short-perch grid. (Philp 2003)

East Langdon (3/-/C)

Nineteenth-century plan: Roads through, and boundaries within, East Langdon village have a predominant SW–NE/NW–SE orientation, with elements generally parallel and perpendicular to each other. Langdon Abbey is 1km to the NW, but there is no similarity in orientation with East Langdon. The wider historic landscape contains long, gently sinuous boundaries, and the regularity of the village may reflect its development within this possible co-axial framework.

Excavations: None identified on ADS.

LiDAR: The 1-m LiDAR coverage stops 250m short of the village.

Aerial photographs: Three adjacent cropmarks of former boundaries are visible on RAF aerial photography to the NE of the village, and these share the same orientation and position as the proposed grid (RAF/106G/UK/1443 30 APR 46 Frame 4246).

Historic maps: None consulted.

Lyminge (–/I A; Blair 2018, fig. 34; present Figure 5.7)
A major royal centre that evolved through the fifth to seventh centuries. The seventh-century phase comprised a great hall complex in courtyard formation, laid out on a short-perch grid. (Thomas 2017)

Minster in Thanet (2/-/B; present Figure 5.17)
Nineteenth-century plan: JB suggested that there might be gridding in the nineteenth-century plan of Minster. The proposed grid is orientated with St Mary's church. While there are many parts of the settlement that do not conform, most obviously the tenements E and W of the abbey, parts of the road network and surrounding field pattern do share this axis. The abbey precinct in particular conforms well, as do field drains to the S and the Durlocks Farm complex. Earthworks on Abbey Green also conform to the proposed grid alignment.

Excavations: None identified on ADS.

LiDAR: There is complete 1-m LiDAR coverage, but it shows few earthworks that might relate to the proposed grid. Unfortunately the fields S of the Abbey and E of St Mary's church have been built over. A distinct linear feature crossing three former fields S of 'Foot Bridge and Sheep Pen' on the 1st edition OS 25-inch map is aligned with the grid but might be a recent footpath. An earthwork extending from an extant field boundary SE of Durlock conforms to the proposed grid.

Aerial photographs: Aerial photographs held in the NMR were consulted but no features of relevance were evident.

Historic maps: The historic map consulted provides no additional information (Minster-in-Thanet (Kent), tithe map, 1839: National Archives, IR 30/17/254).

Staplehurst (3/-/C)
Nineteenth-century plan: There is regularity in the plan of Staplehurst which appears to be set out from a straight N–S-orientated road

through the village. While several boundaries (including the back boundary of tenements fronting the E side of the road) and side lanes are parallel and perpendicular to this axis, there are also many that do not conform. A broader view confirms that the road is Roman, so the plan's regularity could stem directly from its long-term influence on the landscape and not from early medieval gridding.

Excavations: None identified on ADS.

LiDAR: There is 1-m LiDAR coverage for the surrounding countryside, but not for the historic village.

Aerial photographs: Aerial photographs held in the NMR were consulted but no features of relevance were evident.

Historic maps: None consulted.

Leicestershire

Dadlington (1/-/A; present Figure 6.16)
Nineteenth-century plan: The proposed grid is orientated NNW–SSE/WSW–ENE; the greatest correspondence is seen in the SE part of the village, in the vicinity of the manor house and possible village green, where a large gravel pit existed in the nineteenth century. In this area there are some exact right angles where roads, fields and the open ground meet, and field boundaries occur parallel to each other. There are instances of boundary spacings at four-short-perch intervals. Some conformity can also be observed along the W side of the village, though here the long field boundaries are not dead straight and are perhaps more obviously derived from the enclosure of common-field strips. The regularity in the S of the village is notable.

Excavations: None identified on ADS.

LiDAR: No 1-m LiDAR is available.

Aerial photographs: Aerial photographs held in the NMR were consulted but no features of relevance were evident.

Historic maps: The earliest identified is the 1844 tithe map; this provides a few additional boundaries not shown on the 1st edition OS 25-inch map, none of which correspond to the proposed grid (Dadlington, tithe map, 1844: Record Office for Leicestershire, Leicester and Rutland, Ti/88/1).

Desford (1/-/A; present Figure 6.15)

Nineteenth-century plan: The orientation of the proposed grid, as shown on the OS map, conforms to that of the High Street. Numerous roads, tenement boundaries and field boundaries run parallel and at right angles to this, and the great majority conform. There are several places where the four-short-perch multiple finds an exact match, though other elements fall at non-conforming intervals. The parish church of St Martin does not conform, being closer to true E–W than the NW–SE/SW–NE-orientated framework of the historic settlement. It seems likely that the village has expanded N and W along more sinuous routeways, making the settlement look less regular in those areas.

Excavations:
- Land off Leicester Lane 2000: area excavation to the SE of High Street, in the area of proposed gridding (Thomas 2000) revealed a Late Iron Age or Roman ditched enclosure, not orientated with the proposed grid. The earlier geophysical survey and evaluation adds nothing (Butler 1999; Thomas 1999).
- Hunts Lane Geophysics 2010: a large area of magnetic survey 700m W of historic village core revealed few anomalies (Butler 2010).

LiDAR: No 1-m LiDAR is available.

Aerial photographs: Aerial photographs held in the NMR were consulted but no features of relevance were evident.

Historic maps: The early nineteenth-century OS surveyor's drawing (2 inches to 1 mile) shows that Desford was very regular in plan. The other historic maps viewed provide no additional information (Desford, survey of the manor of Thomas Muxloe, 1644: Record Office for Leicestershire, Leicester and Rutland, PP/92; Desford, inclosure, c.1760: Record Office for Leicestershire, Leicester and Rutland, MA/EN/A/89/1; Desford, Barons Park Estate, 1813: Record Office for Leicestershire, Leicester and Rutland, 3D42/M11/1; Desford, tithe map, 1847: Record Office for Leicestershire, Leicester and Rutland, Ti/89/1).

Snarestone (–/–/B)

The earthworks of the deserted medieval village are rectilinear in layout and show plausible conformity to a short-perch grid. There are no evident indications of gridding on the nineteenth-century OS map. (Hartley 1984, fig. 40)

Lincolnshire

Brant Broughton (1/-/A; Blair 2013, fig. 29; present Figure 6.12)
Nineteenth-century plan: JB had already identified potential gridding in the nineteenth-century plan of Brant Broughton. The proposed grid is orientated NNE–SSW/WNW–ESE. A section of High Street conforms to this alignment and is four short perches wide. Many lanes and field boundaries conform to the grid, whether generally or directly. The curving High Street is in contrast to the strongly rectilinear layout, and has probably been imposed upon it. While it would be hard to argue against the strong rectilinearity of the village and surrounding fields, it is just possible that a later episode of planning is the cause: Brant Broughton had a market, and the regular layout might conceivably result from an ultimately unsuccessful attempt at urban planning. It is, however, hard to see why such an exercise would have extended so far into the surrounding fields.

Excavations:
- Guildford Lane 1995: a negative watching brief of foundation trenches for a new building (Archaeological Project Services 1995).
- Church Lane 1997: two undated pits and two undated ditches recorded in the foundation trenches for a new building (Cope-Faulkner 1997). Orientation of ditches not ascertained.

LiDAR: There is extensive coverage of 1-m LiDAR for the village and surrounding landscape. The historic field pattern derives from the enclosure of common fields, with large areas characteristic of parliamentary enclosure. LiDAR surface model shows some areas of ridge and furrow that survive, but also numerous long furlong boundaries that would allow for a fairly accurate reconstruction of the pre-enclosure fieldscape. Ridge and furrow in the N and W of Brant Broughton has the same orientation as the proposed grid. Importantly, there are two areas of Brant Broughton – in the N and S – that have not been built over in the twentieth century, and there the LiDAR shows various earthworks in conformity with the proposed grid. These earthworks appear to be settlement-related rather than ridge and furrow. The southern area is W of St Helen's church and may therefore relate to deserted settlement. That in the N is near the Manor House, and although potentially settlement-related could also be linked to historic landscaping.

Aerial photographs: A cropmark of a former boundary, which turns 90 degrees, is visible on RAF aerial photography to the E of the village:

this shares the orientation and position of the proposed grid (RAF/3G/ TUD/UK/117 03 APR 46 Frame 6294).

Historic maps: The 1838 tithe map adds little to the 1st edition 25-inch map but it does show that the two areas with earthworks on the LiDAR were undeveloped in 1838. One of the earthworks W of the church is a field boundary lost between 1838 and the time of the 1st edition OS 25-inch map (Brant Broughton, tithe award, 1838: Lincolnshire Archives, I205).

Candlesby (2/-/B)

Nineteenth-century plan: There is a distinct rectilinear layout to the core of the village, particularly the road pattern. St Benedict's church is on the orientation of the proposed grid, which is also E–W, so perhaps a coincidence. Candlesby Hall and surrounding field elements conform to the rectilinear pattern, with some indications of the four-short-perch grid.

Excavations: None identified on ADS.

LiDAR: No 1-m LiDAR is available.

Aerial photographs: Aerial photographs held in the NMR were consulted but no features of relevance were evident.

Historic maps: The only relevant map in the Lincolnshire Archives is the 1781 inclosure map. Although possibly stylised, the cartographer conveys the distinct rectilinearity of the roads in the historic village core (Candlesby, inclosure map, 1781: Lincolnshire Archives, CANDLESBY PAR/17/1).

Coleby (3/-/C)

Nineteenth-century plan: JB had noted the potential gridding within the late nineteenth-century village plan and DMV, and had also suggested that excavated ditches might conform to the proposed grid. The further analysis for this project suggested that there are two grid alignments at Coleby, one to the W that focuses on the historic core and includes All Saints church, and one to the E around the vicarage. It seems likely that the latter is a result of parliamentary enclosure, and that no ancient boundaries conform to this eastern grid. The putative western grid – underlying the historic core of Coleby – embodies certain straight and parallel elements, including Church Lane and part of Blind Lane, but some of the conforming field boundaries looks suspiciously late in origin. There are fewer boundaries conforming to the four-short-perch module than in our Category 2 examples.

Excavations: There are no excavations in the village core (the western gridded area). There is a single excavation to the E.

- Rectory Road 1996: two undated ditches, at right angles to each other, might be part of the village topography (Cope-Faulkner 1996); their orientation fits with the eastern grid.

LiDAR: No 1-m LiDAR is available.

Aerial photographs: Aerial photographs held in the NMR were consulted but no features of relevance were evident.

Historic maps: Two maps were identified in the Lincolnshire Archives, one an estate map of 1843 and the other a later reconstruction of the 1760 enclosure award. Neither adds anything to the argument for or against gridding (Coleby, estate map, 1843: Lincolnshire Archives, 2CC 59/12687; Coleby, enclosure award, 1760, reconstructed plan: Lincolnshire Archives, KESTEVEN AWARD 95/4).

Goltho (–/II/ B; Blair 2018, figs 136, 139)

At least three groups of buildings in successive phases of the excavated late Anglo-Saxon aristocratic complex show convincing conformity with short-perch grids, though it is hard from the available evidence to get a clear sense of the overall layout. (Beresford 1987; Blair 2018, 363–9)

Great Hale (2/-/B; present Figure 3.5)

Nineteenth-century plan: A village of rectilinear appearance, dominated by a network of streets in roughly box-like formation. The streets themselves are mostly quite sinuous, but several property boundaries show encouraging conformity with the four-short-perch grid. It is possible that the neighbouring village of Little Hale also reflects some grid-planning.

Excavation:

- Hall Road 2001: multi-period evidence from twelve evaluation trenches, including a prehistoric pit, a 'Saxon' gully and pit and multiple medieval ditches, gullies and pits of twelfth- to fourteenth-century date. The latter is interpreted as expansion and contraction of the village (Rayner 2001). Medieval ditches, as well as undated ditches recorded only on geophysical survey, are seemingly orientated with the proposed grid. Too little of the 'Saxon' gully is recorded to allow a similar observation.

LiDAR: No 1-m LiDAR is available.

Aerial photographs: Aerial photographs held in the NMR were consulted but no features of relevance were evident.

Historic maps: The historic map consulted provides no additional information (Great Hale, tithe map, 1843: Lincolnshire Archives, K689).

Hibaldstow (3/-/C)
Nineteenth-century plan: There is tenuous evidence for gridding in the nineteenth-century plan. The main relevant features are a series of broadly parallel and perpendicular roads to the N of St Higbald's church, but even these are not very straight. There are, across a wider area, some additional lengths of road and field boundaries that conform to the proposed grid, but the overall appearance seems to denote a landscape whose framework derives from the enclosure of open-field furlongs. If there is gridding at Hibaldstow, its vestiges would appear to extend beyond the village core.

Excavations:
- Land at Hopfield 2000: an evaluation 350m south of the parish church revealed considerable evidence for a Late Bronze Age field system, but little else (Allen 2000).

LiDAR: Available 1-m LiDAR covers only the E half of Hibaldstow and the surrounding fields. There has been considerable infill development and settlement expansion, and there are no earthworks of interest showing in any remaining open areas within the historic core. Vestiges of the pre-enclosure field system can be seen as earthworks.

Aerial photographs: Aerial photographs held in the NMR were consulted but no features of relevance were evident.

Historic maps: The 1803 inclosure map shows much the same detail as the 1st edition OS 25-inch map, and contributes little further to the argument for or against gridding. An estate plan of 1861 does not cover the historic village of Hibaldstow (Hibaldstow, inclosure map, 1803(1): Lincolnshire Archives, LINDSEY AWARD 38; Hibaldstow, inclosure map, 1803(2): Lincolnshire Archives, HIBALDSTOW PAR 17; Hibaldstow, estate plan, 1861: Lincolnshire Archives, STUBBS 3/63).

Holton (2/-/C)
Nineteenth-century plan: The framework of roads within and surrounding the historic core have a distinctly rectilinear pattern, which is also reflected in the orientation of various adjacent field boundaries derived from the enclosure of open-field strips. All Saints church is not orientated with the proposed grid (NW–SE/SW–NE), but is on an E–W alignment.

Excavations: None identified on ADS.

LiDAR: No 1-m LiDAR is available.

Aerial photographs: Earthworks relating to the former pattern of enclosed common field strips and associated ridge and furrow are visible on RAF aerial photography, and it is clear from these that some of the regularity within the village is based on the open-field layout. In this case the aerial photography provides negative evidence (RAF/CPE/UK2012 16 APR 47 Frame 3160; RAF/CPE/UK/1880 06 DEC 46 Frame 4252).

Historic maps: None consulted.

Quarrington (–/II/B; Blair 2013, fig.11; Blair 2018, fig. 47.)
The seventh-century phase of an excavated settlement shows persuasive conformity to a short-perch grid, even though the boundary ditches are physically less regular than those on the comparable site at West Fen Road, Ely. (Taylor *et al.* 2003; Blair 2013, 33–4)

Stow (3/-/C; present Figure 3.6)
Nineteenth-century plan: While there is a general impression of regularity in the settlement core, few elements correspond closely to a grid, and this regularity may reflect the expansion of the settlement over former common-field strips. St Mary's church is aligned E–W, whereas the proposed grid has a WSW–ENE axis.

Excavations:
- Old School House 2003: two twelfth-century pits were recorded during groundworks (Brett 2003).
- Church End Farm 2004: a watching brief during groundworks identified no archaeological remains. It was suggested that the site had suffered truncation (Garrett 2004).

LiDAR: The 1-m LiDAR coverage does not add any useful detail.

Aerial photographs: A number of cropmarks of former boundaries, consistent with the format of the historic landscape, are visible on RAF aerial photography on the S side of the village; these share the same orientation and position as the proposed grid (RAF/CPE/UK/2012 16 APR 47 Frame 3128; RAF/541/185 19 OCT 48 Frame 4221).

Historic maps: The 1838 tithe map shows little difference from the 1st edition OS 25-inch map (Stow (Lincs) tithe map, 1838: National Archives, IR 30/20/315).

Welton (2/II/B; present Figure 6.14)

Nineteenth-century plan: There is some conformity to a four-short-perch grid in the E part of this village and DMV, including roads and field boundaries, as well as St Mary's church. The W part of the village plan also shows a degree of regularity, and some excavated ditches that might conform, but alternatively might result from the enclosure of open-field strips.

Excavations:

- 17–21 Lincoln Road 2007: two evaluation trenches revealed Roman features, consisting of a wall in Trench 1 and two ditches in Trench 2. Neither ditch conforms to the proposed grid alignment (Parker 2007).
- 17–21 Lincoln Road 2010: two evaluation trenches in the same area as the 2007 work. Trench 1 revealed Roman material and a possible trackway. Trench 2 revealed no archaeology. There is no relationship between the orientation of the trackway and the proposed grid (Allen Archaeology 2010).
- Cliffe Road 2008: a watching brief during development revealed Saxo-Norman pottery and two thirteenth- to fourteenth-century ditches. The ADS grey literature report does not have a full trench plan; there would appear to be a difference in orientation between the ditches and the proposed grid, though one is described as orientated NW–SE (Pre-Construct Archaeology 2008a).
- Healthlinc House, Cliffe Road 2002: a watching brief of building footings revealed no archaeological features, although a subsoil yielded thirteenth- to fourteenth-century pottery (Cope-Faulkner 2002).
- Healthlinc House, Cliffe Road 2003: a single trench excavated ahead of a new building revealed some Middle Saxon pottery, a pit and gully of late ninth to eleventh-century date, and a medieval/

post-medieval wall. The Late Saxon gully was aligned exactly with the proposed western grid (Albone 2003).

- Healthlinc House, Cliffe Road 2003: monitoring of foundation trenches revealed no archaeological features or deposits (Cope-Faulkner 2003).
- Healthlinc House, Cliffe Road 2007: a single tenth- to twelfth-century ditch was revealed in Area 2, running N–S and orientated with the proposed grid. Other later medieval features were found, including two pits (fourteenth to sixteenth century) and a NW–SW-orientated ditch (late eleventh to twelfth century). The latter is on a different orientation from the proposed grid (Failes 2007).
- Healthlinc House, Cliffe Road 2008: excavation revealed Roman, Late Saxon, medieval and post-medieval archaeology, the majority being of Late Saxon date. Features of this date include ditches, gullies and pits, and it is suggested that this area is close to the contemporary settlement (Cope-Faulkner 2008). There is a good agreement between the orientation of Late Saxon/medieval features and the proposed grid.
- Healthlinc House, Cliffe Road 2011: monitoring and recording during groundworks to extend the property identified no archaeological features or deposits (Garlant 2011).
- Norbeck Lane 1998: evaluation revealed part of a tenth- to eleventh-century post-built building and a thirteenth- to fourteenth-century walled building, as well as various ditches and gullies. Trench 1 exposed Ditch 103 (undated), Gully 105 (tenth century), Gully 113, Ditch 114 and Gully 115 (all undated but pre-eleventh century), and Ditch 109 (post-eleventh century). All linear features except 109 have the same orientation as the proposed eastern grid (Albone 1998).
- Old Vicarage, Norbeck Lane 2008: a watching brief revealed no significant archaeological deposits or features (Pre-Construct Archaeology 2008b).
- Old Vicarage, Norbeck Lane 2009: a watching brief revealed no significant archaeological deposits or features (Hamilton 2009).
- Prebend Lane 2002: trial-trenching revealed no significant archaeological deposits or features (Thomson 2002).
- Sudbeck Lane 1994: trial-trenching of agricultural land S of Sudbeck Lane, outside the village core, revealed no archaeological features, though furrows orientated with the field were noted (Field 1994).
- The Manor, Vicarage Lane 2005: a watching brief revealed only modern features (Brett 2005).

LiDAR: Welton village has seen considerable expansion during the twentieth century, so that the 1-m LiDAR is of little value. There is, however, an undeveloped playing field E of St Mary's church where a linear earthwork conforms to the orientation of the proposed grid.

Aerial photographs: Aerial photographs held in the NMR were consulted but no features of relevance were evident.

Historic maps: The only map identified in the Lincolnshire Archives was the 1773 inclosure map, and copies and tracings of it. This map adds little to the argument for or against gridding, since most boundaries shown on the 1st edition OS 25-inch map were already present in 1773. The exception is a series of buildings and boundaries E of the church that broadly conform to the proposed grid, so the fact that they came into existence after 1773 weakens this case. (Welton, inclosure map, 1773(1): Lincolnshire Archives, LINDSEY AWARD 95; Welton, inclosure map, 1773(2): Lincolnshire Archives, TSJ 12/7; Welton, inclosure map, 1773 (tracing): Lincolnshire Archives, MISC DON 232/2/11.)

London and Middlesex

Lundenwic (not classified; present Figure 5.11)
No grid-planning has been identified in the seventh- to ninth-century emporium, but some of the buildings appear to be based on the long-perch module.

Shepperton (–/II/B; present Figure 6.18)
A small group of excavated ditches appears to conform to the short-perch module, though it is unclear whether the underlying framework comprised strips or a grid. The broader topographical context, as shown on nineteenth-century maps, conforms to the same orientation and might suggest that a larger area was grid-planned. (Poulton 2005)

Westminster Abbey (–/I/A; present Figures 5.18, B.8–B.9)
The church and cloister built by Edward the Confessor are based accurately (apart from a slight deflection of the W and E sides of the cloister) on a long-perch grid. In Appendix B Eric Fernie discusses the potential relationship between gridded and proportional planning.

Norfolk

Attlebridge (–/III/C; Blair 2013, fig. 22)
An excavated tenth-to eleventh-century domestic complex comprising three ranges enclosing a Romano-British monument could be based on a short-perch grid, but the evidence is too limited for a high level of confidence. (Hall *et al.* 1996; Blair 2013, 40–1, 45)

Bergh/Burgh Apton (3/-/C)
Nineteenth-century plan: There is regularity across the field pattern immediately surrounding the village that is not found farther out from the settlement core, although it seems possible that this derives from the enclosure of common-field strips. The settlement at Bergh Apton shows some conformity with the same alignments. There is some potential for the open fields to have been laid out across a pre-existing gridded framework.

Excavations:
* The Stables, Church Road 2013: a single trench was excavated 680m S of the site of Bergh Apton church within farmland. No features of archaeological interest were revealed (Emery 2013).

LiDAR: No 1-m LiDAR is available.

Aerial photographs: Two linear earthworks, set at right angles to each other, are visible to the S of the rectory on RAF aerial photography; both conform to the proposed grid orientation (RAF/CPE/UK/1801 25 OCT 46 Frame 3063).

Historic maps: The 1839 tithe map shows the same layout as the 1st edition OS 25-inch map. The earlier maps also show no difference (Bergh Apton (Norfolk) tithe map, 1839: National Archives, IR 30/23/59; Bergh Apton, 1801: Norfolk Record Office, C/Ca/1/8; Bergh Apton, pre-1806: Norfolk Record Office, NRS 4044).

Field Dalling (3/-/C)
Nineteenth-century plan: Field Dalling is strung along a relatively straight NNW–SSE road, and several boundaries are exactly perpendicular to this. There are few parallel elements, but the road W of St Andrew's church turns 90 degrees to run along the proposed grid. The church is also orientated with the proposed grid rather than E–W. Multiple field boundaries conform to a spacing of four-short-perch units.

Excavations:

- Holt Road 2011: five trenches excavated in advance of housing on the S side of Holt Road, NE of the vicarage, in the area of possible gridding (Crawley 2011). Each trench contained archaeology, which mainly consisted of medieval pits and ditches consistent with former tenements, indicating settlement shrinkage here. The date of most pottery was twelfth to fourteenth century. Individual sherds of Thetford Ware (tenth to eleventh century) were recovered from pit [14] and ditch/ plough-scar [44], but each context also contained later pottery. The orientation of [44] echoes that of the proposed grid, as does that of ditch [10]. Other medieval ditches also broadly conform, but some do not. Parallel ditches running E–W in Trenches 2, 5 and 4 appear to be aligned with extant field boundaries shown in the late nineteenth century.

LiDAR: No 1-m LiDAR is available.

Aerial photographs: A linear cropmark or earthwork visible on the E side of the village and a nearby field boundary both conform to the proposed grid (RAF/106G/UK/1606 27 JUN 46 Frame 2188).

Historic maps: The 1840 tithe map is little different from the 1st edition OS 25-inch map except that the vicarage had not been built and there is an additional field boundary running NNW–SSE about 250m W of St Andrew's church. This boundary appears to conform to the proposed grid. The 1812 map presents no additional information (Field Dalling, tithe map, 1840: National Archives, IR 30/23/207; Field Dalling, 1812: Norfolk Record Office, C/Sca2/71).

Hingham (3/-/C)

Nineteenth-century plan: Potential gridding had been identified by JB. The alignment of the N churchyard boundary (WSW–ENE) is in conformity with other boundaries and roads across the breadth of the settlement, even though several others do not conform. Most conformity can be found N of the church between Chapel Street and The Fairland. The church itself is on an exact W–E alignment. The potential is perhaps a little higher than at other Category 3 sites.

Excavations: None identified on ADS.

LiDAR: No 1-m LiDAR is available.

Aerial photographs: Aerial photographs held in the NMR were consulted but no features of relevance were evident.

Historic maps: The historic maps consulted provide no additional information (Hingham, 1727: Norfolk Record Office, C/Ca 2/2; Hingham, c.1776: Norfolk Record Office, C/Ca 2/4).

Great Ryburgh (not classified)
A recent excavation (plan kindly provided by Tim Pestell) has revealed a seventh-century cemetery with associated buildings. The complex appears to have been laid out on a grid of short perches. No further details were available at the time of going to press.

Sedgeford (3/II/C)
Nineteenth-century plan: The potential for gridding in the nineteenth-century plan of Sedgeford was noted as part of an exercise to place the excavation (below) in its wider context. The proposed grid conforms to the orientation of St Mary's church (E–W) and there are various sections of road and field boundaries that run parallel and perpendicular to this axis. Some key alignments continue across the Heacham River.

Excavations: A small excavated area of a rectilinear eighth- to ninth-century settlement (SHARP 2014, 95–115) shows an encouraging degree of conformity to a short-perch grid, though too little of the site is currently available to make a conclusive case.

LiDAR: No 1-m LiDAR is available.

Aerial photographs: Earthworks forming a rectilinear pattern of land division are visible S of the village on RAF aerial photography, and these coincide with the orientation and expected position of the proposed grid (RAF/106G/UK/1571 07 JUN 46 Frame 4313).

Historic maps: The 1631 Le Strange map shows tenement plots and boundaries N of the church that appear to share the axis of the proposed grid, although as this is a stylised map there can be no certainty. These are again shown in the 1736 map-book. The late maps show a much-altered landscape, and many of the boundaries shown on the 1631 and 1736 maps have been removed during the process of enclosure (Sedgeford, 1631: Norfolk Record Office, Le Strange OC 1; Sedgeford, map book, c.1736: Norfolk Record Office, CHC 11002; Sedgeford, c.1795: Norfolk Record Office, C/Sca 2/249; Sedgeford, c.1797: Norfolk Record Office, C/Ca 3/2).

Shipdham (2/I/A; present Figure 3.9)

Nineteenth-century plan: The potential for gridding at Shipdham was identified by JB, who inferred a SW–NE grid orientated on All Saints' Church, High Street and Mill Street. Numerous straight field boundaries also follow this axis, despite much of the settlement itself being differently aligned. It is worth noting that there is a different orientation evident on the 1st edition OS 25-inch map that is also regular and, while not conforming to the grid proposed by JB, might actually be more interesting as it appears to be represented in the archaeological record over a large area. Possibly there are superimposed grids.

Excavations:

- Church Close 2006–09: several hectares of excavation ahead of proposed residential development revealed settlement evidence and field boundaries from the Early Saxon to the post-medieval periods (Ames and Phelps 2008; Ames *et al.* 2009). Not only do some of the historic boundaries shown on the 1st edition OS appear to have Anglo-Saxon origins, but there is very strong conformity between the excavated remains and the two potential grids. The conforming excavated features seem to cover a wide date-span, from 'Middle Saxon' to the twelfth century, and suggest the possibility that this was an unusually stable grid.
- New Road 2011: watching brief of building foundation trenches identified an undated quarry pit (Murray 2011).

LiDAR: No 1-m LiDAR is available.

Aerial photographs: Earthworks forming a rectilinear pattern are visible SW of the village on RAF aerial photography and these coincide with the orientation and expected position of the proposed grid. So do a second series of linear earthworks visible on the N side of the village over a distance of *c.*400m (RAF/3G/TUD/UK/52 31 JAN 46 Frame 5143).

Historic maps: An early seventeenth-century map is too faint to read clearly. A map of 1807 shows many of the boundaries depicted on 1st edition OS 25-inch maps, though the dead straight boundaries that conform to the proposed grid on the north side of the village around Shrub House are not present on the 1807 map (Shipdham, early seventeenth century: Norfolk Record Office, Hayes and Storr map No 96; Shipdham, c.1807: Norfolk Record Office, BR 276/1/1145).

Thetford, Brandon Road (–/I/A; Blair 2013, fig. 23)

An excavated area of late tenth- to early eleventh-century settlement on the W fringe of the Anglo-Saxon town shows strong evidence of being based on a short-perch grid. The features are sparse and scattered, but the layout of buildings, boundaries and even rubbish pits conforms closely to the grid, suggesting that the site was articulated by light fences that left no archaeological traces. This could be the site of some non-industrial suburban activity such as market gardening. (Dallas 1993; Blair 2013, 42–3, 46)

Watlington (1/–/A; present Figure 3.8)

Nineteenth-century plan: There is regularity across a broad area of roads and fields, but not necessarily in the settlement core itself. We find here a potential grid orientated N–S/E–W that might cover <1km in each axis. Both extant and fossilised landscape components conform to the proposed grid. In various places, boundaries are accurately spaced at multiples of the four-short-perch module.

Excavations:
- 60 Acre Field (2004 and 2008): 1km E of the village and outside of the area of suspected gridding. Evaluation trenching of a cropmark complex suggested the presence of an Iron Age field system (Bown 2004) the orientation of which was different from the suggested grid. This was further confirmed during the excavation of a service trench along the southern side of the field (Ratcliff 2008).

LiDAR: There is complete coverage of 1-m LiDAR for the village and surrounding fields. There has been extensive development in the W part of the village during the twentieth century, so LiDAR in this area has limited value. Much of the E part, however, remains open, particularly to the S and E of St Peter and St Paul's church and around Watlington Hall. In these areas there are apparent earthworks conforming to the proposed grid. During a field visit in December 2013 JB identified various linear earthworks (including broad and apparently ancient hedge-banks) that fit with LiDAR anomalies and others visible on Google Earth.

Aerial photographs: A number of linear cropmarks and earthworks conforming to the proposed grid are visible on RAF aerial photography, both to the SE of the rectory and in the grounds of Watlington Hall (RAF/106G/UK/1427 16 APR 46 Frame 4438; RAF/106G/UK/1606 27 JUN 46 Frame 2334).

Historic maps: The 1839 tithe map shows no additional detail except a single grid-conforming field boundary to the E of 'Windmill' (Watlington tithe map, 1839: National Archives, IR 30/23/613).

Whissonsett (2/I/A; Blair 2018, fig. 109; present Figure 3.11)
Nineteenth-century plan: JB identified the potential for gridding in the nineteenth-century plan and linked that with excavated Middle and Late Saxon archaeology. While there are various elements of the settlement that conform, the best fit is found within the pattern of fields and roads rather than tenements. There is a broad zone surrounding the church where there is now no settlement, but boundaries broadly conform to a rectilinear layout. The church is at the centre of JB's proposed grid, and is orientated with it (E–W).

Excavations:
- Church Close 2004: evaluation trenches revealed Middle to Late Saxon boundary ditches, postholes and gullies, and at least one burial. The area seems to have served as a cemetery in the Middle Saxon period. Occupation declined rapidly post-Late Saxon period (Mellor 2004). Features conform to the proposed grid.
- North View Drive 2010: evaluation revealed Middle Saxon boundary ditches and possible Late Saxon building remains including postholes, a beam-slot and a possible SFB (Trimble and Hoggett 2010). Features conform to the position and orientation of the proposed grid.

LiDAR: No 1-m LiDAR is available.

Aerial photographs: A single linear cropmark N of the village, visible on RAF aerial photography, coincides with the position and orientation of the proposed grid (RAF/3G/TUD/UK/50 31 JAN 46 Frame 6254).

Historic maps: The 1838 tithe map shows additional field divisions NE of the church which might conform to the proposed grid. There are no other marked differences from the 1st edition OS 25-inch map. A plan of 1724 is limited to five fields away from the village and makes no contribution. An 1812 inclosure map shows the same configuration as the 1828 tithe map (Whissonsett (Norfolk) tithe map, 1838: National Archives, IR 30/23/629; Whissonsett, c.1724: Norfolk Record Office, HIL 3/34/27/4; Whissonsett, inclosure map, c.1812: Norfolk Record Office, C/Sca 2/325).

Northamptonshire

Brixworth church (–/I/A; Blair 2013, fig. 2; Blair 2018, fig. 86; present Figure 5.13)
The great Carolingian-style church of *c.*800 stands substantially intact; the plan can be completed from footings excavated on the north side. It is based very clearly and accurately (apart from a deflection at the W end) on a short-perch grid. There is no evidence for gridding in the nineteenth-century plan of the village and fields, though the church occupies the centre of a broadly rectilinear configuration of boundaries. (Parsons and Sutherland 2013; Blair 2013, 24, 26)

Hackleton (2/–/B)
Nineteenth-century plan: JB had noted the regularity of the village plan at Hackleton, proposing a grid of short perches orientated WNW–ESE. The field boundaries are in closest conformity; although the principal road does follow this axis, its course is rather sinuous. The 1st edition OS 25-inch map shows several lines of trees where field boundaries once existed, some of which fit the general orientation, and in some cases the precise position, of the proposed grid.

Excavations: None identified on ADS.

LiDAR: 1-m LiDAR provides some useful additional detail, particularly on the S side of the village where there has been less development (presumably because of the proximity to the river). Not only is there good survival of ridge and furrow, much of which conforms to the orientation of the grid, but there are a number of distinct linear earthworks that might mark relict boundaries, and these too are on the proposed grid orientation. Less convincingly, a number of long furlong boundaries to the E and N of the village might also reflect this axis.

Aerial photographs: A series of earthworks are visible to the N and S of the village core, as well as NE of the village; these are in broad conformity with the proposed grid orientation, and appear to be shrunken settlement rather than simple field boundaries (RAF/CPE/UK/1926 16 JAN 47 Frame 5815).

Historic maps: None consulted.

Little Brington (2/–/B; Blair 2018, fig. 152)
Nineteenth-century plan: In the nineteenth century Little Brington has the appearance of a linear village, focused on a single WSW–ENE-orientated road with tenements perpendicular to it. When a grid is

superimposed it can be seen that there is a broader pattern of regularity, with a rectilinear framework extending out from the linear settlement core to include the enclosed former open fields. In total the area of gridding might cover 500m by 500m.

Excavations: None identified on ADS.

LiDAR: The 1-m LiDAR does not cover the village core. It does show, however, that the orientation of ridge and furrow S of the village is consistent with the axis of the proposed grid.

Aerial photographs: A series of earthworks are visible to the N and SW of the village core, and add additional detail to the regularity seen on the nineteenth-century plan (RAF/CPE/UK/1994 13 APR 47 Frame 2259; RAF/541/341 15 AUG 49 Frame 3174).

Historic maps: A map of 1743 shows good conformity of the settlement, and of furlong boundaries and ridge-and-furrow around it, to a four-short-perch grid (Little Brington, 1743: British Library, Add 78133 F 1; Little Brington, tithe map, 1840: National Archives, IR 30/24/21).

Little Houghton (3/-/C)
Nineteenth-century plan: Various features across the core of the village might conform to a grid, but not enough to make a compelling case. These include St Mary's church, earthworks to the W, much of the road network and some field boundaries. There is no visible correspondence to the short perch (or four-short-perch multiple).

Excavations:
- Bedford Road 2008: two evaluation trenches on land W of St Mary's church. Iron Age and Roman ditches near a moated site (Morris and Walford 2008). The ditches are on a slightly different orientation from the putative grid.

LiDAR: There is 1-m LiDAR data for the central and N parts of the village. Although there has been relatively little twentieth-century development, the open areas in the village show little evidence to support the proposed grid. East of the church, the pattern of ridge and furrow does accord with the proposed grid orientation.

Aerial photographs: Aerial photographs held in the NMR were consulted but no features of relevance were evident.

Historic maps: None consulted.

Nassington (not classified; Blair 2013, fig. 25)
JB suggested that an excavated late Anglo-Saxon building and the standing parish church conformed to two short-perch grids also apparent in boundaries shown on nineteenth-century maps. The other members of the team were not persuaded. (Blair 2013, 49)

Peakirk (3/-/C)
Nineteenth-century plan: The proposed grid is orientated WSW–ENE. St Pega's church is on the same alignment, rather than true E–W. The road network conforms best, though short lengths of property boundary in the immediate vicinity of the church also show some conformity. There is less conformity in the S of the village, where fields are clearly not aligned with the grid. The Car Dyke conforms to the alignment of the potentially grid-based features: if there is a grid, this major linear feature might have been used as the baseline.

Excavations: None identified on ADS.

LiDAR: The 1-m LiDAR coverage does not add any useful detail.

Aerial photographs: Aerial photographs held in the NMR were consulted but no features of relevance were evident.

Historic maps: None consulted.

Peterborough (2/II/A; present Figure 5.15)
The area of the minster precinct as represented on nineteenth-century maps is markedly rectilinear, and shows potential conformity to a short-perch grid. Rectilinearity in the neighbourhood of a Romanesque church and cloister is of course to be expected, but the pattern extends considerably further to the W, E and S. Furthermore, the excavated remains of the late Anglo-Saxon church conform closely to the same grid, which in combination with the map evidence creates a strong case (Irvine 1894 for the excavated remains).

Polebrook (-/II/B; Blair 2013, fig. 7; present Figure 6.2)
A probably high-status seventh-century settlement known from geophysics and cropmarks, backed up by limited excavation, shows a plausible degree of conformity to a short-perch grid; definition of the features is not precise enough to allow complete confidence. There is no evidence for gridding on the nineteenth-century plan. The 1-m LiDAR coverage does not add any useful detail. (Upex 2003; Blair 2013, 27–30)

Preston Deanery DMV (-/-/B; present Figure 3.12)
Nineteenth-century plan: In the nineteenth century Preston Deanery simply had a church and manor house, with no extant village. Apart from the earthworks, there is nothing in the historic landscape to suggest grid-planning.

Excavations: None identified on ADS.

Earthworks: The earthworks of the deserted medieval village have a degree of regularity. The potential for gridding is clear, though establishing which units might have been used is more problematic. There does appear to be conformity with the four-short-perch multiple and the two principal roads are about four short perches in width. The orientation of the earthwork complex and the proposed grid matches that of the parish church, which is a few degrees off E–W.

LiDAR: The 1-m LiDAR coverage shows the same earthworks as the RCHME plan. It also shows earthworks of the associated open field system (wiped away by parliamentary enclosure), parts of which appear to conform to the same orientation as the settlement and may be associated with its grid.

Historic maps: None consulted.

Raunds, Furnells and Langham Road (–/I/A; Blair 2013, figs. 1, 14, 15; Blair 2018, fig. 137; present Figure 6.11)
A large and important excavation of a complex tenth- to eleventh-century settlement, the core of which had emerged by the Conquest as a manor house and church group. There is convincing conformity with a four-short-perch grid (or perhaps successive grids), within which the settlement evolved over several decades. There is, however, no evidence for gridding on the nineteenth-century map. (Audouy and Chapman 2009; Blair 2013, 37–8; Blair 2018, 364–7)

Raunds West Cotton (–/I/A; Blair 2013, figs. 1, 15, 16)
The excavated Late Anglo-Saxon settlement shows convincing conformity with the short-perch module. However, it remains unclear whether the underlying framework comprised strips or a grid. There is no evidence for gridding on the nineteenth-century map. (Chapman 2010; Blair 2013, 38–40)

Sulgrave (2/-/B; Blair 2018, fig. 116)

Nineteenth-century plan: Our grading of Sulgrave was the outcome of a lengthy debate. There is a general appearance of rectilinearity across the site, which is formed by a framework of parallel roads with tenements perpendicular to them. While the roads are not perfectly straight they do fit within the proposed grid. There are also various internal settlement features that conform, as do many of the extant field boundaries surrounding the village core; spaces between conforming boundaries are often compatible with the four-short-perch module.

Excavations: The early eleventh-century fortified enclosure (Davison 1977) does not conform to the proposed grid, and may have been superimposed on it. Nothing else identified on ADS.

LiDAR: Unfortunately the 1-m LiDAR does not extend across the core of the historic village, but only its eastern fringes. Although a number of earthworks show up, nothing obviously conforms with the proposed grid.

Aerial photographs: Aerial photographs held in the NMR were consulted but no features of relevance were evident.

Historic maps: A transcript of a 1789 map was used to produce the plan in Blair 2018, fig. 116.

Thorpe Mandeville (3/-/C)

Nineteenth-century plan: The evidence for gridding within the nineteenth-century village plan is slight, but embraces elements of the road pattern and property boundaries. The parish church is on a different orientation.

Excavations: Nothing identified on ADS.

LiDAR: No 1-m LiDAR data is available.

Aerial photographs: Aerial photographs held in the NMR were consulted but no features of relevance were evident.

Historic maps: None consulted.

Warmington (3/-/C)

Nineteenth-century plan: The oldest part of the village is presumably that along Church Street and around St Mary's church, although here there is no evidence for gridding. The strongest conformity to a grid is found N of the church, near Little Green, although only a handful of field boundaries are aligned exactly. The settlement has clearly spread over a pre-existing framework, but this is perhaps most likely to have been an open-field system.

Excavations: Five archaeological reports for Warmington were found on the ADS, but overall they provide only limited support for a gridded settlement.

- 18–20 Chapel Street, 2011: five trenches were excavated adjacent to Little Green (Taylor 2011). One twelfth- to fifteenth-century ditch runs at 45 degrees to the proposed grid.
- 21 Stamford Lane, 2011: two trenches W of Little Green. eighteenth- to nineteenth-century pits and a single ditch in Trench 2 regarded as possibly Roman (Pozorski 2011; and see below): this ditch [1006] was possibly on a similar orientation to the proposed grid but too little was seen to be sure.
- 21 Stamford Lane, 2012: a larger area excavation of the 2011 site (see above) revealed many post-medieval gravel pits (Trimble 2012). The ditch [1006] that in 2011 was ascribed a Roman date (see above) might actually be sixteenth to seventeenth century.
- Peterborough Road, 2002: geophysics and excavation immediately W and SW of the moated site on the N edge of the village (Meadows 2002). There were extensive eighth- to twelfth-century settlement remains, including ditched enclosures, although some features were unexcavated and so are not phased. There is a sense of rectilinearity within the excavated complex, and some ditches are on the same orientation as the proposed grid.
- Warmington Manor House, 1997: ditched enclosure complex of the tenth to thirteenth centuries (Chapman 1997). This evaluation lay immediately W of the 2002 open area excavation at Peterborough Road. Some ditch alignments conform to the proposed grid, others do not.

LiDAR: Because of the heavy recent development, the 1-m LiDAR coverage does not add any useful detail.

Aerial photographs: Aerial photographs held in the NMR were consulted but no features of relevance were evident.

Historic maps: None consulted.

Northumberland

Beadnall (2/-/B)

Nineteenth-century plan: Although small in size, the arrangement of roads and property boundaries in this nineteenth-century village plan is noticeably grid-like, and on a different orientation from the surrounding fields. There is some correspondence to the four-short-perch module.

Excavations: None identified on ADS.

LiDAR: None available.

Aerial photographs: Aerial photographs held in the NMR were consulted but no features of relevance were evident.

Historic maps: None consulted.

Hexham Abbey (–/I/A; Blair 2013, fig. 3; present Figure 5.3)

The church and associated structures were built by St Wilfrid in the late seventh century; the crypt survives, and much of the rest is known from late nineteenth-century excavations. The complex shows strong and accurate conformity to a short-perch grid. (Cambridge and Williams 1995; Blair 2013, 23–5)

Yeavering (–/I/A; present Figure 5.2)

A royal great hall complex, famous from Bede's account of the activities of King Eadwine and Bishop Paulinus there in the 620s, and from a classic excavation. It is proposed above (Chapter 4) that the first monumental phase was laid out on a short-perch grid, possibly by surveyors sent from Kent. (Hope-Taylor 1977)

Nottinghamshire

Torworth (3/-/C)

Nineteenth-century plan: The rectilinearity of this village can partly be ascribed to an underlying and broadly co-axial layout of E–W-orientated boundaries that are overlain by the main N–S road. However, the core of the village lies to the E of this road, where a series of tenements was laid out either side of a side street. The four-short-perch module is evident in the spacing of various property boundaries, although this is much stronger in the series of E–W boundaries than in those orientated N–S, making it unclear whether the planning was grid-based.

Excavations: None identified on ADS.

LiDAR: No 1-m LiDAR is available.

Aerial photographs: Aerial photographs held in the NMR were consulted but no features of relevance were evident.

Historic maps: None consulted.

Oxfordshire

Bampton (3/-/C; Blair 2013, fig. 28)
Nineteenth-century plan: An area E of Broad Street shows some agreement with a four-short-perch grid, despite a good deal of 'foreground noise' caused by relatively recent features that do not conform.

Excavations: There have been several excavations in other parts of this complex historic settlement (cf. Blair 2018, 238–9), but none relates to the proposed grid.

LiDAR: There is good 1-m LiDAR coverage of the settlement and surrounding fields, including some field and furlong boundaries in broad conformity with the alignment of the potentially grid-planned area. These are, however, some way out from the settlement core, and while it is not impossible that the visible area is a fragment of a much larger grid it seems more likely that it was itself framed within prevailing topographical alignments.

Aerial photographs: Available coverage does not add to the data visible on LiDAR.

Historic maps: Maps of 1789 and 1821 were used to produce the plan in Blair 2013, fig. 28.

Benson (3/-/C)
Nineteenth-century plan: At first sight the meandering road that winds through Benson, and the straight road entering the village from the NW, give the impression of organic development rather than planning. However, when looking beyond this 'foreground noise' there is a common orientation of the church, field and tenement boundaries across the village. The spacing of some of these elements is also consistent with the short perch unit.

Excavations: An early to mid-Anglo-Saxon structure, plausibly identified as a seventh-century 'great hall', has been excavated to the S of the church (McBride 2016). It does not conform to the alignment of the putative grid, which presumably therefore post-dates it.

LiDAR: None consulted.

Aerial photographs: None consulted.

Historic maps: None consulted.

Church Enstone (1/-/A; present Figure 6.7)
Nineteenth-century plan: Much of the framework of the village, including roads and boundaries, conforms to a four-short-perch grid; beyond the village the irregularity and non-conformity of the surrounding landscape starts immediately beyond the village.

Excavations:
- St Kenelm's church 2010: a watching brief identified an earlier medieval phase of the church and three graves. The information adds nothing to the case for gridding (McNicoll-Norbury and Lewis 2010).

LiDAR: No 1-m LiDAR coverage is available.

Aerial photographs: Aerial photographs held in the NMR were consulted but no features of relevance were evident.

Historic maps: None consulted.

Eynsham (2/II/A; Blair 2018, fig. 115)
Nineteenth-century plan: Roads and boundaries within the settlement, and some field boundaries to the NW, show a degree of recurrent conformity with a four-short-perch grid orientated on Mill Street and Abbey Street; any such grid, however, has been heavily overlaid by the high medieval marketplace and small town. What raises this case from the 'possible' to the 'probable' category is the excavation of part of the monastic complex laid out when the abbey was refounded in 1005, which (unlike the later medieval church and cloister) conformed to the same grid: cf. Blair 2018, 318–19.

Excavations:
- 17 Mill Street 2013: a number of medieval features, including ditches, pits and postholes, were recorded during trench evaluation (Dawson and Pine 2013). The linear features have the same orientation as the proposed grid.

- Churchyard extension, 1989–92: multiple Anglo-Saxon and later phases of the monastic complex; they include a rectilinear layout of stone-built ranges ascribed to the 1005 refoundation that conforms to the proposed grid (Hardy *et al.* 2003).
- 3 Thames Street 2008: observation of foundation trenches identified a number of pits, one of which was of eleventh- to twelfth-century date (Cass 2008).
- 13–15 Mill Street 2013: evaluation revealed an undated pit and an infilled pond or stream (Porter 2013).
- 26 High Street 2004: a watching brief identified an 'Anglo-Saxon' pit, a medieval ploughsoil and a post-twelfth-century ditch. Pits of fifteenth-century date were also identified (Moore 2004).
- 36 Newland Street 2008: evaluation identified a twelfth- to fourteenth-century ditch, an undated gully, a large pit and three undated postholes (Millbank 2008). Ditch 4, which was dated to between the twelfth and fourteenth century, has the same general orientation as the proposed grid.
- Abbey Farm Barns 2013: monitoring of service trenches revealed many archaeological features, including eleventh-century ditches (Williams 2013). Owing to limited exposure the orientation of many of the features could not be established, although there does appear to be a N–S trend that does not reflect the orientation of the proposed grid.
- Eynsham Primary School 2010: a watching brief identified a potential late prehistoric ditch (Yeates 2010). The ditch has a similar orientation to the proposed grid.

LiDAR: No 1-m LiDAR is available for the settlement core.

Aerial photographs: Aerial photographs held in the NMR were consulted but no features of relevance were evident.

Historic maps: A map of *c.*1802 was used to produce the plan in Blair 2018, fig. 115.

Iffley (3/-/C)

Nineteenth-century plan: There is limited regularity in the layout of Iffley village. The possible grid is orientated on the main street running N of the church, and this orientation is replicated by some tenement boundaries and field divisions within the surrounding area (e.g. NW of the village). A length of canalised stream SW of the church also conforms.

Excavations: There have been a series of minor interventions (Chadwick 2011; Gilbert 2005; Hammond 2007; Mumford 2009; Taylor 2013), but none provides evidence bearing on the case for grid-planning.

LiDAR: No 1-m LiDAR is available for the settlement core.

Aerial photographs: A linear W–E-orientated earthwork is visible on the NW side of the village, running parallel with a field boundary depicted on the late nineteenth-century map. Both conform to the orientation and position of the proposed grid (RAF/540/673 12 FEB 52 Frame 3358).

Historic maps: None consulted.

Rutland

Glaston (2/II/B; Blair 2013, fig. 24)
Nineteenth-century plan: The pattern of roads, lanes and fields in the N half of the village, particularly in the vicinity of the church, shows plausible conformity to a four-short-perch grid.

Excavations:
- Grange Farm 2002: excavation revealed tenth- to eleventh-century land enclosure, probably representing the northern end of a toft. The enclosure continued in use until the later thirteenth century (University of Leicester Archaeological Services 2002). This is in good conformity with the proposed grid (Blair 2013, 49).
- Coppice Paddock 2007: trench excavation and monitoring of topsoil stripping on the N side of the village revealed no archaeological features or deposits (Hunt 2007). Although there is insufficient detail in the site location map to position the excavation precisely in relation to the historic landscape, it is clear that the features share the same orientation as the proposed grid.

LiDAR: The 1-m LiDAR coverage does not add any useful detail.

Aerial photographs: Aerial photographs held in the NMR were consulted but no features of relevance were evident.

Historic maps: None consulted.

Ketton Quarry (–/II/B; Blair 2013, figs. 19–20; Blair 2018, fig. 139)
A tenth- to eleventh-century sub-aristocratic complex comprising halls, a church and surrounding rectilinear closes. Most of these features

(with the conspicuous exception of the church and its graves) conform plausibly to a short-perch grid. (Blair 2013, 40–4)

Manton (3/-/C)
Nineteenth-century plan: Some boundaries to the N and S of the church conform to the orientation and position of the proposed grid, as does the road running NE–SW to the N of the church. Some roads, while not conforming exactly to the grid, do appear to be four short perches in width.

Excavations:
- Dairy Farm 2006 and 2007: evaluation revealed Late Saxon quarry pits and medieval structures (Tate 2006). Subsequent excavation identified numerous twelfth- to thirteenth-century pits (Tate 2007). While demonstrating the presence of Late Saxon and medieval archaeology, the evidence does not contribute to the case for gridding.
- Hollytop House 2009: three archaeological evaluation trenches revealed two medieval quarry pits (Kipling 2009) that make no contribution to the case for gridding.
- The Priory 2005: a watching brief recorded two alignments of a Saxo-Norman field system, as well as medieval/late medieval structural evidence possibly relating to the Priory (Tate 2005). The Saxo-Norman boundaries do not conform to the orientation of the proposed grid, but the thirteenth- to fourteenth-century ditches do.

LiDAR: Nothing visible on LiDAR that adds to the picture.

Aerial photographs: Aerial photographs held in the NMR were consulted but no features of relevance were evident.

Historic maps: The only historic map identified does not depict the village (Manton, estate of Lord Norton, c.nineteenth century: Record Office for Leicestershire, Leicester and Rutland, MA/R/2).

Whissendine (east) (3/II/B) and *Whissendene (west)* (2/-/B)
Nineteenth-century plan: Two grids are proposed at Whissendine: one for the E half of the village, one for the W half. That on the E is orientated with the parish church, and finds agreement in the layout of boundaries around the Manor House and to the S of the village, despite the main E–W road meandering around. That on the W is orientated with the broadly N–S main road and finds agreement in tenement plots and fields adjacent to it. The regularity extends to the S edge

of the village, where boundaries surrounding the nineteenth-century windmill also conform.

Excavations:
- 5 Melton Road 2006: two evaluation trenches revealed two ditches which yielded early and Late Saxon pottery (Hyam 2006). Ditch 8, which yielded fifth-/sixth- and eleventh-/twelfth-century pottery, shared the same orientation as the proposed western grid.
- Stapleford Road 2007: excavation revealed complex multi-period occupation, including Iron Age settlement, and Late Saxon and medieval pits, structures, ditches and gullies (Browning 2007). A number of the excavated Late Saxon and medieval ditches share the same orientation as the proposed western grid, and in some instances possibly fall on the proposed grid-lines.

LiDAR: The 1-m LiDAR coverage does not add any useful detail.

Aerial photographs: Aerial photographs held in the NMR were consulted but no features of relevance were evident.

Historic maps: The only historic map, dating to 1766, is little different from the later 1st edition OS 25-inch map (Whissendine, plan of estates, 1766: Record Office for Leicestershire, Leicester and Rutland, MA/R/1).

Wing (2/-/B)
Nineteenth-century plan: The principal area of conformity with the proposed grid is N and NW of the parish church. Both Middle Street and Top Street align with the grid, as do a number of boundaries subdividing land within the village. Many buildings are on the same orientation, indicating the dominant axis of tenement plots. The regularity does not extend into the surrounding field pattern.

Excavation: SS Peter and Paul 2009: a limited watching brief revealed no pre-modern archaeological features (Failes 2009).

LiDAR: No 1-m LiDAR is available for the village core.

Aerial photographs: Aerial photographs held in the NMR were consulted but no features of relevance were evident.

Historic maps: A map of 1772 shows the same layout as the 1st edition OS 25-inch map (Wing, inclosure map, 1772: Record Office for Leicestershire, Leicester and Rutland, MA/EN/A/R55/1).

Somerset

Cheddar (–/II/B; Blair 2018, fig. 136)
The excavated site was a royal residential complex. Two successive phases, probably of *c.*950 and *c.*1000, conform plausibly to a long-perch grid. (Rahtz 1979)

Staffordshire

Catholme (–/I/A; Blair 2018, figs. 50, 51; present Figure 5.9)
A complex sixth- to eighth-century settlement focused on a Bronze Age barrow, comprising many buildings within a system of ditched enclosures, evolved over a considerable period but with a broadly stable overall layout. Our analysis has identified a major grid-planned phase and up to two others, all based on short-perch grids. A rectilinear pattern of enclosures S of the site (partly recorded on an early eighteenth-century estate map) does not on its own constitute evidence for grid-planning, but in the light of the excavation it might conceivably represent an extension of the same system. (Losco-Bradley and Kinsley 2002; Blair 2018, 158–61)

Suffolk

Bloodmoor Hill, Carlton Colville (–/III/C; Blair 2013, figs. 1, 10)
A seventh-century settlement comprising rectangular ground-level buildings and sunken-featured buildings, with high-status female graves. JB has suggested that it is based on a short-perch grid; the other members of the team were not persuaded. (Lucy *et al.* 2009; Blair 2013, 30–2)

Brandon (–/I/A; Blair 2018, fig. 46; present Figure 5.12)
An excavated seventh- to ninth-century high-status settlement, probably monastic. Two successive phases of buildings are based very accurately on short-perch grids. (Tester *et al.* 2014)

Bury St Edmunds (3/–/ C; present Figure 5.19)
The monastic precinct and planned town, both probably laid out by Abbot Baldwin (1065–97), share the same alignment and broadly rectilinear configuration. JB has proposed that they are based on a single continuous short-perch grid; the other members of the team were less persuaded.

Fornham All Saints (3/-C)

Nineteenth-century plan: This village plan is notably rectilinear in layout, although this may to a considerable extent result from property boundaries having been laid out parallel and perpendicular to the single long straight main street. The major boundary to the W of the village street does correspond to the four-short-perch module, as do various other stretches of boundary, but this falls well short of a compelling case.

Excavations None identified on ADS.

LiDAR: The 1-m LiDAR coverage does not add any useful detail.

Aerial photographs: Aerial photographs held in the NMR were consulted but no features of relevance were evident.

Historic maps: None consulted.

Ilketshall St Margaret (2/-/B)

Nineteenth-century plan: A rectilinear layout is evident in various elements of this village plan, most noticeably in a pattern of property boundaries that conform to the four-short-perch module in both the SW–NE and NW–SE axes. St Margaret's church also follows the orientation of this putative grid, and thus deviates considerably from a W–E alignment.

Excavations: None identified on ADS.

LiDAR: The 1-m LiDAR shows a series of long straight earthworks, running NW–SE on the S side of the village, which conforms to the orientation of the proposed grid. These earthworks indicate additional long boundaries to those already visible on the 1st edition Ordnance Survey map. There is no LiDAR coverage of the N side of the village.

Aerial photographs: RAF vertical aerial photography shows a series of relict ditches, to the S and E of the parish church, which together make a series of rectilinear enclosures. These do not relate to boundaries visible on the 1st edition Ordnance Survey maps and do conform very well to the position and orientation of the proposed grid (RAF/106G/UK/1716 06 Sep 1946 Frame 3075; RAF/106G/UK/930 16 OCT 1945 Frame 3168).

Historic maps: None consulted.

Kentford (not classified)
A recent excavation (plan kindly provided by Faye Minter) has revealed a settlement of rectangular buildings, perhaps seventh-century, that appears to conform to a short-perch grid. No further details were available at the time of going to press.

Sussex

Broadwater (1/-/A)
Nineteenth-century plan: Property boundaries across the whole village are laid out in a rectilinear fashion, in contrast to the major roads that are stratigraphically later. This regularity continues into the surrounding field systems, suggesting a particularly extensive example of grid-based planning. There is very close correspondence to the four-perch module across the village.

Excavations: None identified on ADS.

LiDAR: The 1-m LiDAR coverage does not add any useful detail.

Aerial photographs: Aerial photographs held in the NMR were consulted but no features of relevance were evident.

Historic maps: None examined.

Burpham (-/II/B; Blair 2013, fig. 1)
A single excavated mid- to late Anglo-Saxon building is apparently based on the short-perch module. (Sutermeister 1976)

Sompting (not classified; present Figure 6.20)
A notably regular case, but an anomalous one: it apparently follows a surveyed framework of strips (based on the four-short-perch module) rather than a grid.

Warwickshire

Fenny Compton (3/-/C)
Nineteenth-century plan: At first sight, this very irregular village shows little sign of planning, but a closer examination of its N and E parts suggests a degree of rectilinearity, reflected in both the roads (some of which have sharp right-angled bends) and property boundaries.

Excavations: None identified on ADS.

LiDAR: The 1-m LiDAR coverage does not add any useful detail.

Aerial photographs: Aerial photographs held in the NMR were consulted but no features of relevance were evident.

Historic maps: The one historic map examined provide no additional information (Fenny Compton, estate map, 1855: Warwickshire Record Office, CR580 box 64).

Kites Hardwick (not classified; Blair 2013, fig. 27)
JB proposed a short-perch grid on the evidence of boundaries shown on nineteenth-century maps, but on re-examination the team rejected this example. (Blair 2013, 49)

Wolvey (3/-/C)
Nineteenth-century plan: There is persuasive use of the four-short-perch module in a series of paddocks to the W of the nineteenth-century village. However, blocks of both 2 × 3 and 3 × 3 modules are evident, so it is unclear whether this represents grid-based planning or simply use of the module. To the E, the village as existing in the nineteenth century had a fairly irregular layout, although several side streets and property boundaries are on the same orientation as the paddocks to the W.

Excavations:
- Church Hill Road 2005: excavation revealed three phases of archaeology: twelfth to thirteenth century, 1250–1300, and fifteenth century. Two perpendicular ditches and a rectangular structure were dated to Phase 1. A reorganisation of land division with a series of ditches occurred c.1250–1300. In the fifteenth century land division was again reorganised and larger ditches were dug across the site (Ramsey 2005).
- Wolvey Hall 2011: evaluation on the W side of Wolvey revealed a variety of post-medieval structural features, but also two thirteenth- to fourteenth-century ditches that were interpreted as field boundaries (Peachey 2011).

LiDAR: No 1-m LiDAR is available.

Aerial photographs: Aerial photographs held in the NMR were consulted but no features of relevance were evident.

Historic maps: A small number of additional boundaries shown on two earlier maps conform to the rectilinear layout (Wolvey, inclosure plan,

1797: Warwickshire Record Office, CR513; Wolvey, tithe map, 1850: Warwickshire Record Office, CR0569 257).

Wiltshire

Bremilham, Cowage Farm (–/I/A; Blair 2013, figs. 5, 6; Blair 2018, fig. 35; present Figure 1.1)
A seventh-century great hall complex of several phases: plotted from cropmarks, with some limited excavation. Two successive phases are evidently based on short-perch grids. (Hinchcliffe 1986; Blair 2013, 27–8)

Yorkshire, East Riding

Flamborough (2/-/B; present Figure 3.10)
Nineteenth-century plan: This village plan appears to have been laid out as E–W-orientated lateral features (both roads and property boundaries) between a series of N–S axes. In places, the complex pattern of roads clearly post-dates an underlying series of boundaries that appear to have been laid out in a grid-like fashion. St Oswald's church is orientated with this putative grid.

Excavations: None identified on ADS.

LiDAR: The 1-m LiDAR coverage does not add any useful detail.

Aerial photographs: RAF vertical aerial photography shows a series of slight rectilinear earthworks in the vicinity of Beacon Farm, particularly on its S side, which conform to the orientation of the proposed grid. On the first edition OS this is marked as the site of an 'old hall' (RAF/613A/BR13/1 20 SEP 51 Frame 5142).

Historic maps: The 1761 map shows a road to the S of Church Farm which conforms to the orientation of the proposed grid. This could be a cartographic error: the road was not present in the late nineteenth century – it cuts through what was then fields – and the map may be depicting the road running S of the church, but in the wrong position. The 1767 enclosure map shows several W–E-orientated boundaries to the N of Beacon Farm that conform to the orientation and position of the proposed grid (Flamborough, 1761: East Riding Archives, DDHU 20/1; Flamborough, inclosure map, 1767: East Riding Archives, IA/64).

Keyingham (2/-/B; present Figure 6.17)
Nineteenth-century plan: The dominant road-plan of Keyingham is irregular, but there seems to be an underlying regularity in the pattern of property boundaries, particularly on the W side of the village. A series of N–S and E–W elements, parallel and at right angles to each other, show some correspondence to the four-short-perch module.

Excavations: None identified on ADS.

LiDAR: The 1-m LiDAR coverage does not add any useful detail.

Aerial photographs: RAF vertical aerial photography shows a series of linear earthworks conforming broadly to the orientation and position of the proposed grid on the SW side of the village. The earthworks appear to define small rectilinear enclosures, and within some of these are traces of ridge and furrow on the same orientation (RAF/CPE/UK/1748 21 SEP 46 Frame 3092).

Historic maps: The tithe map provides moderate support for the hypothesis that Keyingham village was laid out on a grid. It shows a boundary to the SW of the village that aligns with the proposed grid and reflects an earthwork visible on the 1946 aerial photograph (above). The general regularity of the village plan S of the church is also evident (Keyingham, tithe map, 1842: East Riding Archives, PC 18/7/1).

Preston (3/-/C; present Figure 6.13)
Nineteenth-century plan: There is some evidence for an underlying regularity in the central part of the nineteenth-century village plan, in the form of various property boundaries and stretches of road that are orientated broadly ENE–WSW and NWS–SSE. The parish church is also orientated with this putative grid. Some use of the four-short-perch module is evident.

Excavations: None identified on ADS.

LiDAR: No 1-m LiDAR is available.

Aerial photographs: Aerial photographs held in the NMR were consulted but no features of relevance were evident.

Historic maps: The two historic maps consulted provide no additional information (Preston, inclosure map, 1774: East Riding Archives, IA/126 K-6–6; Preston, tithe map, 1848: East Riding Archives, PE 123/86).

Yorkshire, North Riding

Chapel-le-Dale, Brows Pasture (–/II/B; Blair 2018, fig. 52, 53)
Two upland farmsteads, with rough rubble footings, explored by partial excavation and dated to the seventh century onwards. They appear to be based on rows of four-short-perch grids. (Johnson 2013; Blair 2018, 159–63)

Clapham Bottoms (–/II/B; Blair 2018, fig. 52)
An upland farmstead, with rough rubble footings, explored by partial excavation and dated to the seventh century onwards. It appears to be based on a four-short-perch grid. (Blair 2018, 159–63)

Dunnington (2/-/B)
Nineteenth-century plan: Despite the curvilinear pattern of major roads in the N part of the village around the parish church there is a marked rectiliniarity in both roads and property boundaries further S, including Back Lane and Water Lane, which have sharp right-angled bends. Some of this rectilinearity is also seen in property boundaries further N, and the curvilinear Church Lane appears to overlie this more regular arrangement of boundaries. The regularity does not extend into the surrounding field pattern.

Excavations: None identified on ADS.

LiDAR: No 1-m LiDAR is available for the village core.

Aerial photographs: RAF vertical aerial photography shows an earthwork of a relict boundary S of the church that broadly conforms to the proposed grid, and also shows that much of the former ridge and furrow close to the core of the village shares the same orientation (RAF/CPE/UK/1879 6 DEC 46 Frame 4439).

Historic maps: None consulted.

Great Habton (2/-/B)
Nineteenth-century plan: This village plan has a noticeably grid-like layout, with several long, straight N–S axes and a number of boundaries running E–W. There is some correspondence to the four-short-perch module across the whole village, in both the road layout and the property boundaries.

Excavations: None identified on ADS.

LiDAR: No 1-m LiDAR is available.

Aerial photographs: Aerial photographs held in the NMR were consulted but no features of relevance were evident.

Historic maps: The two historic maps consulted provide no additional information (plan of the Lordship of Great Habton, *c.*1770–90: North Yorkshire County Record Office, MIC 2015/114–116; Great Habton, tithe map, 1849: North Yorkshire County Record Office, MIC 2299/450–459).

Kirk Smeaton (2/-/B)

Nineteenth-century plan: A potentially grid-based layout is evident in the nineteenth-century village plan, including a series of sharp right-angled bends in the main E–W street. The rectilinear layout is also evident in minor side roads and property boundaries. Use of the four-short-perch module is evident in various places.

Excavations:
- Plot 3 Went Edge Road 2006: observation during digging of foundation trenches revealed no archaeology (letter from Ian Roberts to Gail Falkingham, 13.03.2006, North Yorkshire Heritage Unit).

LiDAR: No 1-m LiDAR coverage is available.

Aerial photographs: Aerial photographs held in the NMR were consulted but no features of relevance were evident.

Historic maps: The one historic map consulted provides no additional information (Kirk Smeaton, enclosure map, 1810: North Yorkshire County Record Office, PC/HMK).

Whitby (-/II/B; present Figure 5.6)

A substantial area of this major seventh-century monastic site was excavated – very badly – in the early twentieth century, and has been published as a plan reconstructed by Philip Rahtz (Rahtz 1976). Inadequate though this inevitably is (especially in the superimposition of several phases), the buildings and roadways conform persuasively to a short-perch grid. Recent excavations along the headland located features that seem compatible with the same overall layout.

Yorkshire, West Riding

Hooton Roberts (2/-/B)

Nineteenth-century plan: The rectilinear layout of this small nineteenth-century village contrasts strikingly with the more irregular layout of the surrounding fieldscape. Some correspondence to the four-short-perch module is found across the village.

Excavations: None identified on ADS.

LiDAR: No 1-m LiDAR is available.

Aerial photographs: Aerial photographs held in the NMR were consulted but no features of relevance were evident.

Historic maps: None consulted.

Ripon (not classified; Blair 2013, fig. 3)

JB suggested that St Wilfrid's crypt at Ripon, like that at Hexham, was laid out on a module of one short perch; the other members of the team were less persuaded. (Blair 2013, 23–5)

Bibliography

Aalen, F.H.A. 2006, *England's Landscape: The North East*, London: English Heritage.

Albone, J. 1998, Archaeological field evaluation report. Land off Norbeck Lane, Welton, Lincolnshire. Unpublished report: Pre-Construct Archaeology.

Albone, J. 2003, Archaeological evaluation on land at Healthlinc House, Cliff Road, Welton, Lincolnshire. Unpublished report: Archaeological Project Services report 26/03.

Alexander, J. and Pullinger, J. 1999, 'Roman Cambridge: excavations on Castle Hill 1956–1988', *Proceedings of the Cambridge Antiquarian Society* 88, 1–268.

Allen Archaeology 2010, Archaeological evaluation report: Land between 17 and 21 Lincoln Road, Welton, Lincolnshire. Unpublished report: Allen Archaeology Ltd report 2010020.

Allen, M. 2000, Archaeological field evaluation report: Land at Hopfield, Hibaldstow, North Lincolnshire. Unpublished report: Pre-Construct Archaeology.

Allerston, P. 1970, 'English village development: findings from the Pickering district of North Yorkshire', *Transaction of the Institute of British Geographers* 51, 95–109.

Ames, J. and Phelps, A. 2008, An archaeological excavation at land off Church Close, Shipdham, Norfolk. Assessment and Updated Project Design. Unpublished report: NAU Archaeology report 1367a.

Ames, J., Hickling, S. and Morgan, S. 2009, An archaeological excavation at land off Church Close, Shipdham, Norfolk. Unpublished report: NAU Archaeology report 1367b.

Andrews, P. 1997, *Excavations at Hamwic, Volume 2. Excavations at Six Dials*, York: Council for British Archaeology Research Report 109.

Andrews, P., Biddulph, E. and Hardy, A. 2011, *Excavations at Springhead and Northfleet, Kent: I: The Sites*, Sailsbury: Oxford-Wessex Archaeology.

Applebaum, S. 1972, 'Roman Britain', in H.P.R. Finberg (ed.), *The Agrarian History of England and Wales* I(ii), Cambridge: Cambridge University Press, 1–282.

Applebaum, S. 1981, 'The Essex achievement', *Agricultural History Review* 29, 42–4.

Archaeological Project Services 1995, Archaeological watching-brief for a development at Guildford Lane, Brant Broughton, Lincolnshire. Unpublished report: Archaeological Project Services.

Astbury, A.K. 1980, *Estuary: Land and Water in the Lower Thames Basin*, London: Carnforth Press.

Aston, M. and Gerrard, C. 2013, *Interpreting the English Village*, Oxford: Oxbow Books.

Atkins, R. 2013, Medieval to modern remains, St Mary's Field, Gamlingay. Unpublished report: Oxford Archaeology East report 1528.

Audouy, M. and Chapman, A. 2009, *Raunds: the Origin and Growth of a Midland Village AD450–1500. Excavations in North Raunds, Northamptonshire 1977–87*, Oxford: Oxbow Books.

Austin, D. 1987, 'The medieval settlement and landscape of Castle Eden, Peterlee, Co. Durham: excavations 1974', *Durham Archaeological Journal* 3, 57–78.

Austin, D. 1989, *The Deserted Medieval Village of Thrislington, County Durham: Excavations 1973–74*, Lincoln: Society for Medieval Archaeology Monograph 12.

Bailey, R. 1991, 'St Wilfrid, Ripon and Hexham', in C. Karkov and R. Farrell (eds), *Studies in Insular Art and Archaeology*, American Early Medieval Studies vol. 1. Oxford, OH: Miami University, 3–25.

Barber, A. and Riley, R. 2014, Winchcombe Abbey, Winchcombe, Gloucestershire. Archaeological evaluation. Unpublished report: Cotswold Archaeology report 13495.

Barclay, A., Lambrick, G., Moore, J. and Robinson, M. 2003, *Lines in the Landscape: Cursus Monuments in the Upper Thames Valley*, Oxford: Oxford Archaeology.

Barnes, C. 2015, 'Statistics in Anglo-Saxon Archaeology', unpublished MSc dissertation, Department of Statistics, University of Warwick.

Bell, M. 1977, 'Excavations at Bishopstone', *Sussex Archaeological Collections* 115, 1–299.

Bell, T. 2005, *The Religious Use of Roman Structures in Early Medieval Britain*, Oxford: British Archaeological Reports (British Series) 390.

Beresford, G. 1975, *The Medieval Clay-Land Village: Excavations at Goltho and Barton Blount*, London: Society for Medieval Archaeology Monograph 6.

Beresford, G. 1987, *Goltho. The Development of an Early Medieval Manor c.850–1150*, London: English Heritage.

Beresford, G. 2009, *Caldecote: the Development and Desertion of a Hertfordshire Village*, London: Society for Medieval Archaeology Monograph 28.

Beresford, M.W. 1967, *New Towns of the Middle Ages*, London: Lutterworth Press.

Besteman, J.C. and Guiran, A.J. 1987, 'An early peat bog reclamation area in medieval Kennemerland, Assendelver Polders', in R.W. Brandt, W. Groenman Van Waateringe and S.E. Van der Leeuw (eds), *Assendelver Polder Papers 1*, Amsterdam: Albert Egges Van Giffen Instituut voor Prae- en Protohistorie, University of Amsterdam, 297–332.

Biddle, M. and Kjølbye-Biddle, B. 2001, 'Repton and the "Great Heathen Army", 873–4', in J. Graham-Campbell *et al.* (eds), *Vikings and the Danelaw*, Oxford: Oxbow, 45–96.

Bishop, T.A.M. 1948, 'The Norman settlement of Yorkshire', in R.W. Hunt, W.A. Pantin and R.W. Southern (eds), *Studies in Medieval History Presented to Frederick Maurice Powicke*, Oxford: Oxford University Press, 1–14.

Blair, J. 2005, *The Church in Anglo-Saxon Society*, Oxford: Oxford University Press.

Blair, J. 2013, 'Grid planning in Anglo-Saxon settlements: the short perch and the four-perch module', *Anglo-Saxon Studies in Archaeology and History* 18, 18–61.

Blair, J. 2018, *Building Anglo-Saxon England*, Princeton: Princeton University Press.

Blount, T. 1815, *Fragmenta Antiquitatis, or Ancient Tenures of Land*, enlarged edn, London.

Blume, F., Lachmann, K. and Rudorff, A. 1848, *Die Schriften der Römischen Feldmesser (Gromatici Veteres)*, vol. 1, Berlin: Georg Reimer.

Bourin, M. 1995, 'Délimitation des parcelles et perception de l'espace en Bas-Languedoc au Xe et XIe siècles', in E. Mornet (ed.), *Campagnes Médiévales: l'Homme et son Espace; Études Offertes à Robert Fossier*, Paris: Publications de la Sorbonne, 73–85.

Bown, J. 2004, An archaeological evaluation (minimal intervention) at 60 Acre Field, Watlington, Norfolk. Unpublished report: Norfolk Archaeological Unit report 923.

Bradford, J. 1957, *Ancient Landscapes: Studies in Field Archaeology*, London: Bell.

Bradley, R. 2012, *The Idea of Order*, Oxford: Oxford University Press.

Brett, A. 2003, The Old School House, Stow. Archaeological watching brief. Unpublished report: Pre-Construct Archaeology.

Brett, A. 2005, The Manor, Vicarage Lane, Welton, Lincolnshire. Archaeological watching brief. Unpublished report: Pre-Construct Archaeology.

Brewster, T.C.M. and Hayfield, C. 1994, 'Excavations at Sherburn, East Yorkshire', *Yorkshire Archaeological Journal* 66, 107–48.

Brown, M.P. and Farr, C.A. (eds) 2001, *Mercia: an Anglo-Saxon Kingdom in Europe*, London: Leicester University Press.

Brown, T. and Foard, G. 1998, 'The Saxon Landscape: a regional perspective', in P. Everson and T. Williamson (eds) *The Archaeology of Landscape*, Manchester: Manchester University Press, 67–94.

Browning, J. 2007, Archaeological excavation on land of Stapleford Road, Whissendine, Rutland. Unpublished report: University of Leicester Archaeological Services report 2007-066.

Bruce-Mitford, R. 1997, *Mawgan Porth: a Settlement of the Late Saxon Period on the North Cornish Coast*, London: English Heritage.

Brunning, R. 2014, *Somerset's Peatland Archaeology: Managing and Investigating a Fragile Resource*, Oxford: Oxbow.

Bryant, S., Perry, B. and Williamson, T. 2005, 'A "relict landscape" in south-east Hertfordshire: archaeological and topographical investigations in the Wormley area', *Landscape History* 27, 5–16.

Burnham, B.C. and Wacher, J. 1990, *The 'Small Towns' of Roman Britain*, London: Batsford.

Butler, A. 1999, A geophysical survey of land off Leicester Lane, Desford, Leicestershire. Unpublished report: University of Leicester Archaeological Services report 99/30.

Butler, A. 2010, Archaeological and geophysical survey on land at Hunts Lane, Desford, Leicestershire. Unpublished report: Northamptonshire Archaeology report 10/220.

Cambridge, E. 1999, 'The architecture of the Augustinian mission', in R. Gameson (ed.), *St Augustine and the Conversion of England*, Stroud: Sutton Publishing, 202–36.

Cambridge, E. and Williams, A. 1995, 'Hexham Abbey: a review of recent work and its implications', *Archaeologia Aeliana* 5th ser. 23, 51–138.

Campbell, B. 2000, *The Writings of the Roman Land Surveyors*, London: Society for the Promotion of Roman Studies, Journal of Roman Studies Monograph 9.

Canham, R. 1979, 'Excavations at Shepperton Green, 1967 and 1973', *Transactions of the London and Middlesex Archaeological Society* 30, 97–124.

Casa Hatton, R. 2001, Early-mid Saxon activity at land adjacent to No. 12, Hillside Meadow, Fordham: An archaeological evaluation. A192. Unpublished report: Cambridgeshire County Council Archaeological Field Unit.

Cass, S. 2008, 3 Thames Street, Eynsham, Oxfordshire: an archaeological watching brief. Unpublished report: Thames Valley Archaeological Service.

Catteddu, I. 1992, 'L'habitat rural Mérovingien de Genlis', *Revue Archéologique de l'Est et du Centre-Est* 43, 39–89.

Cessford, C. 2004, 'The origins and early development of Chesterton', *Proceedings of the Cambridgeshire Antiquarian Society* 93, 125–42.

Cessford, C. 2005, 'The manor of Hintona: the origins and development of Church End, Cherry Hinton', *Proceedings of the Cambridgeshire Antiquarian Society* 94, 51–72.

Cessford, C. and Mortimer, R. 2003, Land adjacent to 63 Church End, Church End, Cherry Hinton. 607. Unpublished report: Cambridge Archaeological Unit.

Chadwick, A.M. 2011, An archaeological evaluation at Iffley House, Anne Greenwood Close, Iffley, Oxford. Unpublished report: John Moore Heritage Services.

Chaffey, G., Wakeham, G., Leivers, M. and Bradley, P. 2013, 'Bronze Age and Anglo-Saxon occupation at Clement's Park, Southend-on-Sea', *Transactions of the Essex Society for Archaeology and History* 4th ser. 4, 40–58.

Chapman, A. 1997, Archaeological trial excavation of land at Manor House, Warmington, Northamptonshire, January–February 1997. Unpublished report: Northamptonshire Archaeology.

Chapman, A. 2010, *West Cotton, Raunds. A Study of Medieval Settlement Dynamics AD450–1450*, Oxford: Oxbow.

Chapman, P., Chapman, A. and Thompson, A. 2015, 'Anglo-Saxon and Medieval Settlement at the Former Post Office Training Establishment, Wolverton Mill, Milton Keynes', *Records of Buckinghamshire* 55, 75–115.

Christiansen, E. (trans.) 1998, *Dudo of St. Quintin: History of the Normans*, Woodbridge: Boydell Press.

Christy, M. 1921, 'On Roman roads in Essex', *Transactions of the Essex Archaeological Society* new ser. 15, 190–229.

Cockin, M. 2005, A415 Marcham Bypass, Marcham, Oxfordshire. Archaeological evaluation. Unpublished report: Oxford Archaeology report 2712.

Cole, R. 1935, 'The past history of the forest of Essex', *Essex Naturalist* 24, 5–33.

Cole, R. 1939, 'Centuriation in Essex', *Essex Naturalist* 26, 204–20.

Colgrave, B. (ed.) 1927, *The Life of Bishop Wilfrid by Eddius Stephanus*, Cambridge: Cambridge University Press.

Colgrave, B. and Mynors, R.A.B. (eds) 1969, *Bede's Ecclesiastical History of the English People*, Oxford: Oxford University Press.

Collins, M. 2010, Green End Industrial Estate, Gamlingay. An archaeological evaluation. Unpublished report: Cambridge Archaeological Unit report 971.

Commodari, A. 2013, 'Pianificazioni agrarie antiche e medievali nella pianura di Pisa', *Agri Centuriati* 10, 41–56.

Connor, A. 2001, A Middle and Late Saxon property at Fordham Primary School, Cambridgeshire: An archaeological excavation. Unpublished report: Cambridgeshire County Council Archaeological Field Unit report 186.

Cope-Faulkner, P. 1996, Archaeological watching brief of development on land adjacent to Rectory Road, Coleby, Lincolnshire. Unpublished report: Archaeological Project Services.

Cope-Faulkner, P. 1997, Archaeological watching brief of development on land at Church Lane, Brant Broughton, Lincolnshire. Unpublished report: Archaeological Project Services report 50/97.

Cope-Faulkner, P. 2002, Archaeological watching brief of development at Healthlinc House, Cliff Road, Welton, Lincolnshire. Unpublished report: Archaeological Project Services report 53/02.

Cope-Faulkner, P. 2003, Archaeological monitoring during construction at Healthlinc House, Cliff Road, Welton, Lincolnshire. Unpublished report: Archaeological Project Services report 99/03.

Cope-Faulkner, P. 2008, Archaeological excavation on land at Healthlinc House, Cliff Road, Welton, Lincolnshire. Unpublished report: Archaeological Project Services report 60/08.

Cox, S.M. 2009, 'Determining Greek Architectural Design Units in the Sanctuary of the Great Gods, Samothrace: Application of and Extensions to the Cosine Quantogram Method'. Unpublished MSc dissertation, Department of Biostatistics, Emory University.

Cramp, R.J. 1976, 'Monastic sites', in D.M. Wilson (ed.), *The Archaeology of Anglo-Saxon England*, London: Methuen, 201–52.

Crawford, M.H. 2016, 'Johannes the Last Agrimensor ???', in C. Carsana and L. Troiani (eds), *I percorsi di un historikos, in Memoria di Emilio Gabba*, Biblioteca di Athenaeum 58, Como: New Press Edizioni, 216–18.

Crawley, P.E. 2011, Archaeological evaluation at Holt Road, Field Dalling, Norfolk. Unpublished report: NAU Archaeology report 2593.

Creighton, O. and Rippon, S. 2017, 'Conquest, colonisation and the countryside: archaeology and the mid-11th- to mid-12th-century rural landscape', in C. Dyer and D. Hadley (eds), *The Archaeology of the 11th Century: Continuities and Transformations*, London: Society for Medieval Archaeology Monograph 38, 57–87.

Croft, R.A. and Mynard, D.C. 1993, *The Changing Landscape of Milton Keynes*, Aylesbury: Buckinghamshire Archaeological Society Monograph 5.

Crummy, P., Hillam, J. and Crossan, C. 1982, 'Mersea Island: the Anglo-Saxon causeway', *Essex Archaeology and History* 14, 77–86.

Dale, R., Maynard, D., Tyler, S. and Vaughan, T. 2010, 'Carved in stone: a late Iron Age and Roman cemetery and evidence for a Saxon minster; excavations near St Nicholas' church, Great Wakering 1998 and 2000', *Transactions of the Essex Society for Archaeology and History* 4th ser. 1, 194–231.

Dallas, C. 1993, *Excavations in Thetford by B.K. Davison between 1964 and 1970*, Dereham: East Anglian Archaeology 62.

Dalton, P. 1994, *Conquest, Anarchy and Lordship: Yorkshire, 1066–1154*, Cambridge: Cambridge University Press.

Daniels, R. 1990, 'Kilton: a survey of a moorland fringe township', in B. Vyner (ed.), *Medieval Rural Settlement in North-East England*, Durham: Architectural and Archaeological Society of Durham and Northumberland Research Report 2, 33–57.

Daniels, R. 2009, 'The deserted medieval village of High Worsall, North Yorkshire', *Durham Archaeological Journal* 18, 67–98.

Darby, H.C. 1962, *The Domesday Geography of South-East England*, Cambridge: Cambridge University Press.

Darby, H.C. 1977, *Domesday England*, Cambridge: Cambridge University Press.

Davison, A. 1990, *The Evolution of Settlement in Three Norfolk Parishes*, Norwich: East Anglian Archaeology 49.

Davison, A., Green, B. and Millington, B. 1993, *Illington: A Study of a Breckland Parish and its Anglo-Saxon Cemetery*, Norwich: East Anglian Archaeology 63.

Davison, B.K. 1977, 'Excavations at Sulgrave, Northamptonshire, 1960–76: an Interim Report', *Archaeological Journal* 134, 105–14.

Dawson, T. and Pine, J. 2013, 17 Mill Street, Eynsham, Oxfordshire. Unpublished report: Thames Valley Archaeological Service.

Del Lungo, S. 2004, *La Pratica Agrimensoria nella Tarda Antichità e nell'Alto Medioevo*, Testi, Studi, Strumenti 17, Spoleto: Centro Italiano di Studi sull'Alto Medioevo.

Dijkstra, M.E.P. 2011, *Rondom de Mondingen van Rijn & Maas*, Leiden: Sidestone Press.

Dilke, O.A.W. 1971, *The Roman Land Surveyors: an Introduction to the Agrimensores*, Newton Abbot: David and Charles.

Dodgshon, R. 1980, *The Origins of British Field Systems: An Interpretation*, London: Academic Press.

Doyle, K. and Harris, P. 2007, Land off West Road, Gamlingay, Cambridgeshire. An archaeological desk-based assessment and field evaluation. Unpublished report: Archaeological Solutions Ltd report 2120.

Durham, B. 1977, 'Archaeological investigations at St Aldate's, Oxford', *Oxoniensia* 42, 83–203.

Dyer, C. 1985, 'Power and conflict in the medieval village', in D. Hooke (ed.), *Medieval Villages*, Oxford: Oxford University Committee for Archaeology, 27–32.

Eaton, T. 2000, *Plundering the Past: Roman Stonework in Medieval Britain*, Stroud: Tempus.

Edmondson, G. and Preece, T. 2002, Land at Grey's House, Kempston, Bedford. Archaeological field evaluation. Unpublished report: Albion Archaeology report 2002/62.

Egan, S., Peachey, A. and Mustchin, A. 2013, Fox and Hounds, 18 High Street, Kempston, Bedford, Bedfordshire: an archaeological evaluation. Unpublished report: Archaeological Solutions report 4166.

Ellison, A. 1983, *Medieval Villages in South-East Somerset*, Bristol: Western Archaeological Trust Survey No. 6.

Emery, G. 2013, An archaeological evaluation of land proposed for a Ménage at The Stables, Church Road, Bergh Apton, Norfolk. Unpublished report: Norvic Archaeology report 30.

Ennis, T. 2009, Beck Road, Isleham, Cambridgeshire. Archaeological evaluation. Unpublished report: Essex County Council Field Archaeology Unit report 2018.

Ennis, T. 2012, Plot K, Chelmsford Business Park, Springfield, Chelmsford, Essex. Archaeological excavation. Unpublished report: Essex County Council Field Archaeology Unit report 2365.

Ennis, T. 2013, Plot L, Chelmsford Business Park, Springfield, Chelmsford, Essex. Archaeological excavation. Unpublished report: Essex County Council Field Archaeology Unit report 2570.

Ennis, T. 2014, Archaeological excavation. Plot N, Chelmsford Business Park, Springfield, Chelmsford, Essex. A post-excavation assessment and updated project design. Unpublished Archaeology South East report 2013330.

Evans, C. and Ten Harkel, L. 2010, 'Roman Cambridge's early settlement and Via Devana: excavations at Castle Street', *Proceedings of the Cambridge Antiquarian Society* 99, 35–60.

Evans, D.H. and Jarrett, M.G. 1987, 'The deserted village of West Welpington, Northumberland: third report, Part one', *Archaeologia Aeliana* 5th Ser. 15, 199–312.

Everson, P., Taylor, C.C. and Dunn, C.J. 1991, *Change and Continuity: Rural Settlement in North-West Lincolnshire*, London: HMSO.

Failes, A. 2007, Archaeological investigation during construction at Healthlinc House, Cliff Road, Welton, Lincolnshire (WECR 06). Unpublished report: Archaeological Project Services report 24/07.

Failes, A. 2009, Archaeological watching brief on groundworks at SS Peter and Paul Church, Top Street, Wing, Rutland. Unpublished report: Archaeological Project Services report 22/09.

Fairbrother, J.R. 1990, *Faccombe Netherton: Excavations of a Saxon and Medieval Manorial Complex*, London: British Museum Occasional Paper 74.

Fasham, P.J. and Keevill, G. 1995, *Brighton Hill South (Hatch Warren): an Iron Age Farmstead and Deserted Medieval Village in Hampshire*, Salisbury: Wessex Archaeology Report 7.

Fauroux, M. ed. 1961, *Recueil des actes des ducs de Normandie de 911 à 1066*, Caen: Caron.

Fenton-Thomas, C. 2007, 'Excavations at The Gardens, Sprotbrough, South Yorkshire', *Yorkshire Archaeological Journal* 79, 231–310.

Fernie, E. 1978, 'The proportions of the St Gall Plan', *Art Bulletin* 60 (4), 583–89.

Fernie, E. 1979, 'Observations on the Norman plan of Ely Cathedral', in *Medieval Art and Architecture at Ely Cathedral*, London: Transactions of the Annual Conference of the British Archaeological Association 1976, 1–7.

Fernie, E. 1983, *The Architecture of the Anglo-Saxons*, London: Batsford.

Fernie, E. 1985, 'Anglo-Saxon lengths: the "Northern" system, the perch and the foot', *Archaeological Journal* 142, 246–54; also in Fernie 1995, 383–91.

Fernie, E. 1987, 'Reconstructing Edward's Abbey at Westminster', in N. Stratford (ed.), *Romanesque and Gothic: Essays for George Zarnecki*, Woodbridge: Boydell and Brewer, 63–7.

Fernie, E. 1990, 'A beginner's guide to the study of architectural proportions and systems of length', in E. Fernie and P. Crossley (eds), *Medieval Architecture and its Intellectual Context: Studies in Honour of Peter Kidson*, London: Hambledon Press, 229–37.

Fernie, E. 1991, 'Anglo-Saxon lengths and the evidence of the buildings', *Medieval Archaeology* 35, 1–5; also in Fernie 1995, 392–7.

Fernie, E. 1995, *Romanesque Architecture: Design, Meaning and Metrology*, London: Pindar.

Fernie, E. 2002, 'Introduction', in N.Y. Wu (ed.), *Ad Quadratum: the Practical Application of Geometry in Medieval Architecture*, Aldershot: Ashgate, 1–9.

Fernie, E. 2009, 'Edward the Confessor's Westminster Abbey', in R. Mortimer (ed.), *Edward the Confessor, the Man and the Legend*, Woodbridge: Boydell Press, 139–50.

Fernie, E. 2015, 'Norwich Cathedral revisited: spiral piers and architectural geometry', in T.A. Heslop and H.E. Lunnon (eds), *Norwich: Medieval and Early Modern Art, Architecture and Archaeology*, Leeds: Transactions of the Annual Conference of the British Archaeological Association 38, 44–56.

Fernie, E. 2018, 'Éléments des méthodes du dessin utilisées pour les édifices romains et médiévaux', in Marcello Angheben, Pierre Martin and Eric Sparhubert (eds), *Regards croisés sur le monument médiéval: mélanges offerts à Claude Andrault-Schmitt*, Turnhout: Brepols, 93–104.

Fernie, E. and Fearn, T. in press, 'A response to Werner Jacobsen's critique of the use of the square root of two in the St Gall Plan, with a statistical analysis of the techniques employed in the drawing'.

Field, N. 1994, Sudbeck Lane, Welton: archaeological evaluation. Unpublished report: Lindsey Archaeological Services.

Fleming, A. 1988, *The Dartmoor Reaves: Investigating Prehistoric Land Divisions*, London: Batsford; 2nd edn Oxford: Windgather Press, 2008.

Fletcher, T. 2004a, Late medieval features at 1 Cheyney Street, Steeple Morden, Cambridgeshire: an archaeological evaluation. Unpublished report: Cambridgeshire County Council Archaeological Field Unit report 719.

Fletcher, T. 2004b, Medieval ditches at the The New Vicarage, 2 Fulbourn Old Drift, Cherry Hinton, Cambridge: an archaeological excavation. Unpublished report: Cambridgeshire County Council Archaeological Field Unit report 762.

Foard, G. 1978, 'Systematic fieldwalking and the investigation of Saxon settlement in Northamptonshire', *World Archaeology* 9, 357–74.

Foard, G., Hall, D. and Partida, T. 2009, *Rockingham Forest: an Atlas of the Medieval and Early-Modern Landscape*. Northampton: Northamptonshire Record Society General Series 44.

Ford, S., Howell, I. and Taylor, K. 2004, *The Archaeology of the Aylesbury-Chalgrove Gas Pipeline, and the Orchard, Walton Road, Aylesbury*, Reading: Thames Valley Archaeological Services Monograph 5.

Fox, H.S.A. 1981, 'Approaches to the adoption of the Midland system', in T. Rowley (ed.), *The Origins of Open Field Agriculture*, London: Croom Helm, 64–111.

Fox, H. 2012, *Dartmoor's Alluring Uplands. Transhumance and Pastoral Management in the Middle Ages*, Exeter: University of Exeter Press.

France, N.E. and Gobel, B.M. 1985, *The Romano-British Temple at Harlow, Essex*, Gloucester: Alan Sutton Publishing for the West Essex Archaeological Group.

Franceschelli, C. 2008, 'Dynamiques de transmission de la morphologie agraire', *Agri Centuriati* 5, 77–105.

Franceschelli, C. and Marabini, S. 2007, *Lettura di un Territorio Sepolto. La Pianura Lughese in Età Romana*, Bologna: Ante Quem.

Fulford, M. 1990, 'The landscape of Roman Britain', *Landscape History* 12, 25–41.

Gannon, A. 2003, *The Iconography of Early Anglo-Saxon Coinage: Sixth to Eighth Centuries*, Oxford: Oxford University Press.

Gardiner, M. 2009, 'Dales, long lands, and the medieval division of land in eastern England', *Agricultural History Review* 57 (1), 1–14.

Gardiner, M. 2013, 'The sophistication of late Anglo-Saxon timber buildings', in M.D.J. Bintley and M.G. Shapland (eds), *Trees and Timber in the Anglo-Saxon World*, Oxford: Oxford University Press, 45–77.

Garlant, B. 2011, Archaeological monitoring and recording on groundworks at Healthlinc House, Cliff Road, Welton, Lincolnshire, unpublished Archaeological Project Services report 71/11.

Garrett, M. 2004, Church End Farm, Stow, Lincolnshire. Archaeological watching brief. Unpublished report: Lindsey Archaeological Services report 732.

Gem, R. 1992, 'Reconstructions of St Augustine's Abbey, Canterbury, in the Anglo-Saxon Period', in N. Ramsay *et al.* (eds), *St Dunstan: his Life, Times and Cult*, Woodbridge: Boydell Press, 57–73.

Gerrard, C. with Aston, M. 2007, *The Shapwick Project, Somerset. A Rural Landscape Explored*, Leeds: Society for Medieval Archaeology Monograph 25.

Gilbert, D. 2005, An archaeological evaluation at Donnington Middle School, Iffley, Oxford. Unpublished report: John Moore Heritage Services.

Gill, L. 2006, Watching brief: land at 3 to 5 Mill Road Marcham, Oxfordshire. Unpublished report: Archaeological Services and Consultancy Ltd report 766/MMR/2.

Gilmour, N. 2011, Archaeological evaluation at Cherry Hinton Junior School, Cambridgeshire. Archaeological evaluation. Unpublished report: Oxford Archaeology East report 1248.

Gonner, E.C.K. 1912, *Common Land and Enclosure*, London: Macmillan.

Grant, J. and McConnell, D. 2004, Land off Vicarage Lane, Podington, Bedfordshire. Trial trench evaluation. Unpublished report: Archaeological Solutions Ltd report 1615.

Grant, J. and Wilkins, B. 2002, 15–17 Hay Street, Steeple Morden, Cambridgeshire. An archaeological evaluation. Unpublished report: Hertfordshire Archaeological Trust.

Gray, H.L. 1915, *English Field Systems*. Cambridge, MA: Harvard University Press.

Gregson, R. 2012, Land at Home Farm Manor, High Street, Wrestlingworth, Bedfordshire. Archaeological field evaluation and heritage asset assessment. Unpublished report: Albion Archaeology report 2013/25.

Gregson, R. 2013, Land at Home Farm Manor, High Street, Wrestlingworth, Bedfordshire. Archaeological observation, investigation, recording, analysis and publication. Unpublished report: Albion Archaeology report 2013/104.

Gregson, R. and Koziminski, M. 2009, Land at 134 High Street, Kempston, Bedfordshire: a programme of archaeological observation, recording, analysis and publication. Unpublished report: Albion Archaeology report 2005/10.

Grierson, P. 1972, *English Linear Measures: an Essay in Origins*, The Stenton Lecture 1971, Reading: University of Reading.

Grigg, E. 2015, 'Early medieval dykes (400 to 850 AD)', unpublished Ph.D. thesis, University of Manchester.

Grocock, C. and Wood, I.N. (eds) 2013, *Abbots of Wearmouth and Jarrow*, Oxford: Oxford University Press.

Guerreau, A. 1995, 'Remarques sur l'arpentage selon Bertrand Boysset (Arles, vers 1400–1410)', in E. Mornet (ed.), *Campagnes Médiévales: l'Homme et son Espace; Études Offertes à Robert Fossier*, Paris: Publications de la Sorbonne, 87–102.

Haarnagel, W. 1979, *Die Grabung Feddersen Wierde: Methode, Hasbau, Sidelungs- Und Wirtschaftsformen Sowie Sozialstruktur*, Wiesbaden: Franz Steiner.

Hall, D. 1981a, 'The origins of open field agriculture: the archaeological fieldwork evidence', in T. Rowley (ed.), *The Origins of Open Field Agriculture*, London: Croom Helm, 22–38.

Hall, D. 1981b, 'The changing landscape of the Cambridgeshire silt fen', *Landscape History* 3, 37–49.

Hall, D. 1982, *Medieval Fields*, Aylesbury: Shire Books.

Hall, D. 1983, 'Fieldwork and field books: studies in early layout', in B.K. Roberts and R.E. Glasscock (eds), *Villages, Fields and Frontiers: Studies in European Rural Settlement in the Medieval and Early Modern Periods*, Oxford: British Archaeological Reports (British Series) 185, 115–33.

Hall, D. 1995, *The Open Fields of Northamptonshire*, Northampton: Northamptonshire Records Society 38.

Hall, D. 1996, *The Fenland Project, Number 10: Cambridgeshire Survey, Isle of Ely and Wisbech*, Cambridge: East Anglian Archaeology 79.

Hall, D. 2012, 'Field systems and land-holdings', in S. Wrathmell (ed.), *A History of Wharram and Its Neighbours*, York: Wharram: A Study of Settlement on the Yorkshire Wolds 13, 278–88.

Hall, D. 2014, *The Open Fields of England*, Oxford: Oxford University Press.

Hall, J.J., Little, A. and Locock, M. 1996, 'Excavations at Attlebridge, 1989', *Norfolk Archaeology* 42(3), 296–320.

Hamerow, H. 1993, *Excavations at Mucking Volume 2: The Anglo-Saxon Settlement*, London: English Heritage.

Hamerow, H. 2002, *Early Medieval Settlements: the Archaeology of Rural Communities in North-West Europe 400–900*, Oxford: Oxford University Press.

Hamerow, H. 2012, *Rural Settlements and Society in Anglo-Saxon England*, Oxford: Oxford University Press.

Hamilton, L. 2009, An archaeological scheme of monitoring works: Plot 3, The Old Vicarage, Norbeck Lane, Welton, Lincolnshire. Unpublished report: Pre-Construct Archaeology report 447 08–01 Rev A.

Hammond, S. 2007, Iffley House, Anne Greenwood Close, Iffley Turn, Oxford: an archaeological evaluation. Unpublished report: Thames Valley Archaeological Services.

Hardy, A., Dodd, A. and Keevill, G.D. 2003, *Ælfric's Abbey: Excavations at Eynsham Abbey, Oxfordshire, 1989–1992*, Oxford: Oxford Archaeological Unit, Thames Valley Landscapes Monograph 16.

Harmer, R., Peterken, G., Kerr, G. and Paulton, P. 2001, 'Vegetation changes during 100 years of development of two secondary woodlands in abandoned arable lands', *Biological Conservation* 101, 291–304.

Hartley, R.F. 1983, *The Medieval Earthworks of Rutland; A Survey*. Leicester: Leicestershire Museums, Art Galleries and Records Service.

Hartley, R.F. 1984, *The Medieval Earthworks of North-West Leicestershire*. Leicester: Leicestershire Museums, Art Galleries and Records Service.

Hartley, R.F. 1987, *The Medieval Earthworks of North-East Leicestershire*. Leicester: Leicestershire Museums, Art Galleries and Records Service.

Harvey, M. 1978, *The Morphological and Tenurial Structure of a Yorkshire Township: Preston in Holderness 1066–1750*, London: Queen Mary College Occasional Papers in Geography 13.

Harvey, M. 1980, 'Regular field and tenurial arrangements in Holderness, Yorkshire', *Journal of Historical Geography* 6, 3–16.

Harvey, M. 1981, 'The origin of planned field systems in Holderness, Yorkshire', in T. Rowley (ed.), *The Origins of Open Field Agriculture*, London: Croom Helm, 184–201.

Harvey, M. 1982, 'Regular open-field systems on the Yorkshire Wolds', *Landscape History* 4, 29–39.

Harvey, M. 1983, 'Planned field systems in Eastern Yorkshire; some thoughts on their origin', *Agricultural History Review* 31, 91–103.

Harvey, P.D.A. 1989, 'Initiative and authority in settlement change', in M. Aston, D. Austin and C. Dyer (eds), *The Rural Settlements of Medieval England*, Oxford: Blackwells, 31–43.

Haslam, J. 1980, 'A Middle Saxon iron smelting site at Ramsbury, Wiltshire', *Medieval Archaeology* XXIV, 1–68.

Haslam, J. 2003, 'Excavations at Cricklade, Wiltshire, 1975', *Internet Archaeology* 14 http://dx.doi.org/10.11141/ia.14.1.

Hatton, A. 2001, Medieval Features at 69 Mill Lane, Fordham. An archaeological evaluation. Unpublished report: Cambridgeshire County Council Archaeological Field Unit.

Hatton, R.C. 2001, Early-Mid Saxon activity at land adjacent to No. 12 Hillside Meadow, Fordham: An archaeological evaluation. Unpublished report: Cambridgeshire County Council Archaeological Field Unit report A192.

Haverfield, F. 1913, *Ancient Town Planning*, Oxford: Clarendon Press.

Haverfield, F. 1921, 'Centuriation in Essex', *Transactions of the Essex Archaeological Society* new series 15, 115–25.

Hayfield, C. 1984, 'Wawne, East Riding of Yorkshire: a case study in settlement morphology, *Landscape History* 6, 41–68.

Heighway, C. and Bryant, R. 1999, *The Golden Minster: the Anglo-Saxon Minster and Later Medieval Priory of St Oswald at Gloucester*, York: Council for British Archaeology.

Heslop, D. and Aberg, A. 1990, 'Excavations at Tollesby, Cleveland, 1972 and 1974', in B. Vyner (ed.), *Medieval Rural Settlement in North-East England*, Durham: Architectural and Archaeological Society of Durham and Northumberland Research Report 2, 77–106.

Hewson, A.D. 1980, 'The Ashanti weights – a statistical evaluation', *Journal of Archaeological Science* 7 (4), 363–70.

Hickling, S. 2004, Land to the rear of Manor Farm House, High Street, Fen Drayton: an archaeological evaluation. Unpublished report: Cambridgeshire County Council Archaeological Field Unit report 773.

Hill, D. and Rumble, A. (eds) 1996, *The Defence of Wessex: the Burghal Hidage and Anglo-Saxon Fortifications*, Manchester: Manchester University Press.

Hill, D. and Worthington, M. 2003, *Offa's Dyke: History and Guide*, Stroud: Tempus.

Hill, P. 1997, *Whithorn and St Ninian: the Excavation of a Monastic Town 1984–91*, Stroud: Sutton Publishing.

Hilton, R.H. and Rahtz, P.A. 1966, 'Upton, Gloucestershire, 1959–64', *Transactions of the Bristol and Gloucestershire Archaeological Society* 85, 70–146.

Hinchcliffe, J. 1986, 'An early medieval settlement at Cowage Farm, Foxley, near Malmesbury', *Archaeological Journal* 143, 240–59.

Hines, J. and Bayliss, A. 2013, *Anglo-Saxon Graves and Grave Goods of the 6th and 7th Centuries AD: a Chronological Framework*, London: Society for Medieval Archaeology Monograph 33.

Holmes, M. and Walker, C. 2012, An archaeological evaluation of land at Priory Lane, Marcham, Oxfordshire, October 2012. Unpublished report: Northamptonshire Archaeology report 12/182.

Hope-Taylor, B. 1977, *Yeavering: An Anglo-British Centre of Early Northumbria*, London: HMSO.

Horn, W. 1966, 'The dimensional inconsistencies of the Plan of St Gall', *Art Bulletin* 48, 285–308.

Horn, W. and Born, E. 1979, *The Plan of St Gall*, Berkeley: University of California Press.

Huber, F. 2002, 'Der St Galler Klosterplan im Kontext der antiken und mittelalterlichen Architekturzeichnung und Messtechnik', in P. Ochsenbein and K. Schmuki (eds), *Studien zum St Galler Klosterplan II*, St Gall: Historischer Verein des Kantons St Gallen, 233–84.

Huggins, P.J. 1991, 'Anglo-Saxon timber building measurements: recent results', *Medieval Archaeology* 35, 6–28.

Huggins, P.J., Rodwell, K. and Rodwell, W.J. 1982, 'Anglo-Saxon and Scandinavian building measurements', in P.J. Drury (ed.), *Structural Reconstruction: Approaches to the Interpretation of the Excavated Remains of Buildings*, Oxford: British Archaeological Reports (British Series) 110, 21–65.

Huitu, M. and Riska, T. (eds) 1977, *Codex Aboensis*, Helsinki: Suomalaisen Kirjallisuuden Kirjapaino.

Hunt, L. 2005, An archaeological watching brief during groundworks on land adjacent to 6 Main Street, Hartshorne, Derbyshire. Unpublished report: University of Leicester Archaeological Services report 2005-55.

Hunt, L. 2007, An archaeological watching brief at Coppice Paddock, Coppice Farm, Glaston, Rutland. Unpublished report: University of Leicester Archaeological Services report 2007-025.

Hyam, A. 2006, An archaeological evaluation on land to the rear of 5 Melton Road, Whissendine, Rutland. Unpublished University of Leicester Archaeological Services report no. 2006-116.

Irvine, J.T. 1894, 'Account of the discovery of part of the Saxon abbey church of Peterborough', *Journal of the British Archaeological Association* 50, 45–54.

Ivens, R.J., Busby, P. and Shepherd, N. 1995, *Tattenhoe and Westbury: Two Deserted Medieval Settlement in Milton Keynes*, Aylesbury: Buckinghamshire Archaeological Society Monograph Series 8.

Jacobsen, W. 1992, *Der Klosterplan von St. Gallen und die Karolingische Architektur. Entwicklung und Wandel von Form und Bedeutung im Fränkischen Kirchenbau Zwischen 751 und 840*, Berlin: Deutsche Verlag für Kunstwissenschaft.

Johnson, D. 2013, Excavation of two Anglo-Saxon-period farmsteads in Brows Pasture, Chapel-le-Dale, North Yorkshire. Unpublished report: Yorkshire Dales National Park Authority report SYD 13981.

Jones, B. and Mattingly, D. 1990, *An Atlas of Roman Britain*, Oxford: Blackwell.

Jones, R. and Page, R. 2006, *Medieval Villages in an English Landscape: Beginnings and Ends*, Macclesfield: Windgather Press.

Kain, R.J.P. and Oliver, R. 1995, *The Tithe Maps of England and Wales: A Cartographic Analysis and County-by-County Catalogue*, Cambridge: Cambridge University Press.

Kain, R.J.P. and Oliver, R. 2001, *Historic Parishes of England and Wales*, Colchester: History Data Service, http://www.ahds.ac.uk/history/collections/hpew.htm.

Kelly, S. 1995, *Charters of St Augustine's Abbey, Canterbury, and Minster-in-Thanet*, Anglo-Saxon Charters IV, Oxford: Oxford University Press.

Kelly, S. 2009, *Charters of Peterborough Abbey*, Anglo-Saxon Charters XIV, Oxford: Oxford University Press.

Kemp, S. and Spoerry, P. 2002, Evaluation of Iron Age, Roman and Saxon archaeology at the proposed Wellcome Trust Genome Campus Extension, Hinxton, Cambridgeshire. TL5004333 Environmental Statement Technical Annex C. Unpublished report: Cambridgeshire County Council Archaeological Field Unit report 149.

Kendall, D.G. 1974, 'Hunting quanta', *Philosophical Transactions of the Royal Society, London* Series B 276 (1257), 231–66.

Kendall, W.S. 2013, 'Modules for Anglo-Saxon constructions': Appendix to J. Blair, 'Grid-Planning in Anglo-Saxon Settlements: the Short Perch and the Four-Perch Module', *Anglo-Saxon Studies in Archaeology and History* 18, 55–7.

Kenney, S. 1999, Late Saxon settlement on land adjacent to 63 Church End, Cherry Hinton: an archaeological evaluation. Unpublished report: Cambridgeshire County Council Archaeological Field Unit report 163.

Kenney, S. 2001, Undated ditches at Steeple Morden Primary School: an archaeological evaluation. Unpublished report: Cambridgeshire County Council Archaeological Field Unit report A185.

Kenney, S. 2004, A medieval croft at the former allotments, Fordham Road, Isleham: an archaeological evaluation. Unpublished report: Cambridgeshire County Council Archaeological Field Unit report 756.

Kenyon, D. and Watts, M. 2006, 'An Anglo-Saxon Enclosure at Copsehill Road, Lower Slaughter: excavations in 1999', *Transactions of the Bristol and Gloucestershire Archaeological Society* 124, 73–109.

Keynes, S. 1998, 'King Alfred and the Mercians', in M.A.S. Blackburn and D.N. Dumville (eds), *Kings, Currency and Alliances*, Woodbridge: Boydell, 1–45.

Keynes, S. and Lapidge, M. 1983, *Alfred the Great*, Harmondsworth: Penguin.

Kidson, P. 1990, 'A metrological investigation', *Journal of the Warburg and Courtauld Institutes* 53, 71–97.

Kipling, R. 2009, An archaeological evaluation at Hollytop House, Lynden Road, Manton, Rutland. Unpublished report: University of Leicester Archaeological Services report 2009-177.

Kirby, D.P. 1991, *The Earliest English Kings*, London: Unwin Hyman.

Kjølbye-Biddle, B. 1986, 'The 7th-Century minster at Winchester interpreted', in L.A.S. Butler and R.K. Morris (eds), *The Anglo-Saxon Church: Papers on History, Architecture and Archaeology in Honour of Dr H.M. Taylor*, London: Council for British Archaeology Research Report 60, 196–209.

Kjølbye-Biddle, B. 1998, 'Anglo-Saxon Baptisteries of the 7th and 8th Centuries: Winchester and Repton', in *Acta XIII Congressus Internationalis Archaeologiae Christianae* II, Vatican City and Split, 757–78.

Knight, M. 1998, 12 West Street, Isleham, Cambridgeshire. An archaeological evaluation. Unpublished report: Cambridge Archaeological Unit report 246.

Krämer, W. 1951, 'Frühmittelalterliche Siedlung bei Bergheim, Lkdr. Neuburg a.d. Donau', *Germania* 29, 139–41.

Lapidge, M. 2006, *The Anglo-Saxon Library*, Oxford: Oxford University Press.

Lavigne, C. 2002, *Essai sur la planification agraire au Moyen Âge: les paysages neufs de la Gascogne médiévale*, Bordeaux: Scripta Varia 5.

Leigh, D.J. 2008, An archaeological watching brief at Tempsford Hall, Station Road, Temspford, Bedfordshire, July–November 2007. Unpublished report: Northamptonshire Archaeology report 08/041.

Lewis, C., Mitchell-Fox, P. and Dyer, C. 1997, *Village, Hamlet and Field*, Manchester: Manchester University Press.

Licence, T. (ed.) 2014, *Bury St Edmunds and the Norman Conquest*, Woodbridge: Boydell.

Lilley, K.D. 2009, *City and Cosmos: the Medieval World in Urban Form*, London: Reaktion.

Lodoen, A. 2007, St Peter's Church, Wrestlingworth, Bedfordshire. Archaeological watching brief. Unpublished report: Albion Archaeology report 2007/50.

Losco-Bradley, S. and Kinsley, G. 2002, *Catholme: an Anglo-Saxon Settlement on the Trent Gravels in Staffordshire*, Nottingham: Nottingham University Department of Archaeology.

Lucy, S., Tipper, J. and Dickens, A. 2009, *The Anglo-Saxon Settlement and Cemetery at Bloodmoor Hill, Carlton Colville, Suffolk*, Cambridge: East Anglian Archaeology 131.

Luke, M. 2009, Kempston Rural Lower School, Kempston Church End, Bedfordshire. Summary report for archaeological observation and investigations associated with a new hard play area. Unpublished report: Albion Archaeology report 2009/119.

Luke, M., Edmondson, G. and Wells, J. 1999, Cutler Hammer Sportsground. Archaeological field evaluation. Unpublished report: Bedfordshire County Archaeology Service report 1999/33.

Luke, M., Edgeworth, M. and Wells, J. 2000, Land between Box End and Church End, Kempston, Bedford. Archaeological field evaluation. Unpublished report: Bedfordshire County Archaeology Service report 2000/28.

McBride, A. 2016, 'An early Anglo-Saxon great hall at Benson? An alternative interpretation of the excavated evidence', *Oxoniensia* 81, 19–25.

Macaulay, S. 2000, Medieval settlement remains at West Street, Isleham: an archaeological monitoring brief. Unpublished report: Cambridgeshire County Council Archaeological Field Unit report 175.

McCord, N. and Thompson, R. 1998, *The Northern Counties from AD1000*, London: Longman.

McDonald, T. and Trevarthen, M. 1998, Excavations at Station Road, Gamlingay, Cambridgeshire. Interim Site Narrative. Unpublished report: Hertfordshire Archaeological Trust report 317.

McNicoll-Norbury, J. and Lewis, J. 2010, St Kenelm's Church, Church Enstone, Oxfordshire. Unpublished report: Thames Valley Archaeological Services.

Maitland, F.W. 1897, *Domesday Book and Beyond*, Cambridge: Cambridge University Press.

Malcolm, G., Bowsher, D. and Cowie, R. 2003, *Middle Saxon London: Excavations at the Royal Opera House 1989–99*, London: Museum of London Archaeological Service Monograph 15.

Margary, I. 1940, 'Roman centuriation at Ripe', *Sussex Archaeological Collections* 81, 31–41.

Martin, E. and Satchell, M. 2008, *Wheare Most Inclosures be. East Anglian Fields: History, Morphology and Management*, Ipswich: East Anglian Archaeology 124.

Maull, A. 2000, Excavation of a medieval moated enclosure in Tempsford Park, Tempsford, Bedfordshire, 1999. Assessment Report and Updated Project Design. Unpublished report: Northamptonshire Archaeology.

Meadows, I. 2002, Peterborough Road, Warmington, Northamptonshire. Excavations 1998 final report. Unpublished report: Northamptonshire Archaeology.

Medlycott, M. 2011, *The Roman Town of Great Chesterford*, Chelmsford: East Anglian Archaeology 137.

Mellor, V. 2004, Archaeological evaluation on land at Church Close, Whissonsett, Norfolk. Unpublished report: Archaeological Project Services report 128/04.

Miciak, L. and Atkinson, M. 2014, Brays Lane, Rochford Essex: post-excavation assessment report. Unpublished report: Essex County Council Field Archaeology Unit/Archaeology South East report 2014093.

Millbank, D. 2008, 36 Newland Street, Eynsham, Oxfordshire: an archaeological evaluation. Unpublished report: Thames Valley Archaeological Services.

Moore, J. 2004, An archaeological watching brief at The Shrubbery, 26 High Street, Eynsham, Oxfordshire. Unpublished report: John Moore Heritage Services.

Mordue, J. 2012, The Bury, Cemetery Road, Kempston, Bedford Borough: archaeological evaluation. Unpublished report: Cotswold Archaeology report 122347.

Morris, S. and Walford, J. 2008, Geophysical survey and archaeological excavation on land off the Bedford Road, Little Houghton, Northamptonshire. Unpublished report: Northamptonshire Archaeology report 08/81.

Mortimer, R. 2000, 'Village development and ceramic sequence: the Middle to Late Saxon village at Lordship Lane, Cottenham, Cambridgeshire', *Proceedings of the Cambridge Antiquarian Society* 39, 5–33.

Mortimer, R. 2003, Rosemary Lane, Church End, Cherry Hinton. Unpublished report: Cambridge Archaeological Unit report 561.

Mortimer, R. 2007, Land at Coldham's Lane, Cherry Hinton, Cambridgeshire. Evaluation report. Unpublished report: Cambridgeshire Archaeology Archaeological Field Unit report 948.

Mortimer, R., Regan, R. and Lucy, S. 2005, *The Saxon and Medieval Settlement at West Fen Road, Ely: The Ashwell Site*, Cambridge: East Anglian Archaeology 110.

Mould, C. 1999, Hillside Meadow, Fordham, Cambridgeshire. Archaeological Investigations 1998. Post-Excavation Assessment and Research Design. Unpublished report: Birmingham University Field Archaeology Unit.

Mumford, J. 2009, Church of St Mary the Virgin, Iffley, Oxford: archaeological watching brief report. Unpublished report: Oxford Archaeology report 2764.

Murray, J. 1996, Land off Station Road, Gaminglay, Cambridgeshire. An archaeological evaluation. Unpublished report: Hertfordshire Archaeological Trust report 195.

Murray, J. and Vaughan, T. 1999, Land at 69–115 Church End, Cherry Hinton, Cambridge. An archaeological evaluation. Unpublished report: Hertfordshire Archaeological Trust report 487.

Murray, L. 2011, Archaeological watching brief of foundation trenches at New Road, Shipdham, Norfolk. Unpublished report: Archaeological Project Services report 1/11.

Mynard D.C. 1994, *Excavations on Medieval Sites in Milton Keynes*, Aylesbury: Buckinghamshire Archaeological Society Monograph Series 6.

Neal, D.S., Wardle, A. and Hunn, J. 1990, *Excavation of the Iron Age, Roman and Medieval Settlement at Gorhambury, St Albans*. London: English Heritage Archaeological Report 14.

Newboult, J. 2008a, Wrestlingworth Lower School, Church Lane, Wrestlingworth. Archaeological observation, investigation, recording, analysis and publication. Unpublished report: Albion Archaeology report 2008/132.

Newboult, J. 2008b, Ursula Taylor Lower School, High Street, Clapham. Archaeological observation and recording. Unpublished report: Albion Archaeology report 2008/130.

Newton, A. 2006, Archaeological excavations at Fordham Road, Isleham, Cambridgeshire. Unpublished report: Archaeological Solutions report 2090.

Nightingale, M.D. 1952, 'A Roman settlement near Rochester', *Archaeologia Cantiana* 65, 150–9.

O'Brien, L. 2003, Excavations at Kempston Mill, Mill Lane, Kempston, Bedfordshire. Unpublished report: Archaeological Solutions.

O'Brien, L. and Gardner, R. 2002, Land adjacent to 20 Hillside Meadow, Fordham, Cambridgeshire. An Archaeological desk based assessment and trial trench evaluation. Unpublished report: Hertfordshire Archaeological Trust report 1062.

Orderic Vitalis 1969–80, *Historia Ecclesiastica*, ed. M. Chibnall, 6 vols, Oxford: Clarendon.

Page, M. and Jones, R. 2007, 'Stability and instability in medieval village plans: case-studies in Whittlewood', in M. Gardiner and S. Rippon (eds), *Medieval Landscapes*, Macclesfield: Windgather Press, 139–52.

Pakkanen, J. 2004a, 'The temple of Zeus at Stratos: new observations on the building design', *Arctos – Acta Philologica Fennica*, 38, 95–121.

Pakkanen, J. 2004b, 'The Toumba Building at Lefkandi: a statistical method for detecting a design-unit', *The Annual of the British School at Athens* 99, 257–71.

Palola, A.-P. 1997, *Maunu Tavast ja Olavi Maununpoika*, Helsinki: Suomen Kirkkohistoriallinen Seura.

Pallister, A. and Wrathmell, S. 1990, 'The deserted village of West Hartburn, third report: excavation of site D and discussion', in B. Vyner (ed.), *Medieval Rural Settlement in North-East England*, Durham: Architectural and Archaeological Society of Durham and Northumberland Research Report 2, 59–75.

Palliser, D.M. 1993, 'Domesday Book and the "Harrying of the North"', *Northern History* 29, 1–23.

Palmer, J. 1998, 'War and Domesday waste', in M. Strickland (ed.), *Armies, Chivalry and Warfare in Medieval Britain and France*, Stamford: Paul Watkins, 256–76.

Parker, N. 2007, Archaeological evaluation on land between 17 and 21 Lincoln Road, Welton, Lincolnshire. Unpublished report: Archaeological Project Services report 153/07.

Parsons, D. and Sutherland, D.S. 2013, *The Anglo-Saxon Church of All Saints, Brixworth, Northamptonshire*, Oxford: Oxbow.

Partida, T., Hall, D. and Foard, G. 2013, *An Atlas of Northamptonshire: The Medieval and Early-Modern Landscape*, Oxford: Oxbow Books.

Patrick, C. and Rátkai, S. 2011, 'Hillside Meadow, Fordham', in R. Cutler *et al.*, *Five Sites in Cambridgeshire*, Oxford: British Archaeological Reports (British Series) 528, 41–122.

Peachey, M. 2011, Archaeological evaluation on land adjacent to Wolvey Hall, Hall Road, Wolvey, Warwickshire. Unpublished report: Archaeological Project Services report 135/11.

Peterson, J.W.M. 1988, 'Roman cadastres in Britain I (South Norfolk)', *Dialogues d'Histoire Ancienne* 14, 167–99.

Peterson, J.W.M. 1990, 'Roman cadastres in Britain II. Eastern A', *Dialogues d'Histoire Ancienne* 16, 233–72.

Peytremann, E. 2003, *Archéologie de l'Habitat Rural Dans Le Nord de la France du IVe au XIIe Siècle*, Saint-Germain-en-Laye: AFAM.

Philp, B. 2003, *The Discovery and Excavation of Anglo-Saxon Dover*, Dover: Kent Archaeological Rescue Unit.

Pixley, J. and Beswick, I. 2005, The Outdoor Centre, Hillgrounds Road, Kempston, Bedfordshire. Programme of archaeological observation, investigation, recording, analysis and publication. Unpublished report: Albion Archaeology report 2005/28.

Pocock, M. 2006, Springfield Business Park Plots G and H, Chelmsford, Essex. Archaeological evaluation by trial trenching and excavation. Unpublished report: Essex County Council Field Archaeology Unit report 1605.

Pocock, M. and Wheeler, H. 1971, 'Excavations at Escomb Church, County Durham', *Journal of the British Archaeological Association* 3rd ser. 34, 11–29.

Porter, S. 2013, 13–15 Mill Street, Eynsham, Oxfordshire. Unpublished report: Thames Valley Archaeological Services.

Portet, P. 1998, 'La mesure géométrique des champs au moyen age', in G. Brunel *et al.* (eds), *Terriers et Plans-Terriers du XIIIᵉ au XVIIIᵉ Siècle*, Mémoires et Documents de l'École des Chartes No. 62, Paris: École Nationale des Chartes, 244–66.

Portet, P. 2004, *Bertrand Boysset, la vie et les œuvres techniques d'un arpenteur médiéval (v.1355–v.1416)*, Paris: Éditions le Manuscrit.

Poulton, R. 2005, 'Excavations of a Saxon and early medieval occupation site at Saxon County School, Shepperton in 1986', *Transactions of the London and Middlesex Archaeological Society* 56, 45–76.

Powlesland, D. 2014, 'Reflections upon the Anglo-Saxon landscape and settlement of the Vale of Pickering, Yorkshire', in G.R. Owen-Crocker and S.D. Thompson (eds), *Towns and Topography: Essays in Memory of David Hill*, Oxford: Oxbow, 111–23.

Pozorski, Z. 2010, Land at Kempston Mill, Mill Lane, Kempston, Bedfordshire. Archaeological observation, investigation, recording, analysis and publication. Unpublished report: Archaeological Solutions report 3596.

Pozorski, Z. 2011, Land at 21 Stamford Lane, Warmington, Northamptonshire: an archaeological evaluation. Unpublished report: Archaeological Solutions report 3780.

Pre-Construct Archaeology 2008a, Land adjacent to the Welton Family Health Centre, Cliffe Road, Welton, Lincolnshire. Unpublished report: Pre-Construct Archaeology.

Pre-Construct Archaeology 2008b, The Old Vicarage, Norbeck Lane, Welton, Lincolnshire. Unpublished report: Pre-Construct Archaeology.

Preece, T., Luke, M. and Wells, J. 2004, Archaeological salvage investigations at Kempston Box End, Bedfordshire. Provisional summary of results. Unpublished report: Albion Archaeology report 2004/87.

Price, N.S. 2002, *The Viking Way*, Uppsala: Uppsala University.

Querrien, A. 2008, 'Les formes circulaires de l'espace bâti et agricole au moyen âge: tracé, mesure et partage', *Archéologie Médiévale* 38, 123–58.

Rackham, O. 1986, *The History of the Countryside*, London: J.M. Dent and Sons.

Rahtz, P.A. 1969, 'Upton, Gloucestershire, 1964–68', *Transactions of the Bristol and Gloucestershire Archaeological Society* 88, 74–126.

Rahtz, P.A. 1976, 'The building-plan of the Anglo-Saxon monastery of Whitby Abbey', in D.M. Wilson (ed.), *The Archaeology of Anglo-Saxon England*, London: Methuen, 224–5, 459–62.

Rahtz, P.A. 1979, *The Saxon and Medieval Palaces at Cheddar*, Oxford: British Archaeological Reports (British Series) 65.

Rahtz, P.A. and Greenfield, E. 1977, *Excavations at Chew Valley Lake, Somerset*, London: HMSO.

Rahtz, P.A. and Meeson, R. 1992, *An Anglo-Saxon Watermill at Tamworth*, London: Council for British Archaeology.

Ramsey, E. 2005, An archaeological watching brief on land at Altus Windows, Church Hill Road, Wolvey, Warwickshire 2005, Unpublished report: Birmingham Archaeology project number 1286.

Ratcliff, M. 2008, An archaeological evaluation at Sixty Acre Field, Thieves' Bridge Road, Watlington, Norfolk of the Tottenhill S101A sewerage system. Unpublished report: NAU Archaeology report 1838.

Rawes, B. 1979, 'The possibility of Roman land boundaries near Gloucester', *Glevensis* 13, 5–10.

Ray, K. and Bapty, I. 2016, *Offa's Dyke: Landscape and Hegemony in Eighth-Century Britain*, Oxford: Oxbow.

Rayner, T. 2001, Archaeological evaluation of land at Hall Road, Great Hale, Lincolnshire. Unpublished report: Archaeological Project Services report 5/01.

RCHME 1979, *An Inventory of the Historical Monuments in the County of Northampton. Volume II: Archaeological Sites in Central Northamptonshire*, London: HMSO.

RCHME 1981, *An Inventory of the Historical Monuments in the County of Northampton. Volume III: An Inventory of Archaeological Sites in North-West Northamptonshire*, London: HMSO.

Rees, G. 2012, Early medieval occupation and related features at Isleham Recreation Ground, Cambridgeshire: Archaeological excavation. Unpublished report: Oxford Archaeology East report 1369.

Reidy, K. 1997, 'Middle Bronze Age occupation at Great Wakering', *Essex Archaeology and History* 28, 1–11.

Reynolds, A. 2003, 'Boundaries and settlements in later sixth to eleventh century England', *Anglo-Saxon Studies in Archaeology and History* 12, 98–136.

Reynolds, A. and Langlands, A. 2006, 'Social identities on the macro scale: a maximum view of Wansdyke', in W. Davies, G. Hassall and A. Reynolds (eds), *People and Space in the Early Middle Ages AD300–1300*, Turnhout: Brepols, 13–44.

Richmond, I.A. 1963, 'Roman Essex', *Victoria County History of Essex* III, 1–23.

Rippon, S. 1991, 'Early planned landscapes in South East Essex', *Essex Archaeology and History* 22, 46–60.

Rippon, S. 2008, *Beyond the Medieval Village*, Oxford: Oxford University Press.

Rippon, S. 2012, 2012 Olympic Mountain Bike Venue, Hadleigh Farm, Essex: The Evolution of the Historic Landscape. Unpublished report: University of Exeter. <http://hdl.handle.net/10036/4089>.

Rippon, S. 2018, *Kingdom, Civitas, and County: the Evolution of Territory in the English Landscape*, Oxford: Oxford University Press.

Rippon, S., Smart, C., Pears, B. and Fleming, F. 2013, 'The Fields of Britannia: continuity and discontinuity in the pays and regions of Roman Britain', *Landscapes* 14 (1), 33–53.

Rippon, S., Smart, C. and Pears, B. 2015, *The Fields of Britannia*, Oxford: Oxford University Press.

Roberts, B.K. 1987, *The Making of the English Village*, London: Longman.

Roberts, B.K. 2008, *Landscapes, Documents and Maps: Villages in Northern England and Beyond AD900–1250*, Oxford: Oxbow Books.

Roberts, B.K. and Wrathmell, S. 2000, *An Atlas of Rural Settlement in England*, London: English Heritage.

Roberts, B.K. and Wrathmell, S. 2002, *Region and Place. A Study of English Rural Settlement*, London: English Heritage.

Robertson, A. 2006, Springfield Business Park, Chelmsford, Plots C, M and N. Archaeological Evaluation. Interim Summary. Unpublished report: Essex County Council Field Archaeology Unit.

Rodwell, W.J. and Rodwell, K.A. 1986, *Rivenhall: Investigation of a Villa, Church and Village, 1950–77*, London: Council for British Archaeology Research Report 55.

Rudge, A. 2002, Roman remains at 15/17 Hay Street, Steeple Morden, Cambridgeshire. Unpublished report: Cambridgeshire County Council Archaeological Field Unit report A215.

Sawyer, P.H. 1968, *Anglo-Saxon Charters: An Annotated List and Bibliography*, London: Royal Historical Society.

Screeton, A. 2001, 'Skelton village, history and excavation', *Yorkshire Archaeological Journal* 73, 3–18.

Semple, S. 2013, *Perceptions of the Prehistoric in Anglo-Saxon England: Religion, Ritual, and Rulership in the Landscape*, Oxford: Oxford University Press.

SHARP 2014, *Digging Sedgeford: a People's Archaeology*, Cromer: Poppyland Publishing.

Sharpe, M. 1918, 'Centuriation in Middlesex', *English Historical Review* 33, 489–92.

Sheppard, J. 1966, 'Pre-enclosure field and settlement patterns in an English township', *Geografiska Annaler* 48, Series B, 59–77.

Sheppard, J. 1973, 'Field systems of Yorkshire', in A.R.H. Baker and R.A. Butlin (eds), *Studies of Field Systems in the British Isles*, Cambridge: Cambridge University Press, 145–87.

Sheppard, J. 1974, 'Metrological analysis of regular village plans in Yorkshire', *Agricultural History Review* 22(2), 118–36.

Sheppard, J. 1976, 'Medieval village planning in northern England: some evidence from Yorkshire', *Journal of Historical Geography* 2, 3–20.

Sherlock, S.J. 2004, 'Excavations at the Well House, Long Marston, North Yorkshire', *Yorkshire Archaeological Journal* 76, 113–33.

Shoesmith, R. 1982, *Hereford City Excavations Volume 2: Excavations on and Close to the Defences*, London: Council for British Archaeology Research Reports 46.

Silvester, R.J. 1988, *The Fenland Project Number 3: Marshland and the Nar Valley, Norfolk*, Dereham, East Anglian Archaeology 45.

Slater, A. 2011a, Neath Farm Industrial Estate, Cherry Hinton, Cambridge: an archaeological excavation. Unpublished report: Cambridge Archaeological Unit report 1065.

Slater, A. 2011b, Neath Farm Business Park, Chery Hinton, Cambridge: archaeological evaluation. Unpublished report: Cambridge Archaeological Unit report 1004.

Simpson, S.J., Griffith, F.M. and Holbrook, N. 1989, 'The prehistoric, Roman and early post-Roman site at Hayes Farm, Clyst Honiton, *Proceedings of the Devon Archaeological Society* 47, 1–27.

Smith, A., Allen, M., Brindle, T. and Fulford, M. 2016, *The Rural Settlement of Roman Britain. New Visions of the Countryside of Roman Britain Volume 1*, London: Society for the Promotion of Roman Studies, Britannia Monograph 29.

Smith, L. 2010, Horndon on the Hill Primary School, Hillcrest Road, Horndon on the Hill, Essex. Archaeological monitoring and recording. Unpublished report: Archaeological Solutions Ltd report 3664.

Southall, H.R. and Burton, N. 2004, *GIS of the Ancient Parishes of England and Wales, 1500–1850*. UK Data Service. SN: 4828, http://dx.doi.org/10.5255/UKDA-SN-4828-1.

Sparey Green, C. 1987, *Excavations at Poundbury, Volume 1: the Settlement*, Dorchester: Dorset Natural History and Archaeological Society Monograph 7.

Spoerry, P. and Atkins, R. 2015, *A Late Saxon Village and Medieval Manor: Excavations at Botolph Bridge, Orton Longueville, Peterborough*, Bar Hill: East Anglian Archaeology 153.

Stachura, N. 2004, *Der Plan von St. Gallen: Masseinheit, Massstab und Massangaben oder Das Dilemma in Schlafsaal*, Saint-Juste-la-Pendue: CHITAT.

Stocks, H. 2007, An archaeological evaluation at The Whitehouse, 66 Hay Street, Steeple Morden, Cambridgeshire: an archaeological evaluation. Unpublished report: Cambridgeshire Archaeology Archaeological Field Unit report 932.

Sutermeister, H. 1976, 'Burpham: a Settlement Site Within the Saxon Defences', *Sussex Archaeological Collections* 114, 194–206.

Sutherland, M. and Wotherspoon, M. 2002, 17 Hillside Meadow, Fordham, Cambridgeshire. An Archaeological Evaluation. Unpublished report: Hertfordshire Archaeological Trust report 1118.

Tate, J. 2005, Archaeological watching brief during groundworks on land adjacent to The Priory, Priory Road, Manton, Rutland. Unpublished report: University of Leicester Archaeological Services report 2005-91.

Tate, J. 2006, Archaeological evaluation on land at Dairy Farm, Lyndon Road, Manton, Rutland. Unpublished report: University of Leicester Archaeological Services report 2006-013.

Tate, J. 2007, An archaeological excavation and watching brief on land at Dairy Farm, Lyndon Road, Manton, Rutland. Unpublished report: University of Leicester Archaeological Services report 2007-101.

Taylor, A. 2013, 28 Abberbury Road, Iffley, Oxford: archaeological evaluation. Unpublished report: Thames Valley Archaeological Services.

Taylor, A., Malim, T. and Evans, C. 1994, 'Field-work in Cambridgeshire: October 1993–September 1994', *Proceedings of the Cambridgeshire Antiquarian Society* 83, 167–76.

Taylor, C. 1975, *Fields in the English Landscape*, London: J.M. Dent and Sons.

Taylor, C. 1983, *Village and Farmstead*, London: George Philip and Son.

Taylor, C. 1989, 'Spaldwick, Cambridgeshire', *Proceedings of the Cambridgeshire Antiquarian Society* 78, 71–5.

Taylor, C.C. 2002, 'Nucleated settlement: a view from the frontier', *Landscape History* 24, 53–72.

Taylor, E. 2011, Archaeological evaluation at 18–20 Chapel Street, Warmington, Northamptonshire, August 2011. Unpublished report: Northamptonshire Archaeology report 11/170.

Taylor, G. *et al.* 2003, 'An Early to Middle Saxon settlement at Quarrington, Lincolnshire', *Antiquaries Journal* 83, 231–80.

Taylor, H.M. and Taylor, J. 1965, *Anglo-Saxon Architecture*, vol. 1, Cambridge: Cambridge University Press.

Tester, A., Anderson, S., Riddler, I. and Carr, R. 2014, *Staunch Meadow, Brandon, Suffolk: a High Status Middle Saxon Settlement on the Fen Edge*, Bury St Edmunds: East Anglian Archaeology 151.

Thirsk, J. 1964, 'The common fields', *Past and Present* 29, 3–29.

Thirsk, J. 1966, 'The origins of the common fields', *Past and Present* 33, 142–7.

Thomas, A. and Boucher, A. 2002, *Hereford City Excavations Volume 4: 1976–1990. Further Sites and Evolving Interpretations*, Hereford: Hereford City and County Archaeological Trust.

Thomas, G. 2017, 'Monasteries and places of power in pre-Viking England: trajectories, relationships and interactions', *Anglo-Saxon Studies in Archaeology and History* 20, 97–116.

Thomas, J. 1999, An archaeological excavation on land off Leicester Lane, Desford, Leicestershire. Unpublished report: University of Leicester Archaeological Services report 99/72.

Thomas, J. 2000, An archaeological excavation on land off Leicester Lane, Desford, Leicestershire. Unpublished report: University of Leicester Archaeological Services report 2000/44.

Thomas, J. 2008, 'The archaeology of currently occupied medieval rural settlements: evidence from Leicestershire and Rutland', *Medieval Settlement Research* 23, 42–51.

Thomson, S. 2002, Archaeological watching brief of development on land off Prebend Lane, Welton, Lincolnshire. Unpublished report: Archaeological Project Services report 68/02.

Timby, J.R. *et al.* 2007, *Settlement on the Bedfordshire Claylands: Archaeology along the A421 Great Barford Bypass*, Oxford and Bedford: Oxford Archaeological Unit and Bedfordshire Archaeological Council.

Toneatto, L. 1994–5, *Codices Artis Mensoriae: I Manoscritti degli Antichi Opuscoli Latini d'Agrimensura (V–XIX Sec.)*, Spoleto: Centro Italiano di Studi sull'Alto Medioevo.

Trimble, G. 2006, Church Close, Whissonsett, Norfolk: assessment report and updated post-excavation project design. Unpublished report: NAU Archaeology report 1159.

Trimble, G. and Hoggett, R. 2010, An Archaeological Evaluation on Land at North View Drive, Whissonsett, Norfolk. Unpublished report: NAU Archaeology report 1185.

Trimble, R. 2012, 21 Stamford Lane, Warmington, Northamptonshire. Unpublished report: Witham Archaeology report 38.

Tyler, S. and Major, H. 2005, *The Early Anglo-Saxon Cemetery and Later Saxon Settlement at Springfield Lyons, Essex*, Chelmsford: East Anglian Archaeology 111.

University of Leicester Archaeological Services 2002, An archaeological excavation on land at Grange Farm, Main Street, Glaston, Rutland. Unpublished report: University of Leicester Archaeological Services report 2002-131.

Upex, S. 2003, 'A migration period site at Polebrook, Northamptonshire: surveys and excavations up to 2002', *South Midlands Archaeology* 33, 41–51.

Van der Linden, H. 1982, 'History of the reclamation of the western fenlands and of the organisation of keeping them drained', in H. de Bakker and M.W Van den Berg (eds), *Proceedings of the Symposium on Peat Lands Below Sea Level*, Wageningen: ILRI publication 30, 42–73.

Vitruvius 1970, *de architectura*, ed. and trans. F. Granger, Cambridge, MA: Loeb Classical Library.

Von Mises, R. 1918, 'Über die "Ganzzahligkeit" der Atomgewichte und verwandte Fragen', *Physikalische Zeitschrift* 19, 490–500.

Vyner, B. (ed.) 1990, *Medieval Rural Settlement in North-East England*, Durham: Architectural and Archaeological Society of Durham and Northumberland Research Report 2.

Wacher, J. 1995, *The Towns of Roman Britain*, rev. edn, London: Book Club Associates.

Wade-Martins, P. 1980, *Fieldwork and Excavation on Village Sites in Launditch Hundred, Norfolk*, Gressenhall: East Anglian Archaeology 10.

Walker, C. 2008, An archaeological evaluation at Ursula Taylor Lower School, Clapham, Bedfordshire. Unpublished report: Northamptonshire Archaeology report 07/197.

Walker, C. and Maull, A. 2005, An archaeological excavation ay King William Road, Kempston, Bedfordshire, August 2005. Unpublished report: Northamptonshire Archaeology report 05/146.

Ward, G. 1932–4, 'A Roman colony near Brancaster', *Norfolk Archaeology* 25, 373–85.

Watteau, M. 2011, 'La colonisation agraire médiévale en Alentejo (Portugal)', *Études rurales* 188, 39–72.

Watts, L. and Rahtz, P. 1984, 'Upton deserted medieval village, Blockley, Gloucestershire, 1973', *Transactions of the Bristol and Gloucestershire Archaeological Society* 102, 141–54.

Wessex Archaeology 2007, Clements Park, Southend-On-Sea, Essex. Post-excavation assessment report on archaeological excavations for B&Q/Link Road and Comet and updated project design. Unpublished report: Wessex Archaeology (held by Southend-On-Sea Museum).

West, S. 1985, *West Stow, The Anglo Saxon Village*, Ipswich: East Anglian Archaeology 24.

Wickham, C. 2005, *Framing the Early Middle Ages*, Oxford: Oxford University Press.

Williams, G. 2013, An archaeological watching brief at Abbey Farm Barns, Station Road, Eynsham, Oxfordshire. Unpublished report: John Moore Heritage Services.

Williams, R.J. and Zeepvat, R.J. 1994, *Bancroft: A Late Bronze Age/Iron Age Settlement, Roman Villa and Temple-Mausoleum. Volume 2: Finds and Environmental Evidence*, Aylesbury: Buckinghamshire Archaeological Society Monograph Series 7.

Williamson, T. 1987, 'Early co-axial field systems on the East Anglian boulder clays', *Proceedings of the Prehistoric Society* 53, 419–31.

Williamson, T. 2003, *Shaping Medieval Landscapes: Settlement, Society, Environment*, Macclesfield: Windgather Press.

Williamson, T. 2008, 'Co-axial landscapes: time and topography', in P. Rainbird (ed.), *Monuments in the Landscape*, Stroud: Tempus, 123–35.

Williamson, T. 2013, *Environment, Society and Landscape in Early Medieval England. Time and Topography*, Woodbridge: The Boydell Press.

Williamson, T. 2016, 'The ancient origins of medieval fields: a re-assessment', *Archaeological Journal* 173, 264–87.

Williamson, T., Liddiard, R. and Partida, T. 2013, *Champion: The Making and Unmaking of the English Medieval Landscape*, Liverpool: Liverpool University Press.

Wills, J. 2003, Wilderspin Garage, Fen Drayton, Cambridgeshire: an archaeological evaluation. Unpublished report: Cambridgeshire County Council Archaeological Field Unit report 577.

Wilmott, T., in preparation, *Whitby Abbey: Archaeology and History. The Whitby Headland Projects, 1993–2015*, Historic England.

Wilson, D.M. and Hurst, D.G. 1962–3, 'Medieval Britain and Ireland in 1961', *Medieval Archaeology* VI–VII, 306–49.

Wormald, P. 1988, 'Æthelwold and his Continental counterparts: contact, comparison, contrast', in B. Yorke (ed.), *Bishop Æthelwold: his Career and Influence*, Woodbridge: Boydell Press, 13–42.

Wrathmell, S. 2012, *A History of Wharram Percy and its Neighbours*, Wharram: A study of settlement on the Yorkshire Wolds, XIII, York: York University Archaeological Publications 15.

Wright, D.W. 2015a, *Middle Saxon Settlement and Society: The Changing Rural Communities of Central and Eastern England*, Oxford: Archaeopress.

Wright, D.W. 2015b, 'Shaping rural settlements: the early medieval legacy to the English village', *Landscapes* 16 (2), 105–25.

Wymer, J.J. and Brown, N.R. 1995, *Excavations at North Shoebury: Settlement and economy in South-East Essex 1500BC–AD1500*, Chelmsford: East Anglian Archaeology 75.

Yates, D.T. 2007, *Land, Power and Prestige: Bronze Age Field Systems in Southern England*, Oxford: Oxbow.

Yeates, S. 2010, Archaeological watching brief at Eynsham Primary School Beeches, Road, Eynsham, Oxfordshire. Unpublished report: John Moore Heritage Services.

Zadora-Rio, E. 2003, review of Lavigne 2002, *Archéologie Médiévale* 33, 348–51.

Zadora-Rio, E. 2010a, 'Planification agraires de dynamiques spatio-temporelles', *Agri Centuriati* 7, 133–53.

Zadora-Rio, E. 2010b, 'La mesure et la délimitation des terres en Anjou-Touraine (IXᵉ–XIIᵉ siècle): perception et représentation de l'espace', in D. Boisseuil *et al.* (eds), *Ecritures de l'Espace Social: Mélanges d'Histoire Médiévale offerts à Monique Bourin*, Paris: Publications de la Sorbonne, 267–86.

Index

Page-numbers in **bold** indicate illustrations.
English counties are as before 1974.